CISTERCIAN STUDIES SERIES: NUMBER THIRTEEN

STUDIES IN MEDIEVAL
CISTERCIAN HISTORY

CISTERCIAN STUDIES SERIES

Board of Editors

CISTERCIAN STUDIES SERIES: NUMBER THIRTEEN

STUDIES IN MEDIEVAL CISTERCIAN HISTORY

Presented to

JEREMIAH F. O'SULLIVAN

CISTERCIAN PUBLICATIONS

Spencer, Massachusetts

1971

Cistercian Studies Series   ISBN 0–87907–800–6
This volume   ISBN 0–87907–813–8

Library of Congress Catalog Card Number 77–152486

Printed in the Republic of Ireland by
Cahill & Co. Limited, Parkgate Printing Works, Dublin 8

CONTENTS

ABBREVIATIONS

PL   J. P. Migne, *Patrologia Latina,* 222 vols., Paris, 1844–
          1864.

Potthast August Potthast, *Regesta pontificum romanorum,* 2 vols.,
          Berlin, 1874–1875.

Statuta   J. M. Canivez, ed., *Statuta capitulorum generalium
          Ordinis Cisterciensis ab anno* 1116 *ad annum* 1786, 8 vols.,
          Louvain, Bureau de la Revue d'Histoire Ecclésiastique,
          1934–1941.

PREFACE

THE ESSAYS INCLUDED IN THIS VOLUME are presented in honor of Professor Jeremiah F. O'Sullivan who for nearly thirty years taught Medieval History at Fordham University. His principal interest was the history of medieval monasticism, but especially Cistercian monasticism, and over the years he introduced many students to the wisdom of the Rule of St Benedict, the *Carta Caritatis,* the Cistercian *Statuta* and the writings of St Bernard. By his teaching he won the affection of undergraduate and graduate students who recognized him as a man of true learning, integrity, charity and humility. After his retirement in June, 1967, those of us who completed doctoral work under his direction (Professors Brundage, Desmond, Donnelly, Lackner, O'Callaghan, Telesca and Volz) and some friends who have cultivated the same field of study (Professors Constable, Hays and Sommerfeldt) decided that a collection of essays on the themes of medieval Cistercian monasticism would be an appropriate testimony to our affection and admiration.

The essays suggest something of the extraordinary importance of monasticism in the medieval period, dealing as they do with such wide-ranging topics as liturgy, social theory, crusading, military orders, relations between monasteries and bishops, national sentiment, political and economic involvement, conflicts between church and state and, lastly, the character of one great preacher and reformer as seen by another.

We wish to thank Rev Basil Pennington ocso, director of

Cistercian Publications, Spencer, Mass., and the Irish University
Press of Shannon, Ireland, for their kindness in publishing the
volume.

                                        Joseph F. O'Callaghan
Fordham University

DEDICATION

IF, AS IT IS SAID, historians tend to assume the mannerisms, language, and *Zeitgeist* of the period they have studied, this should not perplex anyone in describing Jeremiah F. O'Sullivan. For the Middle Ages was, after all, a period of great variety. And even though Dr O'Sullivan specializes in medieval monastic history —Cistercian history, at that—medieval monks were men for many more seasons than the stereotypes of their personalities would lead us to believe.

Those who have known Dr O'Sullivan can enjoy their own game of attempting to identify the ways in which he reminds them of the age and the institutions he knows best. For my part, I have no difficulty in thinking of him as a forthright, earthy, generous, and humble man, who, unlike Abelard, never boasted, and like Bernard of Clairvaux, knew precisely where he wished to take a stand and took it without regard for the reactions of officials. (For who, in a crisis, could be more official than he? Jeremiah, that is.)

Perhaps more than anything else, Dr O'Sullivan personifies the day when student and teacher communed in a one-to-one ratio. Searching the corners of my memory, I am awed at the amount of time I spent in serious conversation with him during the three years of my graduate study at Fordham between 1938 and 1941. In his office, after class, on the way home, or in his study, we talked at length two or three times a week about medieval history and about my own work. I found no professor more open to a young student's questions than he.

Some years later it occurred to me that I had never spoken with anyone else so much and learned so little about him personally. I knew that Jeremiah was born in Ireland and educated there as well as in Wales and the United States, and that he had received his Ph.D. from the University of Pennsylvania in 1932. Yet he rarely spoke about Jeremiah O'Sullivan; he was more interested in helping young people to become history teachers, or perhaps even historians. He was really a humble scholar, and his wife was a solicitous, gracious, humble lady. It was that simple and uncomplicated.

During the last year or so, I have been amazed to learn how little his colleagues know about Jeremiah's personal history. *Vitae* on him are hard to find. In one directory he laconically admits to being "nat.," a naturalized citizen. He barely notes that he served in the United States Army from 1942 to 1946. This I knew, since he left suddenly for Intelligence school just before my Ph.D. defense. (I spent much of the night before the defense in his study, at the insistence of his wife.) He returned as a lieutenant colonel—with his paratroop boots, unusual artifacts in medieval history classes. Only a year or so ago I learned that he also brought back the Legion of Merit, the Silver Star, and the Bronze Star. Jeremiah left hurriedly again as the Korean War broke, and I filled in for him in some of his courses, thereupon meeting in seminar some of the authors of the essays in this volume. On his return, Jeremiah resumed his work as the leading American student of medieval Cistercian and monastic history.

It is thirty-two years now, almost to the day, since I first met Jeremiah O'Sullivan. Ten years ago, almost to the day, my son met him, sitting before him in a large lecture room set aside for the freshman medieval course in Fordham College. I could track the year-long passage of the Middle Ages in that course as much of my library—even the set of *The Cambridge Medieval History* that Jeremiah gave me in return for reading galleys and page proofs he had to leave behind in 1942, several months before the young man was born—disappeared from home to campus dormitory. Some four years later, when the young man went off to graduate study in history, I suspected the subtle influence of a great teacher in that decision.

This teacher-scholar enjoyed the confidence of his University colleagues, whom he served as departmental chairman, and of his fellow medievalists, whom he served for many years as a member of the Council of the Mediaeval Academy of America. He also won the respect of a generation of graduate students at Fordham, and in 1964 merited the special encomia of the graduating class of Fordham College. Dedicating their yearbook to him, the graduates took pride in saying how grateful they felt toward this man from Queenstown, Ireland, who had professed to them in unassuming ways and illuminating commentaries on the past his commitment to humane studies and to human values.

All of us who studied under Jeremiah O'Sullivan remember this commitment as the measure of the man, but I remember him especially for the brilliant craftsmanship of his seminars. Here, I believe, he was truly at his best, probing, driving, incessantly asking why. Yet no man was kinder when you tired or seemed to feel the loneliness of the long-distance runner. No man was more charitable and concerned about you as a person. For he had lived by an admirable *carta caritatis* of his own. Indeed, as a student I noted the pleasure he took in mentioning the name of that famous Cistercian document.

James S. Donnelly

15 September 1970

THE LITURGY OF EARLY CÎTEAUX

THE LITURGY OF A RELIGIOUS COMMUNITY
is not merely a set of objective cultic rules which must be
carried out by individuals and groups in a mechanical fashion.
In its true form it is a product of the spirit, not an exercise in external
formalism. As such it reveals much about the ideals of a religious
or monastic community, about its way of life and its growth.
Hence its importance in the determination of the history of an
institution and—in the case of this writing—of that of early Cîteaux,
covering the period from its establishment in 1098 to the middle of
the twelfth century.

Works on the subject of the early Cistercian liturgy—particularly
the surveys of Robert Trilhe, André Malet and Joseph-Marie
Canivez and occasional articles in such Cistercian periodicals and
publications as *Cistercienser-Chronik, Collectanea Ordinis Cisterciensium Reformatorum,* and *Analecta Sacri Ordinis Cisterciensis*—are far
from numerous.[1] Generally speaking, they are neither exhaustive
nor do they utilize or consider every aspect of the available material.
Moreover they all proceed from the fixed liturgical legislation of a

---

1. See in particular the bibliographies given in "Cîteaux (Liturgie de
l'Ordre de Cîteaux)," *Dictionnaire d'Archéologie Chrétien et de Liturgie*—
hereafter cited DACL— (Paris, 1907ff.), vol. 3 (1914), p. 1810 f.; Joseph M.
Canivez, "Le rite cistercien," *Ephemerides Liturgicae,* 3 (1949), pp. 281ff.;
Colomban Bock, "Les codifications du droit cistercien," *Collectanea Ordinis
Cisterciensium Reformatorum,* 14 (1952), p. 4, n. 523. Cf. Bernhard Kaul,
"Gelebte Liturgie," *Anima,* 8 (1953), pp. 79–82.

later period—the end of the twelfth century—and attempt to make
retrogressive projections to earlier situations. Finally, in view of the
recent discovery of earlier Cistercian liturgical codes, they are
simply outdated and in need of revision. Aware of all this the
present study wants to offer its contributions in an attempt to hasten
the appearance of a definitive work on this subject of great importance.

The nearly two dozen pioneers of Cîteaux were all from the
Benedictine reform abbey of Molesme in Burgundy founded by
Saint Robert in 1075. At Molesme their monastic life was based on
the general Cluniac pattern in customs and organization, as can be
gathered from the list of monastic offices, the employment of the
priory system, feudal involvements and known contemporary
monastic practices.[2] Recent investigations were able to effect a
further localization by pointing out the indebtedness of the early
Cistercian usages to those of St Benignus Abbey in Dijon which
had founded the Abbey of St Michael in Tonnerre where Robert
of Molesme was abbot before his retirement to the hermitage of
Collan and the subsequent foundation of Molesme.[3]

In his *Historia ecclesiastica* Ordericus Vitalis (d. 1143) recorded the
events at Molesme which led to the establishment of Cîteaux.
While the account is clad in contemporary literary genres, its basic
assertions faithfully reflect the actual state of affairs and the issues at
stake. According to Ordericus, the monks of Molesme had shared
the fate of traditional monachism. They moved away from
Egyptian monastic practices and from the ideals of Saint Benedict,
the Father of western monachism, in a legitimate evolution whose
origins must be sought in the time of the Merovingian kings and
nobles. The latter founded a great number of monasteries and
endowed them with provisions and numerous servants. As a *quid
pro quo* they assigned to the monks the duty of being entirely

2. For more on the subject see Bede Lackner, *The Eleventh-Century Background of Cîteaux*, (Cistercian Studies Series 8).

3. Bruno Schneider, "Cîteaux und die benediktinische Tradition," *Analecta
Sacri Ordinis Cisterciensis*, 17 (1961), pp. 100 and 107ff. Cf. *ibid.*, 16 (1960),
pp. 169ff.

dedicated to reading, to prayers for their benefactors and the celebration of the divine mysteries. The consequence of this turn of events was that the monks withdrew from the rest of the world and shut themselves up in their monasteries where, free from outside intrusion and idle conversation, they observed profound silence and "chanted day and night the psalms of David and other mystical songs to the Creator's praise."[4]

This development went clearly against the ideal of Saint Benedict, who based the monk's life on a happy balance between choral prayer, spiritual reading and manual labor. Increasingly aware of this conflict between contemporary practices and the demands of the Rule of Saint Benedict but unable to resolve it at Molesme, a group of monks eventually left the abbey and after many hardships founded Cîteaux. These monks did not secede because Molesme was in a state of decadence, but because in an age of reform and regeneration they wished to return to the authentic source of monastic renewal, the Rule of Saint Benedict embodying the genuine thoughts of the Father of western monachism.[5] This can be clearly established from the authentic documents of the so-called *Exordium Parvum,* an account of the foundation and early history of Cîteaux, and from the *Exordium Cistercii,* a possibly even older version of the same. They reveal the basic features of the Cistercians' reform endeavor: a return to the strictness of the Benedictine Rule, solitude, poverty, the rejection of traditional monastic observances and a certain exclusive individuality.[6]

This return to the "purity of the Rule," to "monastic purity" and the "rectitude of the Rule"[7] called for a rejection of traditional monastic practices. Archbishop Hugh of Lyons clearly saw this program of the Cistercian founders when he stated in his report to Pope Paschal II that "they left the community of Molesme with their abbot, in order to lead a more rigorous and secluded life following the Rule of Saint Benedict. In the observance of this Rule

---

4. PL 188:639.   5. Lackner, *op. cit.,*   6. *Ibid.,*
7. Kolumban Spahr, "Die Regelauslegung im Neukloster," *Festschrift zum 800-Jahrgedächtnis des Todes Bernhards von Clairvaux* (Wien: Herold Verlag, 1953), p. 26.

they have resolved to abandon the usages of certain monasteries, maintaining that in their weakness they are unable to bear such a great burden."[8] These "traditional" monastic ways found their codification in the reform decrees of Benedict of Aniane (A.D. 817) which decidedly altered the original Benedictine idea and eventually produced the Cluniac *laus perennis* ideal which reduced the monks' life to liturgical and ceremonial functions;[9] hence the Cistercian pioneers' resolve to abandon practices added to the original provisions of the Rule.

The *Exordium Magnum,* written toward the end of the twelfth century by the Cistercian, Conrad of Eberbach, specifies in this connection that, because the first Cistercians decided to observe the divine office in the manner and order established by the Rule of Saint Benedict, they completely rejected the additions that had been made to this office. Therefore they eliminated psalms, prayers and litanies, i.e. everything their "less discreet ancestors had added of their own accord," without authorization, to the original Benedictine *pensum.* Their action was partly motivated by a consideration of human frailty, for in their view additions to the right measure established by Saint Benedict would not aid but actually hurt the monks, since the multiplicity of devotions would lead to tepidity and negligence not only in the slothful, but also in fervent souls.[10]

---

8. *Exordium Parvum,* 12, in Joannes-B. Van Damme (ed.), *Documenta pro Cisterciensis Ordinis historiae ac juris studio* (Westmalle: Typis Ordinis Cisterciensis, 1949), p. 11; trans. Robert E. Larkin in Louis J. Lekai, *The White Monks. A History of the Cistercian Order* (Okauchee, Wis.: Our Lady of Spring Bank, 1953), pp. 251–66.

9. Lackner, *op. cit.,* chs. 1–2.

10. "Et primitus quidem modum et ordinem servitii Dei per omnia secundum traditiones regulae observare decreverunt recisis penitus et reiectis cunctis appendiciis psalmorum, orationum et letaniarum, quae minus discreti patres pro velle suo superaddiderant, quae etiam propter fragilitatem infirmitatis humanae non tam ad salutem quam ad perniciem monachorum esse sagaci consideratione deprehenderunt, dum ob multiplicitatem sui non solum a fastidiosis, sed ab ipsis quoque studiosis omnino tepide et negligenter persolverentur." Bruno Griesser (ed.), *Exordium Magnum Cisterciense sive Narratio de Initio Cisterciensis Ordinis,* 1:20 (Rome: Editiones Cistercienses, 1961), p. 75.

This fidelity to the Rule produced an uncompromising puritanism in the early Cistercians which was in a marked contrast to the then prevalent monastic usages. Hugh of Lyons described it in these words: "The brethren from Molesme and some other monks of the neighborhood do not cease to annoy and disturb them, thinking in the eyes of the world that they are valued less and looked upon with contempt if the world will take notice what exceptional and new kind of monks are living in their midst."[11] Pope Paschal II to whom Hugh addressed these words recognized this feature of the reformers, for (in the so-called *Roman Privilege*) he reminded the Cistercian pioneers: "You must, therefore, remember, sons most beloved and dearest in Christ, that one part of you has left the broad roads of the world, another even the less strict paths of a laxer monastery."[12] In fact he made this "otherness" a condition of papal protection for the new monastery, by decreeing "that the place which you have chosen in order to live in monastic tranquillity, be secure and free . . . and that an abbey may exist there forever and be particularly sheltered through the protection of the Apostolic See . . . as long as you remain in the observance . . . you now follow."[13]

The desire to follow the authentic teachings of the Rule prompted the early Cistercians to undertake a number of community projects, among them in the field of the liturgy. Thus they proceeded to copy the books needed for the celebration of the liturgy and the divine office, prepared a new edition of the Bible, produced a new breviary, reformed their chant and adopted monastic usages which reflected their resolve and their novel way of life.

Work on these projects began in connection with Abbot Robert's recall to Molesme after a brief stay in the new foundation. The modalities of his return were settled by a local council which decided that "with regard to Abbot Robert's chapel and the othei

11. *Exordium Parvum*, 12, p. 11.

12. *Ibid.*, 14, p. 12.

13. Jean A. Lefèvre, "Que savons-nous du Cîteaux primitif" *Revue d'Histoire Ecclésiastique*, 51 (1956), p. 18.

B

things which he took with him upon his departure from Molesme and with which he went to the bishop of Châlons and to the New Monastery, we have ordered that all remain safely with the brethren of the New Monastery. This is with the exception of a certain breviary which, upon the approval of the monks of Molesme, they may keep until the celebration of the feast of Saint John the Baptist so that it may be copied."[14]

The second abbot of Cîteaux, Saint Alberic (1099–1108), continued these undertakings since there is credible evidence that he addressed a letter to Lambert, abbot of Pothières, to solicit his expert opinion about the accenting and spelling of certain Latin words, needed most likely for the correct execution of choral chant.[15]

Also during Alberic's term began the Cistercians' work on a new edition of the Bible. Led by Stephen Harding, it was completed shortly after Stephen succeeded Alberic as abbot. In a preface Stephen explained the underlying principles of this correction, principles the early Cistercians may well have employed in undertakings of a similar nature. In view of "the variance of the different texts" Stephen sought to follow "the more trustworthy text . . . in the belief of its genuineness." To produce an authentic text Stephen consulted learned Jews about the variants, erased "superfluous passages"—parts or verses—and prohibited their reintroduction or the insertion of notes (with the thumbnails) in the text or margin.[16]

During the first half of his reign Stephen was also instrumental in the preparation of a new hymnal. In a letter attached to the latter he revealed that his aim was authenticity, since the Cistercians wished to be "lovers, imitators and propagators" of Saint Benedict, i.e. advocates of "the integrity of the Rule . . . with the greatest possible zeal." Hence the question of what hymns to sing in choir

14. *Exordium Parvum*, 7, p. 9.

15. Jean Marilier (ed.), *Chartes et documents concernant l'abbaye de Cîteaux, 1098–1182* (Rome: Editiones Cistercienses, 1961), pp. 41–46.

16. *Ibid.*, p. 56. A useful bibliography on the subject is offered by Solutor Marosszéki (now Ralph March) in "Les origines du chant cistercien au XIIᵉ siècle," *Analecta Sacri Ordinis Cisterciensis*, 8 (1952), p. 7, n. 2.

could only be decided from what the Rule said on the subject. Since the Rule mentions Ambrosian hymns and Stephen Harding was convinced that the hymns sung at Milan were authentic compositions of Saint Ambrose, he had them copied and brought to Cîteaux. Here they were introduced by the "common consent and decree of our brethren" as Stephen's note reveals. The decision was also made to sing "these alone and no others"; to sing them uniformly, i.e. without change or equivocation; and to make this decision binding not only on their contemporaries, but on their successors as well.[17] Their action is corroborated by William of Malmesbury's testimony stating that the Cistercians "are using the Ambrosian melodies and hymns they were able to secure from Milan"[18] and by Abelard who criticized the Cistercians for abandoning the traditional hymns sung by the whole Church.[19]

In view of their principles the Cistercians also needed a new edition of the antiphonary since "the antiphonaries showed such great variations that no two provinces chanted the same book of antiphons" and, contemporaries felt, "one ought to give thanks to God" if identical copies could ever be found. In this situation the school of Metz, founded around the year 760, recommended itself on account of the antiquity of its tradition, since it had received its antiphonary directly from Rome at an early date, i.e. some two centuries after the death of Saint Gregory. This school was therefore the most renowned in the Middle Ages; it had its own method and was considered an authentic source of the Roman, i.e. Gregorian, chant. In the words of Saint Bernard, "among the things our Fathers, i.e. the Founders of our Cistercian order, have most cherished, was their studious and religious decision to sing in the divine praises only what was attestedly the most authentic." This

---

17. Marilier, p. 55. Cf. Marosszéki, p. 9. C. Waddell has published a critical text in *The Cistercian Spirit (Cistercian Studies Series* 3) p. 206. English trans. M. B. Pennington, "Three Early Documents" in *Cistercian Studies Series* 4, pp. 144f.

18. On William of Malmesbury see also below, p. 16

19. Abelard's remarks are detailed below, pp. 17f.

is why they sent brethren "to transcribe and obtain [a copy of] the antiphonary of Metz, for it was believed to be Gregorian."[20]

Examples of this primitive Cistercian chant are seen in two fragments—*Palat. lat. ms.* 559 and 562—of the Vatican Library. That they are Cistercian is evident from the writing with its "French" notation, from the absence of *quilismas* and from the melodic content. Moreover the so-called "Germanic" intervals which avoid semi-tones are corrected and so is also the *ambitus* (range) of the melodies. As a further proof, changes are made in the text or the melody for textual reasons, to avoid repetitions, and, last but not least, the text fully agrees with other texts of the primitive Cistercian liturgy, notably the Breviary of Saint Stephen.[21]

Because of "the authority of those who chanted it"—an obvious reference of Saint Bernard to the founding Fathers of Cîteaux—this antiphonary remained in use for a number of years in Cistercian houses. Then, i.e. between the years 1132 and 1147 (1148), it was reformed once more, under the auspices of Saint Bernard.[22]

In application of their liturgical principles the Cistercians also edited a new breviary under Stephen Harding, the so-called *Breviarium sancti Stephani* (now *Ms. lat. in oct.* 402 in the library of Marburg, West Germany), dating from approximately 1130, but at any rate not later than 1132. The breviary proper begins on fol. 8 of the manuscript; it starts with the Saturday which precedes the first Sunday of Advent while the Sanctoral begins on fol. 142*v*, with the feast of Saint Stephen the Martyr. The codex numbers 235 folios and ends with a hymn in honor of Saint Martin of Tours. According to Konrad Koch who discovered the manuscript during World War II, the breviary agrees with the structure of the

20. "Prologus in Antiphonarium," 5 *Bernardi Opera,* (ed.), J. Leclercq and H. Rochais, vol. 3 (Rome: Editiones Cistercienses, 1963), p. 515; trans. C. Waddell in *The Works of Bernard of Clairvaux,* vol. 1 (Cistercian Fathers Series 1) p. 161. From this letter are also the preceding quotes of this paragraph. See also Marosszéki, 8 and 16.

21. François Kovács, "Fragments du chant primitif cistercien," *Analecta Sacri Ordinis Cisterciensis,* 6 (1950), pp. 140ff., esp. 150.

22. For this second reform see below, pp. 20ff.

office as outlined by the Rule of Saint Benedict. The sanctoral is shaped by Gallo-Roman influences and, in general, by older traditions. Feasts have only one rank, that of twelve lessons, while the three-lesson offices remain ferial offices, as in the Rule of Saint Benedict. The readings during matins—i.e. the first eight readings on feast days, and the three readings on ferial days—are in most instances excerpts from Scripture. Some feasts of saints, and even great feasts of the temporal—for instance, Christmas, Epiphany, Easter, Ascension, Pentecost—and individual Sundays, however, have patristic readings in the first two nocturns, mostly texts from Gregory the Great, the Venerable Bede, Maximus of Turin, and Haimo of Auxerre. There are such readings from the Church Fathers with some frequency even on ferial days, in place of the continuous reading from Scripture. The ferial office was also retained for the last three days of Holy Week, in a conscious departure from general monastic practices. Saints of a lesser rank have ordinarily a commemoration with a proper oration. Some fifty-seven saints are given a proper office with twelve lessons, while 104 other saints are only commemorated. There are also eight so-called *beatus* saints with no oration of their own but one probably taken from the common of saints. A *beatus* saint is found in the calendar on days when there was already a feast of twelve lessons or a commemoration. Further characteristics are that the *translatio sancti Benedicti* (11 July) is celebrated with the same twelve-lesson office as the feast of the saint on 21 March, and that there is an additional versicle on the feast of the Conversion of Saint Paul and the feast of Saint Lawrence after each antiphon in the First and Second Nocturns. Anniversaries for the deceased and the Commemoration of All Souls on 2 November are not mentioned. Equally absent is the feast of the Holy Trinity. Among the Marian feasts—Purification, Annunciation, Assumption and Nativity of the Virgin Mary—only Assumption has an octave, and among the other saints only Stephen the Martyr, John the Evangelist, the Holy Innocents, John the Baptist, Lawrence and the apostle Andrew. Also the responses and readings display characteristic features different from later practices and revisions, as a full evaluation and discussion of the Bible of Saint Stephen will—hopefully, soon—show.[23]

The influx of vocations, particularly the entrance of Bernard of Clairvaux and his thirty companions in 1113, enabled Cîteaux to make its first foundations. This in turn made it necessary to define the bonds that were to prevail between these monasteries and safeguard the ideals of the Cistercian founders. An appropriate document was drawn up for the purpose which received the name *Charter of Charity (Carta Caritatis)* and in subsequent times underwent a certain evolution. Its earliest extant draft, though primarily concerned with juridical questions, contains also some legislation on liturgical matters. It prescribes, for instance, that all monasteries must have "the usages, chant and books needed for the day and night office and the mass the way the New Monastery (Cîteaux) keeps its usages and books." The reason it gave for this measure was that "there be no discord in our actions, but that we may live with one love, under one Rule and in the same observances."[24] This provision is not animated by a desire to enforce uniformity for the sake of uniformity, at least not in this early Cistercian document. Its underlying motive is mutual love and the practical realization that monks do on occasions visit other Cistercian houses and there participate in the regular exercises.[25] As for the apostolate, the Cistercians were solicitous for all. They wished "to extend their concern to every son of the Church"[26] and did

---

23. Konrad Koch, "Vollständiges Brevier aus der Schreibstube des Hl. Stephan," *Analecta Sacri Ordinis Cisterciensis*, 2 (1949), pp. 146f. and *idem*, "Das Kalendar des Stephan-Breviers," *Cistercienser-Chronik*, 57 (1950), pp. 85ff. For an identification of the readings during Matins and other readings in the office, see Bruno Griesser, "Das Lektionen-und Perikopensystem im Stephansbrevier," *Cistercienser-Chronik*, 71 (1964), pp. 67ff. Cf. also Leodegar Walter, "Das Calendarium Cisterciense einst und jetzt," *Cistercienser-Chronik*, 55 (1948), p. 27.

24. "Volumus ut mores et cantum et omnes libros ad horas diurnas sive nocturnas et ad missam necessarios secundum formam morum et librorum novi monasterii possideant quatinus in actibus nostris nulla sit discordia, sed una caritate, una regula, similibusque vivamus moribus." *Carta Caritatis*, 3, in J. Van Damme, *Documenta*, p. 17.

25. *Ibid.*, 3, p. 17.   26. *Ibid.*, 1, p. 16.

not simply renounce the care of souls; only their special ministration was directed to those within the order. The *Charter of Charity* distinctly stresses this care of souls since its drafters aimed at the promotion of charity and the utility of souls in things human and divine. They "wished to retain the care of their co-abbots' and fellow religious' souls."[27] This is why the *Charter* prescribes that all abbots should meet each year at Cîteaux in general chapter "to make provisions for the salvation of souls: their own and that of their charges."[28] For the nature of their office—as alluded to in the case of the abbot of Cîteaux—was simple "pastoral care."[29] This care is not automatically a life-time charge; its duration is determined by an abbot's fidelity to the Rule and the Cistercian order, and by his active concern for the spiritual progress of the brethren.[30] This concern even takes precedence over the abbot's duty to attend the general chapter at Cîteaux, for the *Charter* explicitly provides that the abbot should stay in his monastery and send a delegate to the chapter if his novices are to be blessed.[31] The *Charter* also settled the question of seniority in the case where several abbots visited the same monastery; it decided in favor of the abbot of the oldest monastery "except if any of them [i.e. abbots] was vested in alb; he then will stand before everyone else and fulfill the tasks of the superior, even if he is of a lesser seniority than all others."[32] This practice of attending choir "vested in alb" on certain occasions belongs to the oldest elements of the Cistercian usages and derives from the Cluniac usages through the monastery of Molesme. It was soon discontinued, however, as its absence in redactions made after the middle of the twelfth century indicates.[33]

In 1119 Pope Callistus II (1119–1124) approved this or an earlier version of the *Charter of Charity* at the request of the Cistercians, to ensure greater peace to the monastery and to improve the safe-

27. *Ibid.*   28. *Ibid.*, 7, p. 16.   29. *Ibid.*, 8, p. 19.
30. "Incorrigibilem a cura pastorali deiciant." *Carta Caritatis,* 8, p. 19.
31. *Ibid.*, 8, p. 18.   32. *Ibid.*, 9, p. 20.
33. Bruno Griesser, "Die 'Ecclesiastica Officia Cisterciensis Ordinis' des Cod. 1711 von Trient," *Analecta Sacri Ordinis Cisterciensis,* 12 (1956), pp. 172ff. See also below, p. 25.

guards of religious discipline. He applauded the religious fervor of the Cistercians and gave papal approval to their establishment, including to "certain statutes you have decreed about the observance of the Rule of blessed Benedict and other matters that seemed necessary to your order and to that place." Confirming these chapters and constitution by apostolic authority the Pope decreed "that they should retain legal force in perpetuity."[34]

Pope Eugene III (1145–1153), a Cistercian on the papal throne, again approved the *Charter of Charity*, and with it the liturgical practices of the order, in 1152. He specifically included the Cistercians' resolve to "observe in every house [of the order] the same observances, the same chant and the same books which are needed for the divine office."[35] Anastasius IV, Hadrian IV and Alexander III reissued Eugene III's bull in almost identical terms, at least as far as the liturgy is concerned.

The earliest known statutes of the order, the so-called *capitula* attached to the *Charter of Charity* in ms. 1711 of the Biblioteca Communale of Trent (nn. 7–26), also legislate about uniformity in liturgical books and related matters. They prescribe that no new abbey should be established without at least twelve monks and without the necessary liturgical books: the psalter; the book of hymns; the book of collects; the antiphonary; the gradual; the Rule; a missal, and the necessary buildings, including the chapel.[36] To preserve a permanent and indissoluble unity between the monasteries, the Rule of Saint Benedict must be interpreted and observed in the same manner by all and "the same books—inasmuch as they belong to the divine office—the same food, the same clothing and, finally, the same customs and usages be found in all

---

34. *Carta Caritatis*, 11, p. 20f.

35. The text is printed in Joseph Turk (ed.) "Cistercii Statuta Antiquissima," *Analecta Sacri Ordinis Cisterciensis*, 4 (1948), p. 122.

36. *Exordium Cistercii cum 'Summa Cartae Caritatis' et Capitulis*, 9, p. 26. Cf. Columbanus Spahr, "De fontibus constitutivis primigenii iuris constitutionalis Sacri Ordinis Cisterciensis," (unpublished dissertation, Lateran University Rome, 1953), p. 57. See also "Instituta monachorum cisterciensium de molismo venientium," in J. Van Damme, *Documenta*, p. 14.

things."[37] This is why "every house shall have the same missal;
book of Gospels; book of epistles; book of collects; gradual;
antiphonary; hymnary; psalter; book of [choir] readings; Rule
and calendar, i.e. martyrology."[38] Everywhere the altar linens and
vestments used at the altar must be without silk, except the stole
and the maniple, and the chasubles must be of one color. In general,
all ornaments, vases and utensils of the monastery must be without
gold, silver or precious stones, except the chalice and the reed
(*fistula*) used for communion—which could be of silver or be gold-
plated, but never of gold.[39] In a similar spirit only painted wooden
crucifixes, i.e. without a *corpus* were allowed.[40] In accordance with
the Cistercians' view of the apostolate, no outsider was to be
admitted to confession, Holy Communion or the conventual
mass, nor was anyone granted burial in their monasteries, except
if a guest or a hired man died within their confines.[41]

A further step in the order's legislation was the redaction of the
Institutes of the General Chapter at Cîteaux, a collection which dates
from before 1152 and is preserved in ms. 31 of the university library
of Laibach. It contains all previous statutes issued by the general
chapters, and has the following, already encountered or additional,
liturgical provisions. To preserve unity, the general chapter
ordered that the Rule of Saint Benedict be interpreted and observed
by everyone in the same manner and that the same books—i.e. the
missal; the book of epistles; the books of Gospels; the book of
collects; the gradual; the antiphonary; the Rule; the hymnary;
the psalter; the book of [choir] readings; and the calendar
(martyrology)—be used in the liturgy, to ensure an identical
observance of usages everywhere.[42] For the same reason, no new
foundation was to be made unless the place in question had the
necessary liturgical books, i.e. the missal; the Rule; the book of
usages; the psalter; the book of hymns; the book of collects; the

37. *Exordium Cistercii*, n. 9. p. 26.   38. *Ibid.*, n. 10, p. 26.
39. *Ibid.*, n. 15, p. 28.   40. *Ibid.*, n. 26, p. 28.   41. *Ibid.*, n. 24, p. 28.
42. "Instituta Generalis Capituli apud Cistercium," 2–3, in J. Turk, "Cistercii
Statuta Antiquissima," *loc. cit.*, p. 16.

book of [choir] readings; the antiphonary; and the gradual, so that the Rule of Saint Benedict could at once be observed in the new establishment.[43] In fidelity to the Rule no additional psalms or prayers were to be said in choir whatever the necessity might be, but in case of an imminent danger another mass or collect could be substituted for the conventual mass or its collect.[44] Because one could not be called a monk and a Cistercian if he sinned against monastic poverty, the Cistercians rejected churches, altars, burials and tithes, i.e. the fruit of someone else's labor.[45] For the same reason their altar linens and the vestments of the ministers of the altar— except the stole and the maniple—had to be without silk, the chasubles of one color, and all ornaments, vessels and utensils of the monastery without gold, silver or precious stones, except the chalice and the reed (*fistula*) which could be of silver or gold-plated, but in no case of gold.[46] It was equally forbidden by the chapter to have golden or gold-plated containers for liturgical books, to cover any codes with a pall made of rich material,[47] or to have cowls (*cuculla*) with fancy sleeves.[48] All Cistercian churches were to be dedicated to Mary, the queen of heaven and earth,[49] but with the exception of painted wooden crosses there were to be no sculptures or pictures in them nor in the workshops, because while one is intent on these, the opportunity for a fruitful meditaion or for religious fervor is lost.[50] The glass, too, had to be plain, i.e. without color, crosses or pictures.[51] Further enactments prohibited that abbots officiate at the consecration of virgins, administer baptism or become godparents.[52] Similarly, if an abbot came late to the office, i.e. arrived after the doxology which follows the first psalm, he was to make a satisfaction at the *gradus presbyterii*, the sanctuary step, as a monk would do, but after that he could proceed to his choir stall without waiting for a signal except if another abbot was present.[53] Traveling abbots were not to take with them a chalice or whatever else they needed for the celebration

43. *Ibid.*, 12, p. 18.   44. *Ibid.*, 51, p. 23.   45. *Ibid.*, 9, p. 17.
46. *Ibid.*, 10, p. 17.   47. *Ibid.*, 13, p. 18.   48. *Ibid.*, 15, p. 18.
49. *Ibid.*, 18, p. 19.   50. *Ibid.*, 20, p. 19.   51. *Ibid.*, 82, p. 27.
52. *Ibid.*, 29, p. 20.   53. *Ibid.*, 49. p. 23.

of the mass, unless they received permission from the general chapter to do so.[54] If a monk was elevated to the episcopate, he had to observe the customs of the order with regard to clothing and the canonical hours, but could wear a mantle of inexpensive linen or sheepskin and a skullcap of a similar material or of coarse wool, if he so wished.[55] The chapter also insisted that a Cistercian monk or a laybrother should not prostrate with his whole body on the chapel floor when praying but talk to God on his knees or standing.[56] Then it specified the days when the monks could receive Holy Communion and gave permission to the ministers of the altar to communicate during the private masses on such occasions.[57] It finally told the monks to sing with manly voices, not with thin, womanish sounds, or in a falsetto, in imitation of the theatrics of buffoons. They should keep the middle range so that their singing may radiate gravity and foster the spirit of recollection.[58]

Further information on the early Cistercian liturgy is furnished by a number of Cistercian and non-Cistercian sources. Foremost among these is the so-called *Exordium Parvum,* an early Cistercian account about the beginning of the order, written probably after the death of Stephen Harding in 1134. It reports that the Cistercians rejected churches, altars, oblations and burials as well as the tithes of other men because Saint Benedict mentioned no such activities and incomes in his Rule and Saint Gregory recorded no such practices in Benedict's life. Besides, it was their wish to be exclusive servants of the Lord and to banish everything that could reflect pride and superfluity, or corrupt their freely chosen poverty, the custodian of all virtues. Hence they also decreed to retain no golden or silver vessels, and to keep only painted wooden crosses, one pair of iron candelabra and thuribles made of copper or iron. Their chalices and

54. *Ibid.,* 59, p. 24.   55. *Ibid.,* 63, p. 25.   56. *Ibid.,* 86, p. 28.
57. *Ibid.,* 46, p. 23. Cf. below, n. 106.
58. "Inst. Gen. Cap.," 75, p. 27. Cf. St Bernard, *Super Cantica, Sermo* 47, in *S. Bernardi Opera,* vol. 2. *Sermones super Cantica Canticorum 36–86* (Rome: Editiones Cistercienses, 1958), p. 66. See also Ailbe J. Luddy, *Life and Teaching of St Bernard* (Dublin: Gill, 1950), p. 257.

communion reeds were made of silver, not gold; they could be gold-plated at the most. They used cruets with nothing in gold or silver on them. Their chasubles, albs and amices were of wool or linen, without gold or silver, and their altar-cloths of plain linen, i.e. without embroideries. The most they would allow in this field was that stoles and maniples could be of silk, but without gold and silver.[59]

Confirming this testimony, William of Malmesbury, the Benedictine author of *Gesta regum Anglorum*, wrote about the Cistercians around the year 1121 that they did not follow the practices of their contemporaries who used gold, jewels, silver, ponderous metals, precious stones, topaz, amethysts and emerald in their services. They had no golden or, in general, glittering priestly vestments, and their walls were without colored painting, because they preferred shining minds to golden vestments; for their primary concern was the improvement of their morals and the purity of their souls. This also explains their untiring zeal in the celebration of the divine office. In observance of the prescriptions of the Rule to perform the day office without artificial light, they so ordered the time of matins that it was light by the time lauds began, and immediately after lauds they chanted the office of prime after which they went to their assigned work. They used the Ambrosian hymns they were able to secure from Milan and made no additions to the divine office, except the Vigils of the Dead. With the exception of the sick no one was ever absent from the canonical hours, including compline, so that the cellarer and the guest master ministered to visitors only after that hour.[60]

If the information of Ordericus Vitalis is correct, when Urban II acceded to the petition of the monks of Molesme and ordered Abbot Robert's return from Cîteaux to his former monastery, he firmly decreed that both Molesme and Cîteaux should choose the usages of

---

59. J. Van Damme, *Documenta,* pp. 13-15. Cf. also Jean de la Croix Bouton, *Histoire de l'Ordre de Cîteaux* (Tirage à-part des Fiches Cisterciennes; Westmalle: Typis Ordinis Cisterciensis, 1959), pp. 63, 72; and C. Spahr, *De fontibus constitutivis,* p. 56.

60. PL 179:1288-1290.

their preference and then keep them firmly in every particular aspect. Thus the monks of Molesme "who followed the general monastic customs" were bidden by the Pope to keep their usages inviolably and never leave their monastery in a search of other observances. And the Cistercians "who profess to keep the Rule of Saint Benedict in all its particulars" were told "never to revert to the usages they now discard with deliberate disdain."[61] Also according to Ordericus, the novelty of their institutions and the canonical rigor of the Cistercians caused many nobles and learned men to join their ranks and rejoice in chanting "triumphant anthems to Christ in the right manner." Moreover, "their doors are always shut and they bury themselves in profound secrecy. They admit no monk belonging to another religious order into their cloister, nor do they allow outsiders to attend Mass or the divine office in their chapel."[62]

An even more important witness of the early Cistercian usages is Peter Abelard's *Letter X.*, addressed to Saint Bernard.[63] It was written in connection with Bernard's visit, between 1131 and 1133, to the convent of the Paraclete ceded by Abelard to Heloise in the year 1129. Heloise saw in Bernard an envoy of heaven whose conferences filled the nuns with joy and increased their dedication. Bernard felt equally rewarded; only one practice displeased him: the substitution of *panem nostrum supersubstantialem* for *panem nostrum quotidianum* in the *Lord's Prayer* on Abelard's suggestion. Heloise confided her sensitivity about Bernard's criticism to Abelard who thereupon undertook to answer the abbot of Clairvaux. He devoted the first part of his letter to justify the change introduced in the *Our Father;* in the second part he launched a strong counter-attack condemning the novel practices of the Cistercians. In the process he furnished a valuable list of early Cistercian usages and thus became one of the most important sources for information concerning the early Cistercian liturgy.

Abelard accused the Cistercians of celebrating the divine office in a manner different from that of all other contemporary monks

---

61. PL 188:640.   62. PL 188:641.   63. PL 178:335–340.

and clerics, and contrary to every tradition, for a number of reasons. They rejected the traditional hymns in the divine office and introduced unknown, hardly known, or, at any rate, unsatisfactory ones in their place. In fact during Vigils they retained one and the same hymn, *Aeterne rerum Conditor* (*Eternal Creator Of All*) throughout the whole year, independently of whether there was a festal or a ferial office. They sang this same hymn even on Christmas Day, on Easter and Pentecost Sundays, and on all other solemn feasts, while the Church at large used a variety of hymns, as the occasion demanded. And, what is more: the Cistercians followed the same practice also in connection with the psalms and other parts of the divine office, since they admitted no variations in respect of the rank of the feast. The Cistercians also omitted the so-called *preces* (said by all houses after the supplication *Kyrie eleison* and the *Our Father*) and the *suffragia sanctorum*, i.e. the invocation (litany) of the saints. Nor did they commemorate Mary, the Mother of God, or any other saint, even though they dedicated their churches in her honor. They inexplicably retained the *Alleluia* in the mass even after Septuagesima Sunday, i.e. until Lent, even though this was against the common practice of the Church. In the office they omitted the Apostle's Creed before prime and compline, but retained the so-called Athanasian Creed on Sundays. Contrary to everyone else's practice in the universal Church they celebrated the office on the last three days of Holy Week in their own fashion, using an invitatory, doxologies, hymns and responses at the various hours. Abelard particularly condemned the chanting of hymns at Vigils during this triduum since hymns in general are expressions of joy whereas one should celebrate the Lord's death in grief. He also faulted the Cistercians for discontinuing almost all the customary processions.[64]

Abelard admitted that in the Cistercians' view these innovations were motivated by a search for what harmonizes best with the spirit and the contents of the Rule of Saint Benedict. They were convinced that they were right when, in carrying out the instruc-

64. PL 178:339f. Cf. Bouton, pp. 145f.

tions of the Rule, they started something new in place of the old.[65]

Like Abelard, Rupert of Deutz (d. 1129–1130) testifies that, contrary to universal practice, the Cistercians kept the *Alleluia* verse even after Septuagesima Sunday, omitting it only after the first Sunday of Lent. He also criticized the Cistercians' habit which seemed to him to be of a "less than white, i.e. dubious and uncertain color," (thus indicating that by making their clothes of coarse undyed linen the Cistercians had returned to the original provisions of the Rule).[66] He found even greater fault with the practice of some Cistercians of abstaining from the daily celebration of private masses, under the pretext of work that had to be done, taking advantage of Saint Benedict's silence on the subject.[67]

Also the Benedictine author who replied to Saint Bernard's *Apologia* around the year 1127—it was probably Hugh of Amiens (d. 1164)—stresses the puritan character of the early Cistercian liturgy in the course of his polemics. Rejecting Bernard's accusation that the Cluniacs' taking a morning sleep was unwarranted, he retorted that the Cistercians have only one reason for not needing such a practice; their Vigils are so short that they have sufficient time for a long night's sleep. For the Cistercians say only the very few psalms prescribed by the Rule, making no additions to matins and abstaining from the recitation of the so-called *psalmi familiares*, the Vigils of the Dead and the chanting of the hymns used by the universal Church. Since their office consists only of a few psalms and not much else, they are able to spend almost the whole night in sleep. In the heat of the argument the author twice states that the Cistercians eliminated all traditional additions to the office, saying only the parts Saint Benedict had prescribed in his Rule.[68]

65. "Si haec vestra novitas ac singularitas ab antiquitate recedat aliorum, quam rationi plurimum et tenori regulae creditis concordare: nec curatis quantacumque admiratione super hoc alii moveantur." PL 178:339.

66. *Super quaedam capitula Regulae divi Benedicti abbatis, libri III*, PL 170:521.

67. *Ibid.*, PL 170:511.

68. "In noctem quoque profundiorem secure poterit dormitio, quia pauculi tantum psalmi quos regula praecipit, nec amplius aliquid est ruminandum in matutinis. Psalmi pro familiaribus, vigiliae pro defunctis gloriosae

In the *Dialogus inter Cluniacensem monachum et Cisterciensem*, written in 1171, the debating Cluniac monk voiced in disapproval to his Cistercian counterpart that the Cluniac prime alone, with its litany and attached prayers, was longer than the entire canonical office of the Cistercians, minus their conventual mass and vespers. The Cistercian speaker justified this situation by referring to his Order's fidelity to the intentions of Saint Benedict who used great moderation in setting up the divine office. While the Cistercians faithfully adhered to this legacy, the Cluniacs have abandoned it and thus became the victims of excess and immoderation. For whatever goes against reason, and the institutes of the great Fathers of monasticism, cannot be called religious devotion. Hence, if additions are made to the number of psalms established by the elders, the monk in choir is likely to think more about when the psalmody will end and rest for his tired body than the usefulness and advantages of prayer.[69]

Meanwhile, i.e. by 1132, the voices grew stronger within the Order to revise the already reformed Cistercian antiphonary, for reasons which were all in line with the postulates of contemporary music theory. The demand grew out of such objections as "grave and multiple inconsistencies," "melodies contrary to the rules of singing," "lack of intensity," "great dissolution," "many errors," "false melodies," "faulty passages," "unlawful licenses," and ineptitude. According to the critics, this caused "sloth and dislike" in its users, "and novices studying the text and the melodies of this antiphonary remained ignorant and fell victims to sloth and drowsiness in the choir."[70]

---

denique quas ecclesia recipit cantilenae minime decantantur; sed puris perrarisque psalmis decursis, totam ferme noctem dormitando consumitis." André Wilmart, "Une reposte de l'ancien monachisme au manifeste de Saint Bernard," *Revue Bénédictine*, 50 (1934), p. 335. Cf. François Kovács, "Rélation entre l'Officium defunctorum fériale et la liturgie cistercienne primitive," *Analecta Sacri Ordinis Cisterciensis,* 7 (1951), p. 81.

69. Edmundus Martène and Ursinus Durand, *Thesaurus Novus Anecdotorum* (Paris: F. Delaulne, 1717), vol. 5, cols. 1599, 1601.

70. "Praefatio seu Tractatus de Cantu seu Correctione Antiphonarii," *Nomasticon Cisterciense,* p. 246 (hereafter cited "Tractatus de Cantu"). Cf. also

Possibly over the objections of Stephen Harding and the first reformers of the Cistercian chant, the general chapter between the years 1132 and 1148 decided that the antiphonary of Metz "must be changed and corrected."[71] The solution envisioned however, was not the adoption of another available antiphonary since nearly all of the latter were "equally faulty," but the revision of the first Cistercian antiphonary, edited by Stephen Harding, on the basis of the manuscript tradition.[72]

The task was entrusted to Bernard of Clairvaux who in turn enlisted the help of "brethren most learned and skilled in the art of singing,"[73] probably that of Guy, abbot of Cherlieu, and of Guy d'Eu, a monk of Longpont, who had been a religious under Bernard at Clairvaux. It is even possible that the abbot of Cherlieu and the monk of Longpont "were the sole correctors of the antiphonary."[74]

In their work the correctors were guided by a number of principles. They first of all sought to restore *modal unity* where a melody began in one mode and ended in another, by concluding the melody in the same mode.[75] Next they stressed the *law of range*, by enforcing the decachord in their chant. The reason for this was "the authority of the Psalter," the endeavor to ensure "equal value to the notes" (so that both lower and higher notes could be heard), and "the problem of notation" posed by the need for supplementary lines where melodies exceeded the decachord.[76] In application of this principle the correctors also prohibited the mixing of authentic (original) and plagal (derived) modes, for such a combination, the result of a faulty composition, led to excessive

---

ibid., p. 245 and "Prologus in Antiphonarium," *Sancti Bernardi Opera*, (ed. J. Leclercq and H. Rochais, vol. 3 (Rome: Editiones Cistercienses, 1963), p. 515; trans. C. Waddell in *The Works of Bernard of Clairvaux*, vol. 1. (Cistercian Fathers Series 1) p. 161.

71. "Prologus in Antiphonarium," p. 515. Cf. Canivez, p. 306.
72. "Tractatus de Cantu," p. 257. See also Marosszéki, p. 129.
73. "Prologus in Antiphonarium," p. 515.
74. Marosszéki, p. 13. For more details see *ibid.*, pp. 10ff.
75. "Tractatus de Cantu," p. 246. Cf. Marosszéki, pp. 49–61.
76. "Tractatus de Cantu," pp. 252ff. Cf. Marosszéki, pp. 62ff.

C

ranges, to melodies ascending and descending against the rules of music.[77] Thirdly, they eliminated the so-called "round b" (b *rotundum*) in their notation in accordance with the rule that "no chant shall be written with a round b if it can be written without it." This forced the reviewers to transcribe a great number of melodies and systematically modify the customary notation.[78] Finally, the correctors made erasures, amputations and simplifications where the chant was "faulty, irregular and unsystematic" and wherever the same text occurred more than once. They felt, in this instance, it was better to eliminate faulty notes rather than to modify them.[79] In R. Trilhe's summation, the aim of the correctors was: (1) to avoid a repetition of the same text; (2) to replace identical passages by other ones; (3) to change the texts which lacked the desired literary genre or were unsuited to be noted in conformity with the demands of music theory; and to suppress texts borrowed from books of the imagination or apocryphal writings.[80] In enforcing these principles they suppressed a number of long vocalizations (*jubilus, cauda*), i.e. entire musical structures, and simplified redundant strophic notes. Since the corrections were "not too numerous, they could easily be made on the manuscripts in use, by erasing the passages that had to be modified. Thus they could also satisfy the demands of Cistercian poverty."[81]

The ideas for these measures came to a great extent from the writings of such theoreticians as Regino of Prüm (d. 915), Odo of Cluny (d. 942), Berno of Reichenau (d. 1048), Guido of Arezzo (d. 1050) and Jean Cotton who lived in the middle of the eleventh century.[82] The first principle of the Cistercian reformers (modal unity) was, for instance, proclaimed and taught by nearly all the theoreticians since the ninth century, though no action was taken on their recommendations. The second principle (range) made its

77. "Tractatus de Cantu," p. 252.
78. *Ibid.*, pp. 248f. Cf. Marosszéki, pp. 70ff.
79. "Tractatus de Cantu," pp. 245f. See also Marosszéki, pp. 73ff.
80. DACL, vol. 3, p. 1782, n. 9.
81. Marosszéki, p. 132.
82. *Ibid.*, pp. 81–87.

appearance only in the middle of the eleventh century. The third
and fourth principles (no "round b" simplification), however, were
not clearly defined by the theoreticians; they were actually formulated by the Cistercian reformers who made general rules of
them.[83]

The end product of this revision was a new antiphonary "different
from that of other churches." Still, the correctors "felt impelled"
to introduce these modifications "contrary to usage," for to them
it was more important "to follow the nature [of a thing] than to
emulate usages"; it was better to make changes "rather than go
against the integrity of nature."[84] And therein lies the difference
between the reform of Stephen Harding and the correction associated with Saint Bernard. Stephen Harding looked for authenticity,
for the true chant of Saint Gregory and saw it in the manuscript
tradition, in the authority of the manuscripts. His antiphonary was
well-rounded, stable and homogeneous, confirmed by authority.
The reformers of the second correction had the same desire for
truth, but in view of the great diversity of the manuscripts they
preferred to follow the experts of music theory who were familiar
with the internal nature of music.[85]

The revision ordered by the general chapter was debated in a
subsequent chapter where the reformers, i.e. the followers of the
theoreticians, presented their first draft. Then in a discussion
between the advocates of the two schools modifications were
agreed upon to find a common ground. Thus, on the insistence of
the old school, many features were "retained from the old antiphonary which were tolerable in themselves, but could be had
much better," as the author of the *Tractatus de Cantu* commented.[86]
The project then received the approval of all. Believed to be
"irreprehensible in both melody and text" and "resplendent with
the integral truth of the rules [of music]," it was "unanimously
received and approved." The chapter also decreed that this corrected
antiphonary be used in all monasteries, i.e. "its text as well as its

83. *Ibid.,* p. 87.   84. "Tractatus de Cantu," p. 257.
85. Marosszéki, p. 129f.   86. "Tractatus de Cantu," p. 257.

music," and prohibited further changes in it "by anyone, in anything."[87]

The effect of this second reform of the Cistercian chant was, first of all, a pronounced *uniformity*, since all room for variation, change and further growth in space and in time had been blocked. Next, the reform imposed a definite *sobriety*. Well defined in all its details, this chant could not face the numerous innovations of the thirteenth and fourteenth centuries with open doors. Besides, the Cistercians of the second reform were children of their age, i.e. of a time when the golden age of Gregorian chant had already come to an end. While on the one hand they still retained a respect for their repertory and desired a definite form of austerity, they had, on the other hand, already lost their keenness for rhythmic nuances and an appreciation for ancient manuscripts. Finally, from a strictly historical and scientific point of view, the reform brought great intentional changes through the elimination of entire melodies and modal alignments, in an application of *a priori* principles over the lead of the manuscripts themselves.[88]

In practice, the chant of the Cistercians was to be—to quote Saint Bernard—"quite solemn, nothing sensuous or rustic. Its sweetness should not be frivolous. It should please the ear only that it might move the heart. . . ."[89]

To ensure the observance of the same customs in all Cistercian houses, the general chapter decreed at an early date that all monasteries must have the same book of usages. A systematic arrangement of these early Cistercian usages began probably between the years 1120 and 1130. In its final form this codification came to be known as *Consuetudines,* a collection which generally includes the so-called *Liber Usuum* or *Ecclesiastica Officia,* the *Instituta generalis capituli,* and the *Usus conversorum.*

87. "Prologus in Antiphonarium," pp. 515f.; "Tractatus de Cantu," p. 245.. See also Marosszéki, pp. 131f.

88. Marosszéki, pp. 132f.

89. Letter to Guy, abbot of Montiéramey, as translated by M. B. Pennington, *The Works of Bernard of Clairvaux,* vol. 1 (Cistercian Father Series 1) p. 181. See also above, n. 58.

The oldest extant text of the *Ecclesiastica Officia* is ms. 1711 of the
Biblioteca Communale of Trent, discovered by Jean Leclercq, and
edited by Bruno Griesser in 1956.[90] The text, comprising some
84 pages (198×128mm), was written in a Cistercian monastery of
northern Italy around the middle of the eleventh century, as can be
determined from an analysis of the handwriting.[91] The origin and
datation of the usages remains unresolved, since there seems to
have been no uniform *Liber Usuum* in 1119. According to B.
Griesser, "It is wholly understandable that around 1119, when the
daughter-abbeys of Cîteaux existed only a few years, the whole
complex of the *Ecclesiastica Officia* was not yet fixed in all its details
or prescribed as a finished collection of statutes. Some practices
may have come into use through oral tradition or daily practice;
in this instance the yearly visitations and the general chapter gave
rise to such a discussion and at the same time guaranteed the unity
of the usages. In other cases there certainly were written traditional
monastic regulations at hand, perhaps taken over, and preserved,
from Molesme. With the steady expansion of the order, a growing
need must have been felt from year to year to have a fixed *corpus*
of liturgical and related statutes, in order to regulate and authorita-
tively describe the daily schedule and yearly life of the monks. It
should not be far from the truth if one places this around the years
1120–1130."[92] Supporting this date is the so-called Breviary of
Saint Stephen, composed before 1132, which has the same antiphons, hymns, invitatories, feasts and antiphonal arrangements as
the *Ecclesiastica Officia*; the second reform of the Cistercian chant
undertaken between 1132 and 1148; the testimony of the oldest
Premonstratensian statutes dating, possibly, from before 1131; and
the introduction of the *officium feriale defunctorum*, on all "non-
twelve-lesson days" around the same time. Also the fact that Trent
ms. 1711 lists only two processions—on Purification of the Blessed
Virgin Mary and on Palm Sunday—is an argument in this connection, since the third procession—on Ascension Thursday—was

90. See above, n. 33.
91. Griesser, "Die Ecclesiastica Officia," pp. 153ff.
92. *Ibid.*, p. 161.

introduced only in 1151, through the instrumentality of Bernard of Clairvaux, as Helinand of Froidmont and Geoffrey of Auxerre, Bernard's secretary and biographer, testify. Finally, the reference to individuals who were "vested in alb" in the monks' choir on certain occasions, e.g. on great feasts, also points to an early date, since the practice—very common in Cluniac monasteries— belonged to the oldest elements of the Cistercian usages which must have reached Cîteaux through Molesme.[93]

The *Liber Usuum* is not an original creation of the Cistercians, but is indebted to and follows the pattern of other monastic *consuetudines* in both form and substance. Like the latter, it seeks a possibly complete regulation of the liturgical year and the monk's daily schedule, particularly his liturgical exercises. It is "a comprehensive work, visibly anxious not to overlook any important field" in its logically arranged 121 chapters. Of these, chapters 1–45 deal, in a continuous sequence, with the liturgical year. The following chapters (46–52) list liturgical regulations of a more general nature (including ordinances on hymns and the Office of the Dead). Next there are prescriptions concerning the mass (chapters 53–66), followed by detailed provisions about the daily schedule (chapters 67–86). Contacts with the outside world, i.e. travel and monastic hospitality, are regulated in chapters 86–88. Chapters 89–101 deal with the care of the sick and with the dying. Those from 102 to 120 describe the duties of the various monastic officials, while the last chapter (121) specified the prayers to be said before and after meals.[94] In general, the *Liber Usuum* displays more clarity and sobriety than other comparable *consuetudines*, by outlining the great fields—e.g. the liturgical year; the daily schedule; the mass; the monastic offices—better than most of its counterparts and by avoiding repetitions with a much greater success. Not wasting words, it lays down the most important monastic principles in a few binding sentences. Strictly legalistic and legislative in nature, it always speaks in the third person, refraining from

---

93. *Ibid.*, pp. 161–74. See also above, n. 33.
94. Schneider, p. 217.

personal comments, introductions and dialogues. Its chapter arrangement proceeds in a strict logical order. From the absence of references to local conditions and colorations, and from the general tone of the provisions, it is easy to conclude that the usages were not meant to be local practices, but destined for many houses. One can also see that individual measures were thought through to see all their implications, that they were the fruit of long experience and reflection.[95]

An analysis of these usages and a comparison with other monastic practices reveals a definite indebtedness of the Cistercians to the Benedictine tradition. Both show a surprising agreement with regard to the great lines of the liturgical year and the daily monastic routine. In addition, the Cistercians purposely retained a number of pre-Cistercian monastic practices—for instance, the allowances made to human nature and the provisions on travel—and regulated minor details in accordance with general monastic traditions. Beyond that, however, they displayed a marked independence from other monastic usages by championing a stricter and more literal interpretation and observance of the Rule, by enforcing a greater simplicity and introducing more restrictions in their usages. Some of these differences were not, however, of a basic nature.[96]

A systematic comparison of individual usages reveals a definite kinship with the "general" Cluniac usages which are equally comprehensive and logical. Both start the liturgical year with the first Sunday of Advent, and have the same sequence of chapters and identical particular usages (e.g. Lent, Holy Week, Easter, procedures in the chapter room, etc.).[97] Some usages are seemingly influenced by imperial monachism; still it would be far-fetched to see in the latter a direct source of the *Liber Usuum*.[98]

Within the general Cluniac tradition, the *Liber Usuum* is definitely related to its Burgundian special forms—i.e. to the usages of St Benignus Abbey in Dijon, Fruttuaria, Bec, and the reform centers of Sigebert—as can be determined from a comparison of the Holy

95. *Ibid.*, p. 95f.   96. *Ibid.*, p. 216.   97. *Ibid.*, pp. 216–41.
98. *Ibid.*, pp. 214ff.

Week services.[99] It also shows occasional agreements with the
Abbey of Cluny in preference to other Cluniac centers in Burgundy,[100] and some similarities with the usages of Vallombrosa.[101]
In the so-called *Agenda Mortuorum*—i.e. the usages dealing with the
illness, death and burial of a monk—Cîteaux, while following, in
a few instances, the traditions of the Abbey of Cluny, often displays
a marked preference for and an extensive agreement with the usages
of Lanfranc and Bec, i.e. the "mixed groups" of Normandy. This
conformity is no definite proof for a direct causal relationship
between the two centers, but may point in such a direction and
could well be substantiated by further research.[102]

It will not be possible to give a full presentation and evaluation of
the *Liber Usuum* in these pages; an outline of its main fields—such
as the mass and the divine office—will have to suffice for our
purpose.

Fourteen chapters (53–66) contain regulations about the mass.[103]
Although Saint Benedict himself did not prescribe a daily high
mass for his monks, the custom of offering such a mass became
soon a general practice in western monachism. While Cluny
celebrated two or three conventual masses, Cîteaux, as a rule, had
only one such mass attended by the community, except on Sundays
and those feast days when the monks did not engage in manual
labor. On all other days, whether they were ferial days or feasts on
which there was work, only one conventual mass was celebrated,
either after prime (in winter), or after terce (in summer). On
feasts of twelve lessons the mass rite was more solemn; then the
celebrant was assisted by a deacon, a subdeacon, and a server who
proceeded from his choir stall whenever needed in the sanctuary.
On ferial days the celebrant had only one assistant, usually a deacon
or a subdeacon, vested in alb.[104]

The early Cistercian mass was not without a number of charac-

99. *Ibid.*, pp. 244–51.   100. *Ibid.*, pp. 251ff.   101. *Ibid.*, pp. 253f
102. *Ibid.*, pp. 73–106.
103. Griesser, "Die Ecclesiastica Officia," pp. 217–30.
104. *Ibid.*, p. 228. See also Bouton, pp. 147f. and Canivez, p. 292f.

teristic features.[105] It began with the *Lord's Prayer*, like every other canonical hour, and was followed, without Psalm Forty-two (*Judica me*), by an ancient form of the *Confiteor*. The *Gloria* and the following *Dominus vobiscum* were intoned at the epistle side of the altar, the *Credo* and the following *Dominus vobiscum* at the Gospel side; only from the Preface on did the celebrant remain in the middle of the altar. The latter did not elevate the sacred species during the consecration, nor did he or the monks in choir—who simply stood facing the altar until the *Lord's Prayer*—genuflect. The kiss of peace was given only to those who received Holy Communion. Communion, always given under both kinds, was obligatory for all brethren on the principal feasts of the year, i.e. Christmas, Maundy Thursday, Easter, and Pentecost. On other occasions—i.e. on Sundays, the feast of the Epiphany, Ascension Thursday, the four principal feasts of the Blessed Virgin Mary, the feast of Saint John the Baptist (24 June), of Peter and Paul (29 June), the solemnity of Saint Benedict (11 July), All Saints, and the dedication of the church—the individual could himself decide whether he wished to go to the Lord's table. Those who for some reason did not receive Communion on Sundays could do so during the week if they so desired.[106]

The mass had its own texts (*Confiteor, Orate fratres*, etc.) and melodies in a number of instances. In their love of simplicity, the Cistercians kept only three melodies for the *Kyrie eleison*, two for the *Gloria* and one for the Creed.

Each day—except on Good Friday, Holy Saturday and the feasts of Christmas, Easter and Pentecost—the Cistercians celebrated a special mass for the deceased religious and familiars of the order. To this they added, probably at a later date, a second daily mass, in honor of the Virgin Mary for all the benefactors of the Order.[107]

Individual priests without official liturgical functions celebrated mass during the time of reading; on feasts of two masses, during

105. *Liber Usuum*, 53, pp. 216–22. See also Canivez, pp. 293f. and DACL vol. 3, pp. 1792ff.
106. *Liber Usuum*, 53, 66, pp. 226 and 229f.
107. *Ibid.*, 21, p. 197. Cf. Bouton, p. 148 and Canivez, pp. 297f.

the Morrow mass (*missa matutinalis*) and, occasionally, even after the offertory of the high mass, i.e. if they had no opportunity to celebrate before that time. They were not obliged and, in fact, did not say (private) mass every day; they omitted it on account of their work load, or for similar reasons.[108]

In the canonical office, which began with the *Pater* and the *Credo*, the Cistercians strictly followed the prescriptions of the Benedictine Rule. Adhering to Saint Benedict's distribution of the psalms, they used the ferial psalms even in lauds and vespers of feasts, though they gave matins its own psalm arrangement on such occasions, in line with the nature of the feast.[109] They took the readings from Scripture and such Church Fathers as Origen, Ambrose, Augustine, John Chrysostom, Leo, Maximus, Gregory and Bede; but while Saint Benedict prescribed Scriptural readings for the First Nocturn, the Cistercians on occasions also used excerpts from homilies in the sanctoral cycle and on Marian feasts.[110] In accordance with the Rule, however, they said Sunday vespers with a single antiphon, and if a feast day occurred on that Sunday, they sang only the first antiphon of the feast with the four psalms. On other days vespers had four antiphons, as prescribed by the Rule. Departing from the Rule, the Cistercians used a *Benedictus* antiphon which they called *in evangelio*, even though Saint Benedict made no reference to it in his Rule. Also, while the Patriarch of Monte Cassino left some freedom to the abbot in the selection of canticles, the *Liber Usuum* settled the question with precise regulations. In the question of hymns, *Jam lucis orto sidere* was sung during prime throughout the entire year. The hymn of terce was *Nunc sancte nobis Spiritus* on Sundays and feasts with no proper hymns; else it varied according to the season or feast, as during the last three days of Holy Week,

108. *Liber Usuum*, 59, pp. 226f. See also Bouton, p. 148; Canivez, p. 295 and above, n. 67.

109. *Liber Usuum*, 68, pp. 230ff. It should be noted here that the versicle *Domine labia mea aperies* is not mentioned in ch. 68. Cf. also Canivez, pp. 297f.

110. *Liber Usuum*, 8, 11, 16 and 39, pp. 183, 185, 188, 190f., 194, 207, 211 and 214. Cf. also Gregor Müller, "Zur Geschichte unseres Breviers," *Cistercienser-Chronik*, 29 (1917), pp. 59f., Canivez, pp. 296f. and Griesser, "Das Lektionen—und Perikopensystem des Stephanbreviers," pp. 73ff.

when *Jam surgit hora tertia* took its place. Sext and none had the same hymns, i.e. *Rector potens* and *Rerum Deus* throughout the year, but the hymn of vespers and compline varied as the occasion warranted.[111]

The *Liber Usuum* confirms William of Malmesbury's assertion that the Cistercians, who retained nothing above the prescriptions of the Rule, recited "the Vigils of the Dead."[112] In fact it prescribes that "the Office of the Dead be said daily," except on feasts of twelve lessons, certain specified days during solemn octaves and the triduum before Easter.[113] The office itself had the same components as the canonical office, though it retained some special features, among them the practice of reciting the Nocturns alternately, i.e. only one at a time, with the first one always at the beginning of the week. The office was originally a community exercise, but in 1157 the general chapter prescribed, if "abbots and monks are away from the community, i.e. on the road or in granges, they may chant (together) . . . the Office of the Dead."[114] In 1186 and 1227 this regulation was extended to the inmates of the infirmary.[115]

Besides this ferial Office of the Dead the *Liber Usuum* also mentions *officia plenaria*, when all three nocturns of the Office of the Dead were recited. They soon disappeared, however, and gave way to the solemn anniversaries of the dead. Trent ms. 1711 lists three such anniversaries: All Souls' Day (2 November); the commemoration of deceased parents, brothers and sisters; and the anniversary of a monastery's deceased abbot. Since no date is given for the last two anniversaries it seems that they were not said on a specific day.[116] It was only around the middle of the twelfth century that

111. *Liber Usuum*, 3, p. 185. Cf. ch. 48, p. 213. See also Bouton, p. 146 and Müller, p. 61.

112. PL 179:1289. See also above, n. 60.

113. *Liber Usuum*, 50, p. 214. See also 19–20, p. 196 and Bouton, p. 146.

114. *Statuta*, vol. 1, p. 60. *Liber Usuum*, 50 and 115, pp. 214 and 275.

115. *Statuta*, vol. 1, p. 105 and vol. 2, p. 56. Cf. Gregor Müller, "Das tägliche Totenoffizium," *Cistercienser-Chronik*, 31 (1919), p.35.

116. *Liber Usuum*, 50, 1, 3, 46 and 98, pp. 214, 183, 184, 211 and 261. Cf. *ibid.*, pp. 170ff. and ch. 52, p. 216f.

the date of the anniversaries became fixed. 11 January was set aside to commemorate the deceased bishops and abbots of the order, 20 November the deceased parents, brothers, sisters and benefactors, and 18 September the deceased confreres and *familiares*.[117]

On the other hand the Cistercians did not originally recite in choir the Little Office of the Blessed Virgin, prescribed by Urban II in 1095 for the success of the first crusade, even though Cluny and the Carthusians had introduced it. This follows from the fact that the Cistercians rejected all additions to the choral office not sanctioned by the Rule[118] and from a statement of the *Exordium Magnum* according to which "it was not yet permissible to recite the hours of the Blessed Virgin publicly" in the time of Abbot Raynald of Cîteaux (1134–1150).[119] In 1157 the general chapter authorized its recitation for those who traveled in a group, and in 1194 for the brethren in the infirmary. But the choral rendering of this office was imposed at a later date.[120]

The *Salve Regina*, a favorite song of the Cistercians, did not at first conclude the liturgical day of the monk,[121] but was chanted only four times a year: during the first vespers of the feast of the Purification (2 February) and the Annunciation (25 March), during lauds on the feast of the Assumption (15 August) and, finally, the second vespers of Christmas. It came to be sung after compline only around the middle of the thirteenth century, and soon developed into a permanent practice.[122]

A comparison of the various "editions" of the *Liber Usuum*, i.e. of Trent ms. 1711 with Laibach ms. 31, shows a definite evolution in the liturgical practices of the Cistercian order. By the end of the twelfth century this evolution culminated in the publication of a *manuscript type*—ms. 114(82) of the Bibliothèque Municipale of

---

117. *Liber Usuum*, p. 171. Cf. Canivez, p. 300.
118. Canivez, p. 300; A. Malet, *La liturgie cistercienne*, p. 53.
119. *Exordium Magnum Cisterciense*, I. 24, p. 95.
120. *Statuta*, vol. I, p. 105 (1157) and p. 171 (1194). Cf. Bouton, p. 146.
121. *Liber Usuum*, 82, p. 246.
122. Canivez, p. 299. Cf. Archdale A. King, *Liturgies of the Religious Orders* (London: Longmans, 1956), p. 112.

Dijon—which contains all the texts and rubrics necessary for the canonical office, the celebration of the mass, and other liturgical and related practices. The note on its first page explains why it was named manuscript type: "This volume contains all the books pertaining to the divine office which must not be different in our order. They were redacted into one volume so that this volume might be an invariable model for the preservation of uniformity and a tool for the correction of diversity in others."[123]

This fixation of Cistercian practices was not absolute, however; subsequent times brought a further evolution. Responsible for this was, in part, the introduction of new liturgical feasts—often at the insistence of popes, cardinals, bishops, other religious orders or secular rulers.[124] Then the general chapter of the order introduced further legislation concerning the mass and liturgical usages in general. Thus it prescribed the elevation of the consecrated host (1152) and of the chalice (1444), and kneeling during the elevation (1232); suppressed communion under both kinds, first for the community (1261), then also for the ministers of the altar (1437); ordered the ringing of the bell during the Preface (1390) and the discontinuation of the *Alleluia* during mass after Septuagesima Sunday (1601). It added new texts and ceremonies in honor of the Blessed Virgin Mary in the office, introduced and rearranged antiphons and, as mentioned, introduced new feasts and offices. It also instituted the practice of excommunicating conspirators, arsonists, thieves, property owners, the enemies of justice, of monastic reform, and of the order in general, in the chapter room on Palm Sunday (1183) and, later, prescribed the recitation of the seven penitential psalms on Fridays.[125] Beginning with the year 1373, the *pontificalia* made their appearance in the order, in opposition to

---

123. Philippe Guignard, *Les Monuments primitifs de la règle cistercienne* (Dijon: Darantière, 1878), title page. Cf. Canivez, p. 276 and DACL vol. 3, p. 2874.

124. Canivez, p. 287.

125. *Statuta*, vol. 8 (Indices). Cf. Malet, p. 52; Canivez, pp. 287, 294; Martène and Durand, *Thesaurus Novus Anecdotorum*, vol. 5, p. 1586, n. 42; and King, pp. 106 and 121.

conciliar legislation of the late eleventh century, and brought new dimensions to its liturgy.[126] Already in the preceding century the general chapter reversed its original prohibition when it granted abbots the right to bless nuns on the day of their profession in a simple ceremony (1231; 1241).[127] In 1260 abbots received the power to confer minor orders on their charges[128] and in 1489 Innocent VIII gave the abbot of Cîteaux the privilege to ordain his monks to the subdiaconate and diaconate (1489).[129] Finally, the invention of printing helped and hastened the appearance of greatly divergent *ordinaria* (collections of rubrics) and breviaries.[130] These factors and a number of related developments not only modified the nature of the early Cistercian liturgy—its Benedictine, eleventh-century and puritan character—but led to great liturgical changes in the order in the seventeenth century.

Bede Lackner so cist

University of Dallas

---

126. Canivez, pp. 287ff. Cf. Lackner, pp. 173 and 175.

127. *Statuta,* vol. 2, pp. 100f. (1231) and p. 231 (1241). Cf. Canivez, p. 305.

128. *Statuta,* vol. 2, p. 462. Cf. King, p. 77.

129. Ms. 311, Montpellier (École de Médicine), fol. 39ff., esp. 54ff. Cf. *Rituale Cisterciense ex Libro Usuum Definitionibus Ordinis et Caeremoniali Episcoporum Collectum* (Westmalle: Typographia Ordinis, 1949), p. 402 (*De ordinatione subdiaconi*) and p. 406 (*De ordinatione diaconi*). Cf. Canivez, p. 289.

130. Canivez, p. 277.

THE SOCIAL THEORY OF
BERNARD OF CLAIRVAUX

BERNARD OF CLAIRVAUX was the leader of
Christendom in the first half of the twelfth century in so
many aspects of the life of the time that it would be difficult
to find a parallel in any similar period. Perhaps more than any other
single event in his life, Bernard's role at the Council of Étampes
reveals the extent of his influence on contemporary society. At this
council Bernard was instrumental in settling the Schism of 1130
and his decision won France for Innocent II.[1] And this was but a
preliminary to Bernard's campaign in Germany, Italy, and Sicily,
a campaign pursued successfully through letters, travels, councils,
and disputations. If in effect Bernard decided who was to be pope
in an age in which religion was as important to society as it was in
the twelfth century, his historical significance is undeniable.

It is not necessary to describe the leadership which Bernard
exercised; that has often been done. His role in launching the Second
Crusade is well known. Many scholars have shown Bernard's great
contribution to theology and his influence on its development.[2] His
letters show Bernard as the preceptor of popes and the conscience
of kings. In short, Bernard was the leader in so many aspects of

---

1. Arnold of Bonneval, *Sancti Bernardi abbatis Clarae-Vallensis vita et res
gestae (Vita prima), Liber secundus* 1, 3, PL 185:270.

2. A good general survey of Bernard's contributions to theology can be
found in E. Vacandard, "Saint Bernard," *Dictionnaire de théologie catholique*,
2, 761–82. A more complete picture may be obtained from *Saint Bernard
théologien: Actes du Congrès de Dijon, 15–19 Septembre 1953 (Analecta Sacri
Ordinis Cisterciensis, 9*; 2nd ed., Roma, 1954), *passim.*

early twelfth-century culture that it is impossible to examine his age without studying him. How, then, did Bernard view the society which he led?

Bernard's social theory is a part of his ecclesiology since he thought of society in terms of the place of each of its elements in the life of the Church. My intention here is to investigate this social theory with special reference to Bernard's theory of the stations of life.

Of course, Bernard included the monastic way of life in his view of society. Bernard was a monk and his joy in his monastic profession was contagious; he remarked to his monks on one occasion:

> Dearest brothers, you are walking in the way that leads to life, in the way, direct and undefiled, which leads to the holy city, to "that Jerusalem which is above, which is free, which is our mother." The ascent, I must say, is difficult seeing as this road runs straight up to the very summit of the mystical mountain: yet its shortness in comparison with other roads renders it, if not absolutely easy, at any rate the least difficult of all. But you, my children, with a joyousness, are not content to walk up this steep incline—you rather run to the top, because you are free from impediments and girded for the journey, because you bear no heavy burdens on your backs.[3]

Bernard's joy in the monastic life was a result of his conviction that in this way he was following the counsel of Christ to ". . . sell what you have . . . and come follow me."[4]

It was at Clairvaux that Bernard felt the greatest joy in his vocation:

> . . . [Here the novice] is no longer an inquisitive onlooker, but a devout inhabitant and an enrolled citizen of Jerusalem; but not of that earthly Jerusalem to which Mount Sinai in Arabia is joined, and which is in bondage with her children, but of that free

---

3. *De diversis, sermo* 22, 1, PL 183:595.

4. Mt 19:21. Bernard used this text to emphasize the merits of the monastic life in his *De diversis, sermo* 27, 3, PL 183:613.

Jerusalem which is above and the mother of us all. And this, if you want to know, is Clairvaux. She is the Jerusalem united to the one in heaven by whole-hearted devotion, by conformity of life, and by a certain spiritual affinity.[5]

However, Bernard's enthusiasm for Clairvaux and for his Order did not exclude an appreciation of other monastic foundations or of different forms of conventual life. Bernard's relations with Cluny have been discussed often, but generally with an eye to his criticism of the Cluniac way of life.[6] Hermans maintains, however, that Bernard's best known work on the Order of Cluny, his *Apology*, was written rather to praise it than to detract from its glory.[7] Although there are some very important criticisms of Cluny in Bernard's writings, still it must be granted that he thought very highly of the life of the Order:

How can I, the most miserable of men "dressed in rags and tatters and living in holes in the ground" be said to judge the world, and what would be more intolerable than to criticize the most glorious Order of Cluny and impudently slander holy men who live in it such praiseworthy lives?[8]

It was not only the Cluniacs to whom Bernard offered his friendship; other Benedictine monasteries,[9] the canons regular, including

5. *Epistola* 64, 1–2, PL 182:169–70.

6. See M. D. Knowles, *Cistercians and Cluniacs: The Controversy Between St Bernard and Peter the Venerable* (London, 1955).

7. ". . . Apologie dus niet *tegen* de Cluniacensers maar veeler *voor* de Cluniacensers." Vincentius Hermans, "De H. Benardus en de stichters van Cîteaux," *Sint Bernardus van Clairvaux: Gedenkboek door monniken van de noord—en zuidnederlandse Cisterciënser abdijen samengesteld bij het achtste eeuwfeest van sint Bernardus' dood,* 20 *Augustus* 1153–1953 (Rotterdam, 1953), p. 44.

8 *Apologia,* 1: 1, PL 182:899. This work is also found in the excellent new edition of Bernard's works now appearing. See Bernard of Clairvaux, *Opera* (ed. Jean Leclercq *et al.;* Rome, 1957–), vol. 3, p. 81. This edition will hereafter be cited as *Opera.* A complete English translation will be found in *The Works of Bernard of Clairvaux,* vol. 1, Cistercian Fathers Series 1.

9. See Jean de la Croix Bouton, "Bernard et les monastères bénédictins non clunisiens," *Bernard de Clairvaux* (Paris, 1953), pp. 219–49.

D

the Order of Premonstratensians and the Victorines,[10] the Gilbertines,[11] and also the hermits,[12] including the semi-eremetical Carthusians,[13] received help or encouragement from him. Bernard justified his cordial relations with religious not of his Order with this reasoning:

> It is impossible for all orders to hold one man or for all men to hold one order. . . . Thus it is written: "In my Father's house there are many mansions." Just as there are many mansions in one house in that case, so in this case there are many orders in one Church. . . . Further, their unity consists here as there in one charity; their diversity, however, consists in the multifold division of orders and operations. . . .[14]

Bernard approved of the various orders not only because of the variety of activity which they undertook, but also because of the individual spiritual and psychological needs of the men who filled their ranks:

> Diverse diseases call for diverse remedies and stronger call for stronger. . . . Therefore I praise and love all orders, wherever in the Church one can live piously and justly.[15]

The fact that Bernard acknowledged that there were different paths to salvation and various legitimate occupations within the religious life is important. Since he made these distinctions in this area of

10. See Jean de la Croix Bouton, "Bernard et les Chanoines Réguliers," *Bernard de Clairvaux*, pp. 263–88 and "Chanoines et abbayes cisterciennes au temps de saint Bernard," *Ibid.*, Appendix 3, pp. 543–47; François Petit, "Bernard et l'Ordre de Prémontré," *Ibid.*, pp. 289–307; and Henry-Bernard de Warren, "Bernard et l'Ordre de Saint-Victor," *Ibid.*, pp. 309–26.

11. Francis Giraudot and Jean de la Croix Bouton, "Bernard et les Gilbertins," *Bernard de Clairvaux*, pp. 327–38.

12. Joseph Grillon, "Bernard et les ermites et groupements érémitiques," *Bernard de Clairvaux*, pp. 251–62.

13. See the two cordial letters which Bernard wrote to the prior and other religious of the Grand Chartreuse, *Epistola* 11 PL 182:108–115 and *Epistola* 12, 182:115–16.

14. *Apologia*, 3:5 and 4:8, PL 182:901 and 904. *Opera*, vol. 3, pp. 85, 88.

15. *Ibid.*, 4:7–8, PL 182:903. *Opera*, vol. 3, p. 88.

greatest concern to him, we might profitably search his writings for a theory of the states of life in general.

Indeed, Bernard made an explicit comment on the legitimacy of the various elements in the social structure of his time, by comparing this life on earth to a sea:

> This large, extensive sea . . . is traversed by three types of men, each by his own means crossing safely. The three are Noah, Daniel, and Job, of whom the first crossed by ship, the second by a bridge, the third by a ford. These three men signify in turn the three orders of the Church. Noah guided the ark, in which I perceive immediately the form of the Church of the just, so that it did not perish in the flood; Daniel, a man of longings, gave himself up to abstinence and chastity, this is the order of penitences and strivings which free one for God alone; Job, also, dispensing well the goods of this world in the married state, symbolizes the faithful laity rightly possessing earthly things.[16]

Bernard identified the three orders of society more explicitly in the following way:

> . . . [The fountain of mercy] is common to all, "for in many things we all offend," and consequently have need of the fountain of mercy to wash away the defilement of our transgressions. "All have sinned," says the Apostle, "and need the glory, that is, the mercy, of God"; and to whichever order we may belong, whether we are prelates, virgins, or married men, "if we say that we have no sin, we deceive ourselves and the truth is not in us." Therefore, since no one is free from stain, the fountain of mercy is necessary for all alike; Noah, Daniel, and Job ought to run to its waters with the same eagerness.[17]

All of these stations of life, according to Bernard, not only required the mercy of God, but were also able to produce heroes of the faith:

---

16. *De diversis, sermo* 35, 1, PL 183:634. *Opera,* vol. 5, pp. 288–89.

17. *In nativitate Domini, sermo* 1, 7, PL 183:118–19. *Opera,* vol. 4, p. 249. See also *Apologia,* 3:5, PL 182:901 (*Opera,* vol. 4, pp. 84–85) and *De diversis, sermo* 9, 3, PL 183:566 for references to these three Old Testament figures whose lives symbolized the states of life.

What suffering can you refuse to submit to when you see so many persons of both sexes and of every age and condition, not only enduring with patience but eagerly welcoming all manner of torments for Christ? Consider the immaturity of boyhood, the fiery ardor of youth, the tenderness of virgins, the feebleness of age, the helplessness of decrepitude; turn your eyes to any state of life you please, you shall everywhere discover a multitude of heroes hastening with fortitude towards the martyr's crown.[18]

Thus Bernard's social theory allowed a prominent place for three different ways of life, that of the prelate, the monk, and the married person. The second of these has been described sufficiently; however, it would be appropriate to investigate the life of the prelate and of the married man, as Bernard saw them, in order to identify them more explicitly and discover their significance for his theory.

Bernard's attitude toward the bishops of his time was one of great respect. However, his respect was not only for the virtue of his episcopal friends but also for their office; he wrote, for example, to Thurstan, Archbishop of York, the following admonition against his becoming a monk:

I praise your desire for quiet and your wish to rest peacefully in the Lord. But the reasons you give do not seem to me in themselves sufficient for abandoning your pastoral care, unless perhaps (which I am sure is not the case) you have committed some grave sin or have obtained the permission of the Holy See, for I am sure you are not ignorant of those words of the Apostle: "Are you married to a wife? Then do not seek to be free of her." No promise such as you say you have made can be binding on a bishop so as to impede the ministry to which he is called. It seems best to me, if I can say so without prejudice to the wiser opinions of wise men, that you should stay where you are and exhibit in a bishop the dress and life of a monk.[19]

When one considers the vigor with which Bernard described the virtues of the monastic state, his attempt to restrain Thurstan's

---

18. *De diversis, sermo* 40, 9, PL 183:652.
19. *Epistola ad Turstinum Eboraci archiepiscopum* (319), 1–2, PL 182:524.

eagerness to join it illustrates well Bernard's evaluation of the
active life of the prelate. Bernard showed in this case that he considered that a bishop received a "calling" and that this calling was
from God. He wrote to Bruno, who had been offered the archiepiscopal see of Cologne:

> You ask my advice, most illustrious Bruno, whether you should
> yield to those who would raise you to the episcopate. But what
> mortal would venture to decide such a matter? Perhaps God
> calls you, and then who would dare to dissuade you? Perhaps he
> does not call you, and then who would dare to persuade you?
> But whether or not he does call you, who can tell except the
> Spirit, who can search even the hidden things of God, or one to
> whom God himself might perhaps reveal it?[20]

Bernard considered the office of bishop sacred. He also saw the
active life as conducive to the salvation of the person in it:

> ... Every one who in this life shows himself so benevolent and
> beneficent, who tries to converse with such kindness among men
> that instead of keeping for himself the graces he receives, he
> devotes them all without exception to the common use, con-
> sidering himself, as St Paul, a debtor alike to friends and enemies,
> "to the wise and the unwise," possesses the "best ointments" of
> contrition, devotion, and piety. Because persons of this descrip-
> tion are useful to all, and humble in all, therefore are they loved
> above all both by God and man, and the fragrance of their
> virtues "shall be in benediction."[21]

However, even though Bernard spoke of the active life with
specific reference to the episcopate, he included all of the secular
clergy, and, indeed, the regular clergy devoted to the active life, in
his praise of this state. He wrote, for example, an admonition to
Oger, a Canon Regular, which resembles his warning to the
Archbishop of York:

> Either you should not have undertaken the care of souls at all, or,
> having undertaken it, you should on no account have relin-

---

20. *Epistola ad Brunonem Coloniensem electum* (8), 1, PL 182:105.
21. *In Cantica Canticorum, sermo* 12, 2:5, PL 183:830. *Opera*, vol. 1, p. 63.

quished it, according to those words: "Are you married to a wife? Then do not seek to be free of her." . . . . You have preferred your own will to the designs of God, choosing quiet for yourself rather than the work for which he has selected you.[22]

Bernard's positive attitude toward the life of action in the world included an approval in principle of the transfer of monks from their contemplative life to the active life; he wrote to his monks at Clairvaux the news of the elevation of the monk Baldwin to the purple:

> Pressed for time and with ebbing strength, my words are broken by tears and sobs, as our dear brother, Baldwin, who has taken down this letter for me, can testify. He has been called to serve the Church in another post.[23]

The "tears and sobs" Bernard shed were not for Baldwin, but because of his own absence from Clairvaux. Bernard's sorrow that his own labors kept him from the contemplative life makes his support of Baldwin's transfer from the monastic to the active life all the more impressive. Bernard did oppose the elevation of another Cistercian, Hugh, to the cardinalate. But this protest was not against transferral from the monastic to the active state but rather specifically against the suitability of Hugh's elevation.[24] In short, Bernard was not only enthusiastic about the life of the monk but considered the active ministry of the secular clergy to be a valid calling.

The discussion of Bernard's theory of the married state is still more revealing of the fundamental principles of his views on society. There is no doubt that Bernard did not consider the continence required of the monastic and active states a necessary condition for salvation:

> Therefore, also, a woman "shall be saved through childbearing" if she continue in faith; and the infant shall be saved by the

22. *Epistola ad Ogerium canonicum regularem* (87), 3 and 5, PL 182:213–14.

23. *Epistola ad monachos suos Clarae-Vallenses* (144), 4, PL 182:302.

24. *Epistola ad dominum papam Eugenium* (273), 2, PL 182:479.

regeneration of holy baptism. The adult who cannot observe continence shall be redeemed with the thirtyfold fruit of conjugal virtue.[25]

However, Bernard did not merely reserve a sort of sociological limbo to the married person. He held that marriage was a state of great importance and involved great blessings; in replying to the assertions of heretics that the marriage of a widow was unlawful, Bernard asked:

Why do you restrict the abundant benediction bestowed on marriage and narrow to the virgin alone that which is allowed to all her sex?[26]

Bernard wrote many letters to those in the lay life—never, as far as I know, criticizing the station of the recipient; for him virtue was a more important index to the worth of a man than his status.[27] This attitude found a theoretical as well as a practical expression; the following statement to his monks shows his insistence on this point:

Virginity is a praiseworthy virtue, but humility is more necessary; and if you are invited to keep the one, you are commanded to practice the other. . . . You can be saved without virginity, but not without humility. The humility, I say, which mourns over the loss of virginity is pleasing to God; but without humility, I am bold to say, not even the virginity of Mary would have been so. . . . If Mary had not been humble, the Holy Spirit would not have rested upon her. It is then evident that she conceived by the Holy Spirit just because, as she herself declared: "God regarded the humility of his handmaiden," rather than because of her virginity: and I conclude without doubt that it was rather by her humility than by her virginity (where both were pleasing) that she pleased God and was chosen by him.[28]

25. *In Cantica Canticorum, sermo* 66, 4:10, PL 183:1099. *Opera*, vol. 2, p. 185.
26. *Ibid.*, 2:5, PL 183:1096. *Opera*, vol. 2, p. 181.
27. See the *De moribus et officio episcoporum*, 2:4, PL 182:812–14.
28. *Super "Missus est," homilia* 1, 5, PL 183:59.

On a less exalted level, but with perhaps even more persuasiveness, Bernard revealed his regard for the dignity of married life by the following preface to a letter:

> Bernard, Abbot of Clairvaux, to his dear friends Mar and his wife, that they may love each other. . . .[29]

However, to limit Bernard's characterization of the lay life to a discussion of his view of the legitimacy of marriage is to restrict his thought to a too literal interpretation of the classification which he generally used to describe this state. Bernard's doctrine of the lay life was more complete. His letter to Mar and his wife, for example, contains the earnest advice to assist the poor:

> It is very certain that sooner or later you will lose whatever possessions you have, unless you send them on ahead to heaven by the hands of the poor . . . . You have not far to look for those who will bear your treasure there, for they who will faithfully do so are at your door, not one but many. God has multiplied their miseries at this time so as to give you an opportunity of laying up treasure in a place of endless joy and inviolable security.[30]

Thus Bernard thought wealth legitimate if used properly; riches, in his view, could be the occasion of the spiritual development which was for him the criterion of the worth of any human activity:

> . . . Let not the rich of this world imagine that the brethren of Christ possess only the goods of heaven, because they hear the Master saying, "Blessed are the poor in spirit, for theirs is the kingdom of heaven." Let it not be thought, I repeat, that heavenly treasures alone are held by these poor, because they alone are mentioned in the promise. Earthly things, too, are possessed by them who, "as having nothing, possess all things." They do not beg for them, as the involuntarily poor, but they own them as lords, and the more truly lords of them the less they desire them. In fact the whole world is the treasure of the faithful soul. The

29. *Epistola ad Mar et uxorem ejus* (421), PL 182:629.
30. *Ibid.*

whole world I say, because both its prosperity and its adversity are equally her servants and cooperate with her for good.[31]

Bernard was, as Bruno James points out, content to work within the feudal framework of his age.[32] Bernard's social theory did not emphasize the lower classes; it rather emphasized the responsibilities of the upper class in which he was born[33] and to whose members most of his letters were directed.[34]

Bernard praised not only the good use of possessions, but also the dedication of the ordinary occupations of the laity to their proper end. Moreover, he held that the laity had a function in society as necessary as the functions of the monk and the secular clergy. Bernard criticized the attempted expedition to the Holy Land of Abbot Arnold of Morimond:

> And if he says that he wishes to keep the observances of our Order in that land and for this reason has taken with him a crowd of the brothers, who would not be able to see that what is wanted there is soldiers to fight, not monks to sing and pray![35]

This indicates that Bernard considered that the monastic way of life was inadequate in areas of activity in which lay persons were proficient. Bernard's attitude is shown by his support of the Templars;[36] since the Templars were members of an Order dedicated to a task that was religious only in its ultimate purpose, it is safe to include them in the general classification of the laity. Thus,

---

31. *In Cantica Canticorum*, *sermo* 21, 4:7, PL 183:875-76. *Opera*, vol. 1, p. 126.

32. Bruno S. James, *St Bernard of Clairvaux: An Essay in Biography* (London, 1957), p. 87.

33. Jean Richard, "Le Milieu familial," *Bernard de Clairvaux*, pp. 9-15.

34. Congar considers that Bernard thought of the laity primarily in terms of the nobility. See Yves Congar, "Die Ekklesiologie des hl. Bernhard," *Bernhard von Clairvaux, Mönch und Mystiker: Internationaler Bernhardkongress, Mainz, 1953 (Veröffentlichungendes Instituts für europäische Geschichte, Mainz, 6;* Wiesbaden, 1955,) p. 89.

35. *Epistola Clarae-Vallensium ad Caelestium* (359), PL 182:561.

36. He wrote for them, for example, his *De laude novae militiae ad Milites Templi*, PL 182:921-49. *Opera*, vol. 3, pp. 213-39.

Bernard thought that if the activities of lay people were done with a good intention they were thereby justified.

Bernard's division of society into three classifications, each with its own duty and, hence, its own justification, is of great importance because it shows that Bernard made clear and self-conscious distinctions between functions in society which did not exclude any of them. This division of functions was accompanied by an ethical factor which weighed the actions of a man as good or evil according to his role in society. This ethical distinction was explicitly stated by Bernard:

> Now so that you may understand me you must know that there are some things wholly good and others wholly evil. . . . Then there are the in between things, neither good nor evil, and these can be indifferently, either well or ill, commanded or forbidden. . . . As examples of them I give fastings, vigils, reading, and the like. But you must know that some in between things can often become either wholly good or wholly evil. Thus marriage is neither enjoined nor forbidden; but once contracted it cannot be dissolved. What, therefore, before the nuptials was clearly an in between thing, after them becomes, for the persons married, a thing wholly good. Likewise, whether a secular person should hold property or not is a matter of indifference; but for a monk it is wholly evil, for he is not permitted to hold property at all.[37]

An interesting example of a practical application of ethical distinctions which Bernard based on his social theory is his attitude toward the decoration of churches. In his *Apology* Bernard made the following reference to Cluniac architecture:

> But these matters are small things; I come to greater abuses. Of the enormous size of their oratories, their great height, their superfluous breadth, their sumptuous polished marbles and curious paintings which, while they distract the eye, impede the recollection of those who should be praying, I have nothing to say. For me it all savors of the worship of the Jews in the Temple.[38]

37. *Epistola ad Adam monachum* (7), 4, PL 182:95–96.
38. *Apologia*, 12:28, PL 182:914. *Opera*, vol. 3, p. 104.

On the other hand, he wrote the following to the people of Rome:

> Consider for what reason, for what purpose, by whom and for
> whose benefit, you have only lately squandered all the revenues
> and ornaments of your churches. Whatever gold or silver could
> be found in the vessels of the altar, on the sacred images them-
> selves, has been torn off and carried away by impious hands. How
> much of all this have you still got in your purses? But the
> beauty of the Lord's house has been irretrievably lost.[39]

On the one hand Bernard criticized the ornamentation of churches
and in the other case maintained that ornamentation contributed to
the beauty of the Lord's house. Bernard made the reasons quite
clear in his *Apology*:

> A monk myself, I will ask you my brother monks what a pagan
> poet asked his fellow pagans: "Tell me, you priests of God, to
> what purpose the gold in your holy places?" And I say: Tell me,
> poor men (if indeed you are poor), what is the gold doing in your
> holy places? We monks are differently situated than bishops; they
> have a duty to their people not all of whom are spiritual, and they
> must try to stir up their devotion by material things. But whose
> devotion do we hope to stir up by ornaments of gold and
> silver . . . we who have left the world and everything precious
> and splendid?[40]

Bernard thus made important ethical and even aesthetic distinctions
on the basis of his social theory.

Bernard's social theory is more important than many others, for
he played a most influential role in his society. This leads us to ask
the question: how is it that a monk could play such a role? How is
it that a man dedicated to withdrawal from the world could have so
much influence on the world? My contention is that Bernard could
lead Europe to a crusade, decided who its leaders were to be and how
they were to act, and influence what its inhabitants were to believe,
because his life embodied many ideals of his age, some of which had

---

39. *Epistola ad Romanos* (243), 4, PL 182:439.
40. *Apologia*, 12:28, PL 182:914–15. *Opera*, vol. 3, pp. 104–105.

not even crystallized until his coming. The ideals of early twelfth-century Europe were largely unified around other-worldly values. Thus it was possible' for one man, who as a monk embodied those ideals most perfectly, to give expression to many of the dominant norms of the society, including that society's view of itself. Because of his genius Bernard was able not merely to reflect his society's values, but to explicate them by forceful expression.

John R. Sommerfeldt

Western Michigan University

A REPORT OF A LOST SERMON BY ST BERNARD
ON THE FAILURE OF THE SECOND CRUSADE

AMONG THE STORIES in a collection of *exempla* found in British Museum Ms Royal 7. D. i. is a brief account of the return of King Louis VII and his barons from the Second Crusade:

> Narratur de rege Francie Lodoluico et baronibus suis quod cum in bello contra sarracenos ab ipsis fugati ad terram suam redirent confusi, in tantum ex hoc grauabantur quod quasi desperabant quia non completa est tunc in eis facta scriptura que dicit: *Quomodo persequebatur unus mille* et cetera (Deut 32:30). Quod cum audiret beatus Bernardus occurrit eis et cepit eis predicare ab isto uersu, themam suum accipiens: *Deus auribus nostris* et cetera (Ps 43:2). *Nunc autem repulisti et confudisti nos, et non egredieris deus in uirtutibus nostris* (Ps 43:10) id est exercitibus, ut quando unus fugabat. x. mille et cetera (Deut 32:30), et asseruit ipsos tunc fuisse fugatos a saracenis, duplici demonstrata, una causa est quia plus sperabant de uiribus suis, quam de dei adiutorio, et frangit deus omnem superbum (Is 2:12), alia causa est quia repulit eos dominus in terra, ut ex hoc attendent sola celestia esse querenda. Quo audito, miro modo rex et barones sui per predicationem uiri dei confortati sunt et per fidem bene firmati.[4]

There is no reason to believe that this story is ltierally true, since the manuscript was written in England in the late thirteenth century

---

1. British Museum Ms Royal 7. D. i, f. 63*v*. The text is printed as it appears in the manuscript, except for capitalization, the substitution of modern for medieval punctuation marks, and the expansion of abbreviations (of which not all, however, are clear).

and the collection of *exempla* was put together, probably by an
itinerant preaching friar, after 1254, that is, over a century after
the Second Crusade.[2] In addition, St Bernard is not known from
other sources to have preached to the crusaders after their return.
The two reasons given by Bernard for their failure, however, suggest that the tale is based upon an authentic tradition. While they
do not correspond precisely to the views expressed by Bernard in
De consideratione and the letters written immediately after the
crusade,[3] they clearly reflect the attitudes found among Cistercians
at the time and could hardly have been made up a century later.
The *exemplum* is therefore of interest not only as evidence of
crusading attitudes in the mid-thirteenth century but also as an
addendum to my article on "The Second Crusade as Seen by
Contemporaries" and to other studies on Bernard's crusading
thought which were published in connection with the octocen-
tenary of his death and subsequently.[4]

These works emphasize Bernard's view of the crusade as a
pilgrimage undertaken by each crusader for the welfare of his soul.
The crusade for Bernard, as Delaruelle said, was "a liturgy before
being a strategy or a policy," "an effusion of divine grace bringing
remission of sins," and an "affair of the interior life, of the salvation

2. Cf. George F. Warner and Julius P. Gilson, *British Museum: Catalogue of
Western Manuscripts in the Old Royal and King's Collections* (London, 1921)
vol. i, p. 185.

3. Cf. Giles Constable, "The Second Crusade as Seen by Contemporaries,"
Traditio, 9 (1953) p. 267.

4. See in particular, André Seguin, "Bernard et la seconde croisade,"
Bernard de Clairvaux (Commission d'histoire de l'ordre de Cîteaux, 3; Paris,
1953) pp. 379–409; Eugène Willems, "Cîteaux et la seconde croisade," *Revue
d'histoire ecclésiastique,* 49 (1953) pp. 116–51; Edmond Pognon, "L'échec de
la croisade," *Saint Bernard: Homme d'Église* (Témoignages: Cahiers de le
Pierre-qui-Vire, 38–39; Paris, 1953) pp. 47–57; Étienne Delaruelle, "L'idée
de croisade chez saint Bernard," *Mélanges Saint Bernard* (XXIVe Congrès de
l'Association bourguignonne des Sociétés savantes: Dijon, 1953; Dijon, 1954)
pp. 53–67; Y. Congar, "Henri de Marcy, abbé de Clairvaux, cardinal-
évêque d'Albano et légat pontifical," *Analecta monastica,* 5 (Studia Anselmiana,
43; Rome, 1958) pp. 1–90; and E. O. Blake, "The Formation of the 'Crusade
Idea'," *Journal of Ecclesiastical History,* 21 (1970) pp. 11–31.

of the soul aspiring to communion with the sufferings of Christ."[5]
It was "a personal engagement to penitence"[6] and "a penitential
progress aimed at individual regeneration."[7]

Bernard's view of the failure of the crusade was likewise fundamentally moral and personal although it has been variously interpreted by recent scholars. Some have said that he placed the
responsibility for the crusade on Pope Eugene III and King Louis
VII; others, that he blamed the crusaders themselves.[8] In the *De
consideratione*, however, while referring to the papal command to
preach the crusade, Bernard clearly stated that the command came
from God through the pope;[9] and although he spoke briefly of the
crusaders' iniquities and punishment,[10] he basically accepted the
disaster as an example of the inscrutable workings of the ways of
God, of which the goodness must be taken on faith. "We all know
that the judgments of God are true," he wrote, "but this judgment
is so deep that I should seem to myself not unjustified in calling
him blessed who is not scandalized thereat."[11] According to
Delaruelle, Bernard was not "disconcerted" by the failure because
it proved a source of spiritual gain,[12] but both his own works and
those of his followers show that in fact he was deeply troubled by
the outcome of the expedition he had done so much to promote.[13]
It reinforced, however, his view of the interior and individual

5. Delaruelle, pp. 58, 66.

6. Congar, p. 80, who also stressed the essentially monastic character of the
crusade.

7. Blake, p. 29.

8. Seguin, p. 406; Delaruelle, p. 59; and Constable, p. 267, citing (among
other previous writers) George B. Flahiff, *"Deus Non Vult:* A Critic of the
Third Crusade," *Mediaeval Studies*, 98 (1947) p. 164, n. 12.

9. *De consideratione,* 2. 1, in *Sancti Bernardi . . . opera omnia* (Paris, 1839)
vol. 1, p. 1021 C. A few lines later he said that Moses spoke to the Israelites by
divine command (col. 1022 B).

10. *Ibid.,* 2. 2, col. 1022 C.

11. *Ibid.,* 2. 1, col. 1022 A; cf. Constable, p. 275.

12. Delaruelle, col. 59.

13. Cf. Constable, pp. 266–67. Willems, p. 146, said that Bernard was so
discouraged that he temporarily even doubted the authenticity of his mission.

nature of the crusade. "For Bernard," Delaruelle said, "one went
on a crusade not to kill but to be killed."[14] The Cistercian Abbot
John Casa-Maria wrote to Bernard that God had turned evil into
good by winning the salvation of many defeated crusaders.[15] That
a spiritual victory was thus won by a temporal defeat was the
attitude generally taken by Cistercians to the failure of the crusade.[16]

This is the view found in the *exemplum* printed above. Bernard,
having heard of the despair of the returned crusaders, who thought
they had been abandoned by God, (and having perhaps also heard
of the reproaches directed against himself[17]) hurried to them in
order to restore their flagging faith. The report of his sermon does
not derive from *De consideratione* or any other known work concerning the crusade, where he used different, though parallel,
Biblical citations, but it follows the same general line of reasoning.
Taking as his text that God has "cast off and put us to shame and
goest not forth with our armies," Bernard explained, first, that
God had punished the pride of the crusaders for relying on their
own strength rather than his aid and, second, that he had rejected
them on earth so that they might learn that their salvation was in
heaven.

These explanations may be compared with other contemporary
e actions to the disaster.[18] One, which is only briefly mentioned in
my article on "The Second Crusade as Seen by Contemporaries,"
is in the Dialogue of the monk, William of St Denis. In reply to a
question from William as to why "hardly anyone survived from
so great a multitude of men and the army of two very powerful
kings and [why] those who escaped the sword and famine returned
without any result," his companion Geoffrey cited a long passage
from Seneca's *De beneficiis*, concerning the defeat of Xerxes in
reece, and then said that the same reasons accounted for the

14. Delaruelle, p. 59.
15. Willems, p. 147; Constable, pp. 270–71; and Congar, p. 82.
16. Cf. Willems, p. 148.
17. Cf. Constable, pp. 266–77.
18. *Ibid.*, 166–67.

defeat of the crusaders.[19] Hubert Glaser, commenting on this passage in his article on William of St Denis, wrote that "the wreck of the crusade was for him a matter of strategy, not, as for Bernard, a result of conduct of life or an emanation of divine justice."[20] The contrast between William and Bernard in this respect, however, should not be overstressed. For while it is true that Seneca discussed the naturalistic considerations of terrain and military tactics; he also attributed Xerxes's defeat to over-confidence and the bad advice of flatterers, and this was probably the point that William (like other users of this passage in the twelfth century[21]) had in mind.[22]

Another point of view is found in the *Life* of the hermit Wulfric of Haselbury, which was written by Abbot John of Ford about 1185–1186 but which records an apparently contemporary conversation concerning the crusade between Wulfric and his friend Alvred de Lincolnia. Wulfric expressed his disapproval of the whole enterprise and cited in particular the judgment on it of God, "Who abandoned the false pilgrims, shaved the heads of the proud, and shamed the great men of the world because they sought not the Lord in truth but polluted the way of pilgrimage in idols."[23] The crusade, Wulfric suggested, was doomed to failure from the beginning owing to the false spirit of the participants. His attitude

19. André Wilmart, "Le dialogue apologétique du moine Guillaume, biographe de Suger," *Revue Mabillon*, 32 (1942) p. 107.

20. Hubert Glaser, "Wilhelm von Saint-Denis," *Historisches Jahrbuch*, 85 (1965) p. 296. He went on to say that for William contemporary history was a matter of human will and wisdom.

21. Klaus-Dieter Nothdurft, *Studien zum Einfluss Senecas auf die Philosophie und Theologie des zwölften Jahrhunderts* (Studien und Texte zur Geistesgeschichte des Mittelalters, 7; Leiden-Cologne, 1963) pp. 106–7. On the popularity of the *De Beneficiis* in the twelfth century, see also L. D. Reynolds, *The Medieval Tradition of Seneca's Letters* (Oxford, 1965) p. 112.

22. Elsewhere in his discussion of the crusade, William also put greater emphasis of the moral aspects and divine intervention: cf. Constable, p. 271.

23. Maurice Bell, ed., *Wulfric of Haselbury by John, Abbot of Ford* (Somerset Record Society, 47; n. p., 1933) chap. 86, p. 112, and, on the date of composition, p. xviii. I overlooked this interesting source in the article cited in note 3 above.

E

Giles Constable

is clearly a long way from that of Bernard, but it also shows a basically moral and personal approach to the crusade. It helps therefore to illustrate the wide range of contemporary opinions about the expedition and its failure.

Giles Constable

Harvard University

A TRANSFORMED ANGEL (X 3.31.18):
THE PROBLEM OF THE CRUSADING MONK

STABILITY IS A CORNERSTONE of the monastic life. No monastic virtue was more strongly commended by St Benedict than was stability, no vice more forcibly condemned than willful wandering by a monk.[1] The monk's permanent residence in his cloister was of the essence of his profession. Exhortations to monks that they remain in their cloisters are a commonplace of monastic writers and ecclesiastical legislators. The monk out of his monastery is like a fish out of water, according to one often cited authority.

Although it was obviously necessary or desirable for monks on some occasions to absent themselves from their cloisters, this was a situation which those who governed monastic communities sought to control most strictly. The crusade, however, was one enterprise which drew twelfth and thirteenth-century monks quite regularly out of their monasteries and involved them in occupations which were startlingly incongruous with the monastic ideal.[2] This

---

1. St Benedict, *Regula monachorum,* c. 1, 51, ed. P. Schmitz (Maredsous, 1955) pp. 38, 113. Even earlier, in 451, the Council of Chalcedon, can. 14, had made it clear that monks were expected to remain in their communities and that they were not to travel about on either secular or ecclesiastical business.

2. Monks were noticed by contemporaries as participating in all of the significant crusading expeditions from the first one in 1095 onward. Normally their participation seems to have consisted mainly in acting as spiritual counsellors and in praying for the success of the crusading armies—*la stratégie spirituelle,* as Paul Rousset called it. The extent of monks' participation in the

paper will examine the regulations and guidelines which, at least
in theory, governed the participation of monks in crusade expeditions.

The participation of monks in the crusade was a natural out-
growth of their participation in pilgrimages, which they often
joined and sometimes led, as is well known.[3] Although the crusade
was counted as a species of pilgrimage, there was concern at the
highest levels of the medieval Church about the abuses which
might arise from the participation of monks in them. St Anselm,
for one, testified to this concern in a letter to some monastic
colleagues:

> I hear, dearest friends, that you wish to go to Jerusalem. Let me
> tell you, first of all, that this wish of yours has no good origin. It is
> contrary to your profession, for you have promised before God
> to remain fixed in the monastery in which you took the monastic
> habit. And it is contrary to the obedience owed to the Apostle,
> who, with his great authority, ordered monks not to take on this
> journey, save for some religious person who might be useful in
> governing the Church of God and instructing the people.
> And even such a person should not go save at the advice of and
> under obedience to a prelate. I was present when the Apostle
> declared this policy.[4]

St Anselm's admonition reflected the policy, in fact, of the father
of the crusades, Pope Urban II, who clearly sought to restrict the

---

crusades, however, has never been studied, although it would seem to merit
some attention.

3. The development of the pilgrimage tradition and its connection with
the crusade is briefly reviewed in my *Medieval Canon Law and the Crusader*
(Madison, 1969) pp. 3–18. On the participation of monks in pilgrimages see
especially Dom Jean Leclercq, "Mönchtum und Peregrinatio im Frühmittel-
alter," *Römische Quartalschrift*, 55 (1960) pp. 212–25.

4. St Anselm, *Epist.* 130 in PL 159:165. A generation later, Peter the
Venerable was likewise concerned about the participation of monks in the
crusade and in other pilgrimages, a theme which recurs in several of his
letters. See *Epist.* 51, 80, 83, 144, in *The Letters of Peter the Venerable,* ed.
Giles Constable, 2 vols. (Cambridge, Mass., 1967), vol. 1, pp. 151–52, 214–17,
220–21, 353–60.

participation of monks and clerics in the first crusade by requiring that they receive the prior consent of their abbots and bishops before enlisting in the crusading expeditions.[5]

The attitude which St Anselm described remained the normative one up to the time of Pope Innocent III, when a sharp change in papal policy took place. Writing to the bishops of the Western Church in 1213, Innocent radically liberalized the existing law governing the crusade vow. No longer was the prior permission of an eccelsiastical authority to be required when taking the vow to go on crusade. According to the new ruling, anyone at all might, if he chose, commit himself morally and legally to participate in the crusade. Having done so, he might then be relieved of his obligation by the pope or his delegate, should it seem advisable that he not participate personally in the action of the crusade.[6] This change in papal policy altered the recruitment and organization of crusade armies in many basic respects.[7] It also altered the juridical situation of the crusading monk.

In the first place, the new regulations made basic revisions in the twelfth-century law of the Church, the intent of which had been clear: a monk had no right to make any vow, including a pilgrimage or crusade vow, without his abbot's consent. This had been the position stated by Gratian (himself a monk) and by the authorities on whom he relied.[8] The commentators on the *Decretum* generally accepted Gratian's position, but some of them considered that there should be a distinction between the right to make a vow and the right to fulfill a vow once it had been made. The former, they thought, was a right which a monk enjoyed, but it was his abbot's

5. Pope Urban's policy is described by Robertus Monachus, *Historia Iherosolimitana* 1.2 (*Recueil des historiens des croisades, Historiens occidentaux*, vol. 3, pp. 729–30), and also in Urban's letter of 19 September 1096 to the people of Bologna, in H. Hagenmayer, *Epistulae et chartae ad historiam primi belli sacri spectantes* (Innsbruck, 1901), pp. 137–38.

6. Innocent III, *Registrum* 16.28 (PL 116 :819–20); Potthast, no. 4,725.

7. The general legal effects of this change are discussed at length in *Medieval Canon Law and the Crusader*, pp. 69–114, as well as by Palmer A. Throop, *Criticism of the Crusade* (Amsterdam, 1940), pp. 83–94.

8. *Decretum Gratiani* C. 20 q. 4 c. 2 and d. p. c. 3.

prerogative to decide whether the vow ought to be discharged or not. If the abbot should decide that the vow ought not to be discharged, the monk was absolved from the obligation created by his vow.[9] This was initially the position of Innocent III, as he stated it in a decretal letter issued early in 1198, just a week after his coronation.[10] It is this refinement of votive doctrine, originating in the legal faculty at Bologna (where Innocent himself had been trained), which formed the basis of Innocent's policy concerning the crusade vow.

Crusade vows were very much on Innocent's mind during the opening years of his pontificate. This can be seen from the series of his decretal letters on this matter which was incorporated in the great decretal collection of Gregory IX, where more than half of the decretals dealing with vows bear the inscription of Innocent III.[11] In his early decretals, Innocent regarded the making of crusade vows by clerics (presumably including monks) as something less than desirable,[12] although he did not flatly forbid them and seemed to regard them as licit and valid once made. He clearly thought it preferable that the vows of clerics be redeemed by payments or other forms of aid to the Holy Land, than that the vows be fulfilled.[13] A few years later, in 1201, he defined his position on this matter more precisely. The guideline to be considered in such

9. Such a construction seems to be implied by the anonymous author of the *Summa Parisiensis* to C. 20 q. 4 c. 2 (ed. T. P. McLaughlin, Toronto, 1952), p. 198. The position is considerably clearer in the *Summa decretalium* of Bernardus Papiensis 3.29.5 (ed. E. A. T. Laspeyres, Regensburg, 1860), p. 114. The *glossa ordinaria* to C. 20 q. 4. c. 2 ad v. *uouerit* held that even vows made before entering the monastery were not be to fulfilled without the abbot's permission, an opinion often cited by later authors as well. The *glossa ordinaria* to the various collections of the *Corpus iuris canonici* is cited throughout this paper from the printed version in the Venice, 1615, edition in 4 vols.

10. *Liber extra* (cited hereafter as *X*) 3.34.6; Potthast, no. 4.

11. See the table of decretals in my paper, "The Votive Obligations of Crusaders," *Traditio*, 24 (1968) p. 95.

12. *X* 3.34.7 (15 March 1198): "Ipsum etiam uotum, quod ex sui for ma sanctum et honestum erat, ex persona uouentis minus licitum uidebatur."

13. Thus in 1198 he wrote, in a section of the decretal cited above but not included in the excerpts chosen for the *Liber extra:* "Minus etiam uotum illud terre orientali uidetur expediens, que plus pugnatorum subsidium quam

matters, he now wrote, was the usefulness of the particular person in the recovery of the Holy Land. Rather than ruling out the licitness of the vows of a whole class of persons, the pope now preferred to treat each case individually. Clerics—including monks—might be authorized to go to the Holy Land if it was clear that they would be useful to the crusading army as preachers or counsellors or if they were rich and would bring numerous warriors in their train. Otherwise, they should not go, even if they had vowed to do so. Rather, they should redeem their promises by making a donation in aid of the Holy Land; unless, of course, the journey had been imposed upon them as a penance for their sins.[14] At this point, Innocent was not so much concerned with the fact that monks were making crusade vows as he was with the criteria for determining whether they should fulfill vows of this kind. By 1213, as was said before, the shift in Innocent's policy was complete. The right to make the vow was conceded; but its fulfillment was restricted by reasonably precise rules and guidelines.[15]

By the end of Innocent III's pontificate it appears that papal policy concerning this subject was clear. It is therefore rather startling to find that the canonical writers of the thirteenth century took so little notice of the changes which Innocent III had made.

---

clericorum, quos et officium et dissuetudo reddit imbelles, ministerium articuli necessitate requirit, quamuis orationibus tuis et aliorum terra illa uehementer indigeat. . . . Credebatur etiam quod terre orientali magis accederet, quod si in tuis et tuorum clericorum procuratoribus fueras impensurus secundum alicuius religiosi arbitrium transferretur in subsidium bellatorum."

14. *X* 3.34.9 (Sept. 1201): "De clericis uero duximus respondendum quod cum clericatus officium eos reddat inhabiles ad pugnandum, nisi uel consilio strenui uel officio predicationis instructi aut magnatum sint obsequio deputati aut usque adeo diuites fuerint et potentes ut in expensis suis aliquos secum ducere ualeant bellatores, magis ab eis expedit redemptionem accipere quam ad uotum illos cogere prosequendum, si necessitas exigit uel utilitas persuadet. Hec autem de uouentibus dicimus, non de his quibus labor peregrinationis in penitentia est iniunctus."

15. Set forth especially in *X* 3.34.7. The glossator, with justice, notes that the position is distinctly odd: "Nota hic ab initio unum mirabile, quod ius commune est ut dispensetur in uoto terre sancte et tamen eius executio nulli permittitur, nisi cum papa specialiter committat."—*glos. ord.* to *X* 3.34.9 ad v. *secundum*.

Time and time again they hark back to the older, pre-Innocentian position. "There are some persons," wrote St Raymond of Peñafort, "who do not have a free power to make vows, so that a monk cannot make a vow of fasting or pilgrimage or anything else; and if he does so he may not carry it out without the permission of his abbot, lest the brethren be scandalized that one person should wish to go beyond the common norm."[16] Similar denials of the monk's right to make the crusade vow, much less fulfill it, were uttered by other decretalists.[17] Hostiensis, in many ways the greatest of them all, was clearly suspicious of the monk who felt inspired to make a pilgrimage vow: "It is to be feared," he wrote of such a monk, "that the spirit of Satan may have taken on the appearance of an angel."[18] Hostiensis was equally clear in his belief that monks were completely inhibited from making vows, save with the permission of their religious superiors.[19]

What is so remarkable in all of this is that the decretalists could so unanimously have hardened their faces against the monk's right to make a vow when, in the opening words of one of the decretals in the very same title of the *Liber Extra* on which they were commenting, there was an explicit assertion that everyone, without exception, was free to make a vow.[20]

16. *Summa de casibus* 1.8.4 (ed. Verona, 1744), pp. 59–60.
17. E.g. Goffredus de Trani, *Summa super titulis decretalium* to X. 3.34 (ed. Lyons, 1519), fol. 153*vb-ra* and particularly Innocent IV, *Apparatus* to X. 3.34.4 (ed. Frankfurt, 1570), fol. 429*ra-rb*: "Item irritatur uotum potestate inferioris, nam monachus uotum facere uel complere non potest sine licentia superioris, siue sit abstinentie, siue peregrinationis, siue quodlibet tale unde posset prebere uiam uagandi, uel scandalizandi fratres, uel minuendo obsequium debitum, 20 q. 4 monacho; imo etiam si ante ingressum monasterii uouisset non tenetur soluere, arg. c. scripture, 23 q. 5 noluit; si autem uoueret dicere unum psalmum, uel aliquam orationem, ubi nihil mali potest contingere, seruet uotum, est enim sibi licitum plus mereri." The last statement is eloquent in its implications for Innocent IV's view of the monastic vocation.
18. *Summa aurea*, Lib. 3 tit. De uoto et uoti redemptione (ed. Lyons, 1537) fol. 177*ra*.
19. *Idem*: "Monachus equidem non potest uotum facere per quod ipsum sine licentia abbatis claustrum exire oporteat."
20. X 3.34.6: "Licet uniuersis liberum sit arbitrium in uouendo, usque adeo tamen solutio necessaria est post uotum. . . ." Further, in X 3.34.11,

Canonical opinion on this matter had come round the full circle when Joannes Monachus (d. 1313) set forth a gloss on the question of whether monks ought to be allowed to make the pilgrimage to Rome in order to receive the Holy Year indulgence. Although Joannes included in his discussion a number of arguments to show that participation in a pilgrimage was perfectly compatible with the religious life, he finally concluded that a monk had no right to go on any pilgrimage, however pious and pacific, unless his abbot felt that it was likely to be spiritually profitable and, accordingly, granted permission for the journey.[21]

Two observations are in order at this point. First, it may be instructive to compare the development of the canon law governing the crusade vows of monks with the law governing the crusade vows of married men.[22] The situation of these two groups was more closely parallel than might at first glance appear. Both were groups of persons whose decision to go on crusade had a direct bearing on their relationship—moral, spiritual, and legal—with another person, whether real (as in the case of a husband and his wife) or moral (as in the case of a monk with his superior and community). The relationship in both cases grew out of a promise. In both cases the common teaching of the canonists up to the time of Innocent III was that an individual of either category could not make a vow without the consent of the other person involved. In both cases Innocent III sought to change the previously existing rules so as to make it easier for anyone who so desired to make the crusade vow. The change with regard to married men was more precisely spelled out and more radical in its effects than it was with regard to monks; for, in September 1201, in the decretal, *Ex*

Honorius III, writing in 1216, made it quite clear that the prior of a religious house required no special permission to make a crusade vow and that he might participate personally in a crusade expedition so long as he was certain that his church would not be endangered by his absence.

21. Gloss to *Extrav. comm.* 5.9.1 ad v. *confitebuntur*. This view prevailed and continues to be reflected in the current discipline of the Church; see *Codex iuris canonici*, can. 606.

22. On the crusade vows of married persons see my paper "The Crusader's Wife: A Canonistic Quandary," *Studia Gratiana*, 12 (1967) pp. 425–42.

multa, Innocent specifically provided that husbands might make the crusade vow and fulfill it without the consent of their wives.[23]

No such special privilege was granted to monks who wished to go on crusade without the consent of their abbots, although monks were surely included among those who were affected by Innocent's more general instructions about the making of the crusade vow, as has been argued above. The difference between the treatment of married men and the treatment of monks on this matter seems to reflect Innocent's *Realpolitik* regarding the crusade. The knights who might be expected to furnish effective military service on the crusade were likely to be married. Hence special and explicit provisions to encourage their service on the crusade were in order, even if this broke with a well established legal and moral tradition of the Church. The need for the services of monks on the crusade was far less immediate and pressing. Hence, while they might be encouraged in a general way by Innocent's policy to volunteer their service on the crusade, the encouragement was neither so explicit nor so forcible as that given to married laymen.

A second observation has to do with the treatment of these two categories by the canonists. The writers who commented on the decretals were notably conservative in their treatment of the crusade and pilgrimage vows of monks. Although the texts which they glossed would have supported some wide-ranging conclusions about the freedom of monks to make crusade vows, those conclusions were not drawn. It is probably no coincidence that a similarly conservative attitude is evident in the commentaries on *Ex multa* and that in both cases the ultimate result was to abrogate the innovations which Innocent III had tried to introduce into the discipline of the Church in its treatment of the crusade vow.

James A. Brundage

University of Wisconsin-Milwaukee.

23. X 3.34.9. In addition to the references given for this decretal in my earlier paper, cited above, it should now be noted that it is also calendared by C. R. and M. G. Cheney in *The Letters of Pope Innocent III (1198-1216) Concerning England and Wales,* (Oxford, 1967) no. 350, pp. 57-58.

THE ORDER OF CALATRAVA AND THE
ARCHBISHOPS OF TOLEDO
1147–1245

IN LESS THAN A CENTURY the Castilian kings Alfonso
VIII (1158–1214) and Fernando III (1217–1252) completed the
reconquest and initiated the colonization and christianization
of the extensive territory lying between the Tagus and the Guadalquivir rivers. Both the military Order of Calatrava and the archbishops of Toledo took an active part in these tasks. Until the
establishment of bishoprics in Andalusia in the thirteenth century
most of the region south of the Tagus fell within the limits of the
Toledan see. At the same time, the central sector, forming much of
the modern province of Ciudad Real, belonged by royal grant to
the Order of Calatrava. By virtue of its affiliation with the Order of
Cîteaux Calatrava claimed exemption from archiepiscopal jurisdiction. Inevitably then, quarrels ensued concerning the tithe, the
erection of churches, the appointment of clergy, and secular
problems such as boundaries, rights of pasturage, woodcutting
and the like. For these reasons the archbishops had to seek a *modus
vivendi* with the Order. This aspect of the Castilian reconquest
merits greater attention than it has hitherto received; the purpose of
this paper, therefore, will be to study the conflicts which arose
between the knights and the archbishops during the century from
the Christian reconquest of Calatrava in 1147 until the general
accord reached by the parties in 1245.

In 1085 Alfonso VI conquered Toledo and restored the archiepiscopal see, but without defining its southern boundary.[1] Sixty-five miles directly south of Toledo, on the left bank of the Guadiana river, stood Calatrava, a principal base for Muslim attacks upon the royal city of Castile. In January 1147 Alfonso VII conquered Calatrava and in jubilation gave the mosque to Archbishop Raimundo of Toledo, who transformed it into a church and appointed ten clerics to serve it. The king also ceded a tenth of royal revenues (tolls, fines, etc.) in Calatrava to the archbishop (13 February 1147).[2] Thus the see of Toledo acquired indisputable rights in the future seat of the Order of Calatrava. The administration of these rights was entrusted to the archdeacon of Calatrava.

Within ten years Calatrava was exposed to the possibility of attack by the Almohads, and the knights of the Temple, to whom Alfonso VII had entrusted the defense, asked to be relieved of that responsibility. In these critical circumstances King Sancho III, who had just succeeded his father, welcomed the offer of Raymond, Abbot of the Cistercian monastery of Fitero in Navarre, to defend the beleaguered fortress. In January 1158 the king granted Calatrava and all its appurtenances to Abbot Raymond and his successors to hold in perpetuity "and to defend it against the pagans, the enemies of the cross of Christ."[3] While Archbishop Juan of Toledo offered indulgences to those who would cooperate in the defense, the abbot

1. Urban II confirmed Archbishop Bernardo as primate of Spain and authorized him to restore sees recovered from the Muslims. Subsequent pontiffs confirmed these privileges. See D. Mansilla, *La documentación pontificia hasta Inocencio III* (Rome, 1955), nos. 24–27, pp. 39–45. Also J. F. Rivera Recio, *La iglesia de Toledo en el siglo XII (1086–1208)* (Rome, 1966).

2. Madrid, Archivo Histórico Nacional, Sign. 987 B, *Becerro de Toledo*, fols. 45r–45v; Sign. 996 B, *Becerro de Toledo*, fols. 83r–83v, and Biblioteca Nacional, Sign. 13042-Dd-61, *Cartas y bulas para Toledo*, fols. 82r–83v. See also *Chronica Adefonsi Imperatoris*, ed. Luis Sánchez Belda (Madrid, 1950), *passim*, and *Anales Toledanos I*, in *Espana Sagrada*, ed. Enrique Flórez, 51 vols. (Madrid, 1754–1779), vol. 23, p. 510. This collection will be cited hereafter as *ES*. Alfonso VII gave a *fuero* to Calatrava later in the year; unfortunately it exists only in a very corrupt form in Archivo Histórico Nacional, Sign. 1341 C–1350 C, *Registro de Escrituras de la Orden de Calatrava*, 9 vols., vol. 1, fol. 4r. Henceforth I will cite this collection as *RE*.

3. *Bullarium Ordinis Militiae de Calatrava* (Madrid, 1761), p. 2. Cited hereafter as *BC*.

gathered his monks at Calatrava and assembled a band of warriors, some of whom embraced the religious life. In this way the military religious Order of Calatrava came into being.[4]

Six years later, García, the first recorded master of Calatrava, obtained a *vivendi forma* from the Cistercian general chapter, thus establishing a bond with the Order of Cîteaux which continued throughout the Middle Ages.[5] Pope Alexander III gave his approbation on 25 September 1164 and exempted the knights from episcopal jurisdiction and from the duty of paying tithes on lands which they cultivated or used for pasturage.[6] In the next decade the Order developed rapidly. Royal donations gave the Order a firm footing in the Tagus valley, extending from Maqueda west of Toledo to Zorita, northeast of the city.[7] Other possessions were acquired throughout Christian Spain but in general the Order's most important holdings were in the modern provinces of Ciudad Real, Toledo and Guadalajara. This was precisely the area which pertained to the archdiocese of Toledo. Naturally Archbishop Cerebruno (c. 1167–1181) and his successors were concerned lest their jurisdiction within the Order's estates be diminished.

In view of the energetic character of Martín Pérez de Siones, master of Calatrava from about 1170/1172 to 1182, the fears of the archbishop were not unwarranted. Pope Alexander III found it necessary to admonish the master ("since you are professed to the Order of Cîteaux") to render to the archbishop that reverence and obedience customarily expected of Cistercian abbots. Although

4. Rodrigo Jiménez de Rada, *De rebus Hispaniae,* 7.14 in *Hispania Illustrata,* ed. A. Schott, 4 vols. (Frankfurt, 1603–1609), vol. 2, pp. 118–19. See my study, "The Affiliation of the Order of Calatrava with the Order of Cîteaux," *Analecta Sacri Ordinis Cisterciensis,* 15 (1959), pp. 178–183.

5. *BC,* pp. 3–4.

6. *BC,* pp. 5–6. The reservation of papal authority (*salva sedis apostolicae auctoritate*) indicated exemption from episcopal visitations, synods, interdicts, excommunications, tithes, etc. See J. B. Mahn, *L'Ordre cistercien et son gouvernement* (Paris, 1945), pp. 128–148 and Georg Schreiber, *Kurie und Kloster im 12. Jahrhundert,* 2 vols. (Stuttgart, 1910), vol. 2, pp. 99–100.

7. For royal charters given to Calatrava see Julio González, *El reino de Castilla durante la época de Alfonso VIII,* 3 vols. (Madrid, 1960), especially vols. 2–3.

this letter bears only the date 29 January at Anagni, it probably should be referred to the year 1174.[8]

One of the major points at issue between the archbishop and the Order was the tithe. In granting exemption to the knights in 1164, Alexander III had used the general formula beginning, *sane laborum*, which implied a total exemption for all lands cultivated by the Order or used for pasturage.[9] But if lands which traditionally owed tithes to archdiocesan churches passed into the hands of the Order, the archdiocese would be deprived of substantial revenues. Apparently Alexander III did not intend to contribute in this way to the impoverishment of the Toledan see. Writing to the master of Calatrava and the prior of the Hospital in the province of Toledo on 10 October 1175, he demanded that they show proper reverence and obedience to the archbishop and his suffragans. In particular he insisted upon the preservation of traditional episcopal rights over the tithe and the appointment of clergy in villages belonging to the Orders or acquired by them in the future, unless such rights were yielded by the bishops or conceded by the Holy See. If the Orders ignored this command, the pope promised to uphold any sentence imposed upon the peasants settled on their estates or upon their churches by the archbishop and his suffragans.[10]

8. The text in *Cartas y bulas para Toledo,* fol. 88r–88v, is published in the appendix. Alexander III was in residence at Anagni in January 1160, 1161, 1174, 1176, 1178. Since the Order did not receive approbation until 1164, the years 1160, 1161 may be eliminated. The general tone of the letter is similar to one of 10 October 1175 on the same subject and for this reason I think it should be dated in 1174.

9. *BC*, pp. 5–6: "Sane laborum vestrorum quas propriis manibus aut sumptibus colitis, sive de nutrimentis animalium vestrorum nullus a vobis decimas aut primitias exigere presumat." *Labores* were cultivated lands which had paid tithes in the past; *novales* were lands newly placed under cultivation from which tithes had not been collected previously. Mahn, p. 107 points out that Alexander III's formula included exemption for both *labores* and *novales*.

10. *Cartas y bulas para Toledo,* fols. 90r–91v. The text is published in the appendix. See also J. Delaville Le Roulx, *Cartulaire général de l'Ordre des Hospitaliers de St Jean de Jérusalem,* 4 vols. (Paris, 1894–1906), vol. 1, no. 485, p. 334.

In effect this decision seriously limited the exemption granted to the Order of Calatrava in 1164. Presumably the knights would not be subject to the payment of tithes on lands from which no tithe had been collected in the past; but on older tithable lands they would not enjoy an exemption unless the archbishop consented to it. Similar difficulties had arisen between the Cistercians and the bishops; for this reason the Cistercians decided to acquire only lands never subject to the tithe and, in the case of tithable lands, to seek agreements with the bishops to whom the tithe was owed.[11]

Alexander III urged such a solution to the controversies between the Order of Calatrava and the Portuguese bishops. King Afonso I Henriques of Portugal (1128-1185) had requested the pope's advice concerning the refusal of the Orders of Calatrava and Santiago to pay tithes to the Portuguese bishops. In his reply, which Erdmann has dated *circa* 1179-1181, the pope declared that the knights of Calatrava, because of their profession to the Order of Cîteaux, were exempt from payment on their cultivated lands; but he urged the king to arrange an amicable composition between the knights and the bishops and he promised to confirm it. On the other hand, he forbade the knights of Santiago to withhold tithes formerly paid to the bishops, as this was contrary to the papal charter confirming their foundation.[12]

A few years later the Order of Calatrava and the archbishop of Toledo concluded an agreement of the type suggested by the pope. Prior to that, however, relations between the knights and the archiepiscopal authorities had become embittered. Upon the death of Archbishop Cerebruno in 1181, the chapter of Toledo sent to the Archbishop-elect, Pedro de Cardona, Cardinal priest of San Lorenzo in Damaso, who was then in Rome, a report detailing complaints against the Order.[13] According to this document, after Cerebruno's death, the Order had seized the estates and tithes in

11. *Statuta*, vol. 1, pp. 86-87.

12. Carl Erdmann, *Papsturkunden in Portugal* (Berlin, 1927), no. 81, p. 254. See also Derek W. Lomax, *La Orden de Santiago 1170-1275* (Madrid, 1965).

13. Pedro de Cardona was chancellor of Castile but while in Rome on royal business Alexander III decided to make him a cardinal; Lucius III

Calatrava and the neighboring villages belonging to the arch-diocese by virtue of Alfonso VII's charter of 1147. The knights had also forbidden the archdeacon of Calatrava to build a church in the cemetery nearby as the people had requested; the knights claimed that the archdeacon previously had given them the cemetery together with a church which had formerly been a mosque. On the contrary, the chapter argued that the church and the cemetery (which had been consecrated for Christian burials after the bones of the dead Muslims had been thrown out) belonged to the see of Toledo. Finally, it was alleged that the Order had prohibited the people of Calatrava from bequeathing any property to the churches where they had been baptized and where they would be buried or to sell any property to the archdeacon. The latter was forbidden to purchase property or to receive bequests *quod est mirabile dictu.* The tenor of these complaints seems to indicate that the Order was determined to harass the archdeacon until he was driven from Calatrava and archiepiscopal rights there were abolished.

Considering the Order's attitude, the chapter appealed to Alfonso VIII, who expressed his astonishment at this usurpation of Toledo's rights. Writing to the master on 12 July 1181, he demanded restitution and commanded the faithful to continue paying tithes to the churches in which they had been baptized.[14] Summoned before the chapter, the master read a papal bull, probably Alexander III's privilege of 1164 conferring exemption on the Order. But then "moved by the shame of the people of Calatrava and of our citizenry who were present, in fraud and deceit," the master made an agreement with the chapter. But rather than observe it, he persuaded Alfonso VIII to intervene once more. The king proposed an accord on 29 September 1181 which he believed acceptable to both parties.

---

actually did so. On 25 December 1180 he was elected as archbishop of Toledo. Rivera Recio, pp. 200–202. The chapter's report to him is found in *Becerro de Toledo,* Sign. 996 B, fols. 82*v*–83*v* and is published here as an appendix.

14. González, vol. 3, no. 928, p. 622, has published the letter.

In the future the archbishop would receive a third of all tithes of bread, wine and livestock in the villages acquired by the Order. The knights would retain the remaining two-thirds as well as other ecclesiastical rights, such as the appointment of parish clergy. On the other hand, the clergy serving churches on the Order's lands would be subject to the visitation, correction and censure of the archbishop of Toledo. The knights consented to these arrangements and commissioned Rodrigo Gutiérrez, the royal *mayordomo*, to act for them in ratifying the pact; the king asked the chapter to send several discreet persons to do likewise.[15] On the same day he notified the *concejo* and *alcaldes* of Calatrava of the proposed agreement.[16]

Refusing to approve the pact without archiepiscopal consent, the chapter urged Pedro de Cardona to inform the pope of the excesses of the Order of Calatrava and of the Order of Santiago, which also claimed exemption from archiepiscopal jurisdiction. The canons expressed the hope that the archbishop-elect, armed with papal privileges, could "extirpate from the roots the enormities" of both Orders. In return for papal confirmation of rights in Calatrava the archdeacon of Calatrava promised an annual payment of fifty gold pieces to the archbishop-elect.[17] Evidently Pedro de Cardona brought the situation to the attention of Pope Lucius III who, on 6 March 1182, announced his intention to investigate the immunities claimed by the military Orders.[18] Within a few months, however, Pedro de Cardona died before he could be consecrated and installed (26 June) and toward the end of the year Martín Pérez de Siones ceased to hold the mastership of Calatrava.

---

15. *Ibid.*, no. 932, pp. 624–25.   16. *Ibid.*, no. 933, p. 625.

17. *Becerro de Toledo*, Sign. 996 B, fol. 83*v*. The chapter complained that the knights did not even wish to give a third of the tithes to Toledo as provided by the king, and they retained the whole of the tithes of Malagón, a village north of Calatrava. The knights of Santiago claimed a papal privilege allowing them to erect churches, to appoint and remove clergy and to receive the holy oils from any bishop. See Lomax, *La Orden de Santiago*, pp. 185–98.

18. González, vol. 1, p. 440, citing the *Liber privilegiorum Toletanae ecclesiae*, vol. 1, fol. 43*v*.

F

These changes perhaps contributed to a more harmonious relationship between the new archbishop, Gonzalo Pérez, and the new master, Nuño, who concluded an agreement on 7 December 1183 in the king's presence. In substance it followed the lines which he had proposed in 1181, but it emphasized especially archiepiscopal rights in Calatrava itself. In all villages populated by the Order between the Sierra de Orgaz and the Puerto del Muradal (roughly the northern and southern limits of the province of Ciudad Real), the knights would receive two-thirds and the see of Toledo, one-third, of the tithes of produce and livestock and of fines for sacrilege. Within the district of Calatrava, however, the archdiocese would receive the tithes of all produce and of the vineyards which the parishioners of Calatrava held. If a taxpayer living in Calatrava committed sacrilege in the estates of the Order, the archbishop would be entitled to remit the entire fine; but if the perpetrator was not a resident taxpayer in Calatrava, the archbishop would receive only his share of the fine, namely, one-third. The clergy named by the Order to serve parish churches were to be presented to the archbishop or his vicar for confirmation or rejection; for any just cause the archbishop could remove a cleric. The clergy were obliged to attend archdiocesan synods, to observe all interdicts, to render a procuration to the archbishop or his vicar according to the customs of the archdiocese, and to conserve archiepiscopal rights in all things.[19]

For many years the compromise of 1183 laid to rest overt controversy between the see of Toledo and the Order of Calatrava. But the preceding quarrels probably convinced Master Nuño of the necessity of strengthening the Order's position. Thus in September 1187 he attended the Cistercian general chapter and requested that Calatrava be incorporated fully into the Order of Cîteaux.[20] In this way the knights could claim, without any legal doubt, all the rights of the Cistercian Order. The assembled abbots consented and affiliated Calatrava with the abbey of Morimond.[21] At Ferrara

19. *BC*, p. 20; *RE*, vol. 1, fol. 84r; *Becerro de Toledo*, Sign. 996 B, fol. 17v.
20. *Variorum ad Innocentium III Epistolae*, PL 217: 283.
21. *BC*, pp. 20–21.

on 4 November 1187 Nuño obtained Pope Gregory VIII's confirmation.[22] The bull specified the liberties enjoyed by the Order, viz., the right to celebrate divine services privately in time of interdict; to erect oratories and chapels, *sine manifesto dispendio vicinarum ecclesiarum*; to bury fellow knights and *familiares* in these oratories; to prohibit anyone to erect chapels, oratories or churches within parochial limits on land acquired by the Order from the Muslims; to present clerics to serve the Order's churches to the diocesan bishop, who, if he found them worthy, had to commit the care of souls to them; in spiritual matters the clergy were responsible to the bishop, but in temporal affairs, to the Order; the right to request from any bishop in communion with the Holy See, the holy oils, the consecration of altars and basilicas and the ordination of clerics. Lastly, the pope confirmed the Order's exemption from the payment of tithes.[23] The incorporation into the Order of Cîteaux and the papal bull of 1187 went far toward defining precisely the status of the Order of Calatrava.

The renewal of Muslim aggression at the close of the twelfth century threatened both Calatrava and the archbishopric. In 1195 after inflicting a crushing defeat on the Castilians at Alarcos, the Almohads occupied the most important fortresses belonging to the Order, including Calatrava itself. About two years later the knights reestablished their headquarters at Salvatierra well in advance of the Castilian frontier.[24] In this precarious situation the master obtained from Pope Innocent III a confirmation of Gregory VIII's bull (28 April 1199) and the ties with Cîteaux were also reaffirmed.[25] Although Salvatierra fell to the Almohads in 1211, the Christian counter-offensive of the following year culminated in the great

22. *BC*, pp. 22–25.

23. On 22 September 1189 Alfonso VIII confirmed his father's donation of Calatrava, defining with some exactitude the limits of the district. The southern boundaries were set at El Viso del Marqués on the east and Pedroche on the west. González, vol. 2, no. 534, pp. 915–17.

24. See my article, "Martín Pérez de Siones, Maestre de Salvatierra," *Hispania*, 22 (1962), pp. 163–70.

25. *BC*, pp. 30–35.

victory of Las Navas de Tolosa which broke the power of the Almohads and opened the road to Andalusia to Christian arms. Reestablished at its original seat at Calatrava, the Order obtained a new confirmation of its privileges from Innocent III (20 May 1214).[26]

The disintegration of the Almohad empire enabled Fernando III, aided by the Order and the archbishop, to conquer the great cities of Andalusia. With the capture of Seville in 1248 the Castilian frontier reached beyond the Guadalquivir river. The newly acquired territories were distributed among those who had collaborated in the reconquest and episcopal sees were reestablished at Jaén, Córdoba, Seville, etc., to further the christianization of the area.[27] Although Calatrava shared handsomely in the partition of Andalusia, the nucleus of its power remained in the *campo de Calatrava*. No longer a frontier province menaced by the ravages of the enemy, the area began to enjoy a more settled and prosperous existence and probably experienced a substantial population increase.[28] In view of these changed conditions the agreement concluded by the Order and the archbishop of Toledo in 1183 seemed no longer satisfactory.

The see of Toledo was now presided over by one of the great prelates of medieval Castile, Rodrigo Jiménez de Rada (1208–1247). Scholar, historian, royal counsellor, he was endowed with great energy and undertook to reaffirm all the rights of his see, beginning with the primacy.[29] Although he had words of high praise for the

26. *BC*, pp. 42–46. See my article, "Sobre los origenes de Calatrava la nueva," *Hispania*, 23 (1963), pp. 495–504.

27. See Julio González, *Las conquistas de Fernando III en Andalucía*, (Madrid, 1945) and his *El Repartimiento de Sevilla*, 2 vols. (Madrid, 1951). Innocent III, on 20 December 1213, allowed Archbishop Rodrigo of Toledo to administer reconquered bishoprics until they received their own bishops. Mansilla, no. 512, pp. 552–53.

28. Jaime Vicens Vives, *Historia económica de España* (Barcelona, 1959), pp. 149–51.

29. See Innocent III's bull of confirmation, March 4, 1210. Mansilla, no. 422, p. 439. Javier Gorosterratzu, *Don Rodrigo Jiménez de Rada* (Pamplona, 1925). Among the possessions listed as belonging to the see of Toledo or in

services rendered in defense of Castile by the knights of Calatrava and Santiago,[30] he did not hesitate to resist their encroachments upon or denial of his rights as archbishop. His long controversy with the Order of Santiago (1231–1243), recently studied by Derek Lomax,[31] was paralleled by a similar dispute with the Order of Calatrava. Litigation between the archbishop and the Order extended over a long time and eventually reached Rome. In 1236 Pope Gregory IX remarked that the controversy had been in progress before various judges for more than ten years, but it had not even reached the *litis contestatio*. At issue were archiepiscopal rights to the tithe, the erection of churches, revenues in Calatrava and other places within the limits of the archdiocese, and the like.[32]

In recent years the Order had obtained further clarification of its rights from Rome. Pope Honorius III, for example, commanded all prelates to observe the Order's privileges and forbade any papal legate to excommunicate, suspend or interdict the knights without his express command. This prohibition was aimed undoubtedly at Archbishop Rodrigo who had been named papal legate and given the responsibility of organizing a crusade against the Moors in Spain. The legate was also forbidden to take any monetary procuration from the Order. In addition the pope forbade parish clergy to demand the *mortuarium* from those entering the Order; with respect to the tithe he declared that the Order did not have to pay tithes for noval lands, that is, lands brought under cultivation since the Fourth Lateran Council (30 January 1221).[33] Gregory IX

---

which the see had property rights were the church of Calatrava; the tenth of the royal rents in Santa Olalla, Maqueda and Escalona; the towns of Talavera, Alfamín, Maqueda, Santa Olalla, Olmos, Canales, Madrid, Alcalá, Guadalajara, Hita, Peñafora, Uceda, Salamanca, Buitrago, Calatalifa, Escalona, Zorita, Calatrava, Almoguera and Alcolea.

30. *De rebus Hispaniae*, 7.27, vol. 2, p. 125, contains a poetic passage praising Calatrava.

31. Derek W. Lomax, "El arzobispo don Rodrigo Jiménez de Rada y la Orden de Santiago," *Hispania*, 19 (1959), pp. 323–65.

32. *Les Registres de Grégoire IX*, ed. L. Auvray, 6 vols. (Paris, 1896–1955), no. 3374, vol. 2, cols. 500–502.

33. *BC*, pp. 52–55.

also extended his protection to the knights and confirmed their right to conduct religious services privately in their frontier churches during a general interdict.[34]

When the suit between the archbishop and the Order came to the pope's attention the Order was undergoing an internal crisis of some importance. King Fernando III had complained to the pope that the prior of Calatrava, a Frenchman appointed recently by the abbot of Morimond, was ignorant of the customs of the country and had thrown the Order into a turmoil. The pope instructed the abbot to correct the situation and promised to send the archbishop of Toledo and the bishops of Segovia and Cuenca to conduct an investigation (14 December 1235).[35] The abbot of Morimond and the Cistercian general chapter upheld the prior,[36] but whether the archbishop and his colleagues intervened in the matter is not known.

In any case tension within the Order continued. A group of knights and clerics protested to the pope that their master had usurped his office and by his wrongdoing had nearly destroyed the religious life of the community.[37] The master in question probably was Fernán Pérez; though his name is not included in the catalogues of masters, he is recorded in two royal charters of 1234 and 1235.[38] The charges against him may have been motivated by his acceptance of the prior appointed by the abbot of Morimond, but there is insufficient information on which to base a judgment. In response to the appeal directed to him Gregory IX appointed the bishops of Osma, Segovia and Baeza to reform the Order in head and members (18 September 1236).[39] What action they took, if any, is unknown.

34. *BC*, pp. 63–65.

35. Gorosterratzu, no. 121, pp. 447–48. *Registres*, no. 2861, vol. 2, cols. 212–213, does not give the text.

36. Angel Manrique, *Annales Cistercienses*, 4 vols. (Lyons, 1642–1649), vol. 4, p. 528; *RE*, I, fols. 97–98, gives a Spanish text of this document. *Statuta*, vol. 2, p. 145.

37. Manrique, vol. 4, p. 527. *Registres*, no. 3320, vol. 2, cols. 475–476 gives only a resumé. The complainants included two future masters, Martín Ruíz (1238–1240) and Fernán Ordóñez (1245–1254), five clerics and six knights.

38. *RE*, vol. 2, fols. 165, 170.   39. Manrique, vol. 4, p. 527.

Meantime, to end the controversy between the archbishop and the Order, "lest it become immortal," the pope had commissioned the Cistercian abbot of Valdeiglesias and his prior to cite the master and knights to appear in Rome by Pentecost, 1236.[40] Although the archbishop personally came to the *curia*, the Order failed to send anyone and after forty days had elapsed the archbishop demanded that the Order be denounced as contumacious.[41] A knight of Calatrava, who described himself as a special envoy rather than a procurator, eventually appeared before the papal auditor, the cardinal-bishop of Ostia, and argued that no process could be instituted against the Order because a legitimate citation had not been received. He pointed out that the master and knights were absent on public business *pro servitio Jesu Christi* and that those entrusted with the citation had refused to present a copy of the papal rescript. He also urged that the case be committed to judges in Spain so that the master could participate personally in the Order's defense. In justification of these arguments it should be pointed out that the knights were occupied in the siege and capture of Córdoba from January to June 1236. Fernando III also interceded with the pope on their behalf, and Gregory IX acquiesced in part by refusing to take action against the Order; but he did instruct the archdeacons of Segovia and Cuéllar and the cantor of Segovia on 6 November 1236 to summon the master and knights to appear before him by the feast of the Assumption in the following year.[42] The Order's representative took advantage of his visit to Rome to obtain papal confirmation *in communi forma* of the Order's possessions; to placate the procurator of Toledo who contradicted the Order's claims, the pope declared that the legitimate rights of that see would not be prejudiced in any way (28 November).[43]

40. I have not been able to locate the text of this commission which is mentioned in later papal letters. Gorosterratzu, no. 124, p. 448, mentions a papal citation to the Order, dated 7 January 1236.

41. *Registres*, no. 3374, vol. 2, cols. 500–502; Gorosterratzu, no. 132, pp. 451–452.

42. *Registres*, no. 3374, vol. 2, cols. 500–502; Gorosterratzu, no. 133, p. 452.

43. Madrid, Archivo Histórico Nacional, *Documentos eclesiásticos de Calatrava*, no. 30; Manrique, vol. 4, p. 529; Gorosterratzu, no. 134, p. 452.

Early in the next year Gregory IX confirmed the abbot of
Morimond's right to appoint the prior of Calatrava (5 January)
and admonished Fernando III not to interfere with the abbot's
jurisdiction (12 February).[44] By 15 August 1237 the Order
apparently responded to the papal summons and sent a procurator
to defend its interests before the auditor, Cardinal Sinibaldo. The
procurator tried to delay the proceedings in every way and then
on the pretext that the master of Calatrava had died, he left the
hearing without permission.[45] The master's name is not mentioned
but it was probably Fernán Pérez. In relating these events in 1239
Gregory IX noted that after the master's death he was succeeded
by the *comendador mayor* who had been present when the summons
was delivered. There was no excuse therefore, for the procurator's
abrupt withdrawal.[46] Pérez probably died in late 1237 and was
succeeded by Martín Ruíz whose name is first recorded on 23 May,
1238.[47]

On the request of the archbishop's procurator, the pope commissioned the archdeacons of Segovia and Cuéllar and the abbot of
Sotos Albos (29 January 1239) to compel the Order to respond
within two months to each article in the *libellus* of Toledo's complaints compiled by Cardinal Sinibaldo.[48] In the meantime the
Order complained of harassment by the archbishop, charging that
his subordinates (in violation of the spirit, if not the letter, of the
Order's exemption) excommunicated, interdicted or suspended
persons having dealings with the knights. The pope forbade these
abuses (30 March 1240).[49] A few months later (4 May) he wrote

44. Manrique, vol. 4, p. 529; *BC*, p. 68.

45. *Registres*, no. 4717, vol. 2, cols. 1212–1214; Gorosterratzu, no. 142,
pp. 456–57.

46. *Ibid.*

47. Madrid, Archivo Histórico Nacional, *Documentos particulares de
Calatrava*, 98; *RE*, vol. 2, fol. 196r.

48. *Registres*, no. 4717, vol. 2, cols. 1212–1214; Gorosterratzu, no. 142,
pp. 456–57.

49. *BC*, pp. 70–71; Gorosterratzu, no. 157, pp. 461–462. The same bull
was sent on 20 April 1240 to the archbishop of Braga and his suffragans.
See Lomax, *La Orden de Santiago*, p. 16.

his last letter concerning this legal hassle. An attempt by the bishops of Segovia and Osma to reconcile the parties had failed and the judges delegated by the pope had threatened to excommunicate the Order's procurator, and the master too, if a response were not given to the allegations contained in the *libellus*. Taking up the challenge, the Order appealed to the pope who instructed the abbot of San Pedro de Arlanzón and the archdeacons of Lara and Palenzuela to calm these troubled waters and to remit the case again to the judges appointed in the previous year.[50]

What action they took is unknown as there is no further documentation concerning this suit for the next five years. In 1243 the archbishop and the Order of Santiago settled their long-standing dispute and this probably facilitated the resolution of the archbishop's quarrel with Calatrava. The agreement concluded on 7 May 1245 by Archbishop Rodrigo and Fernán Ordóñez, master of Calatrava, reflects the willingness of both sides to compromise.[51]

A review of the articles contained in the *libellus* will reveal the essential complaints of the archbishop and will demonstrate the extent to which the Order eventually gave him satisfaction. At the outset the archbishop charged that the knights "who say they belong to the Cistercian Order" did not render canonical obedience and reverence to him as they ought, though they did so occasionally. He seemed particularly distressed because the Order failed to pay tithes. He alleged, for example, that the Order usurped the third of the tithe destined for the repair of churches in Calatrava la vieja but did not use it for that purpose.[52] As compensation he demanded 200 marks. The knights also failed to pay tithes on mills at Toledo, Calatrava, Maqueda, San Silvestre, Cogolludo, Zorita, Aceca and other places; yet he conceded that in those places from time immemorial he and his predecessors had exercised jurisdiction over the churches and the Order had received holy oils and chrism

---

50. *BC*, pp. 71–72; Gorosterratzu, no. 158, pp. 462–63.

51. *BC*, pp. 78–82. See Lomax, *Hispania*, 19 (1959), pp. 323–65.

52. Fernando III took a third of the tithe (*tercias reales*) to finance the reconquest. See Demetrio Mansilla, *Iglesia castellano-leonesa y curia romana en los tiempos del rey San Fernando* (Madrid, 1945), pp. 56–58.

from him and had presented clerics to him for ordination and had paid the third of the tithe to which he was entitled. As compensation for failure to pay tithes on the mills he demanded 1,000 marks. He also declared that even though the Order's tenants paid him half the tithe and were prepared to pay the other half, the Order forbade them to do so. Thus he asked an additional 1,000 marks compensation.

In more than thirty villages in the *campo de Calatrava* he charged that the Order unlawfully held churches to which it had no right whatsoever and collected their revenues and refused to acknowledge his rights as archbishop, except to give him a third of the tithe.[53] He demanded the restoration of those churches with all their appurtenances and endowments and full freedom to exercise his archiepiscopal rights. As compensation for past losses he asked 3,000 marks. In many of the same villages the Order acknowledged his jurisdiction but did not pay tithes.[54] As restitution he demanded 2,000 marks and an additional 2,000 for failure to pay tithes in Maqueda, Zorita, Cogolludo, Almoguera, Aceca, Alfondiga, and Huerta in the Tagus valley. He also alleged that the Order seized revenues in Calatrava la vieja which belonged to him by royal grant and he asked 1,000 marks restitution.

Finally, the archbishop charged the knights with disturbing his possession of the castle of Milagro, with having despoiled him of property between Azuheruela and Villafranca, and of violating the boundaries between Calatrava la vieja and Azuheruela.[55] He com-

53. The villages were Guadalerzas, Fuente del Emperador, Malagón, Villarrubia, Jétar, Curenga (Ureña), Daimiel, Calatrava la vieja, El Pozuelo, Villafranca, Benavente, La Fuente de Porzuna, Corral Rubio, Piedrabuena, Ferrera, Caracuel, Calabazas, La Cañada, Almodovar, Puertollano, El Encinar del Rey, Corral Rubio de Jabalón, El Viso, Alcudía, Villamarciel, Castellanos, La Calzada, Ferran Munoz, Valverde, Aldea del Rey, Fuente el Moral, Fuente el Moral de Darazotan.

54. The list is the same as in the previous note with these exclusions: Guadalerzas, Malagón, Calatrava la vieja, Benavente, Piedrabuena, and Caracuel.

55. Archbishop Rodrigo built the castle of Milagro on the limits of the modern provinces of Ciudad Real and Toledo. In a charter of 6 November

plained that the Order imposed undue exactions and burdensome tolls upon his clergy and tenants and even forbade them to acquire property or to make wills. The Order also established tolls and new markets where they had not been customary and so prejudiced his rights.

The agreement reached by the archbishop and the Order in 1245 resolved some of these difficulties, but ignored many of the specific charges and did not provide any monetary compensation. With respect to the tithe, the Order agreed that the archbishop was entitled to a third of all tithes in parish churches in the Order's estates in the modern province of Ciudad Real. He would also have a third of the tithe and of first fruits from the Order's tenants. The Order would use the other two-thirds for the maintenance of the clergy and the repair of churches. Free will offerings and burial fees also belonged to the Order. Fines for sacrilege would be divided equally between the Order and the archbishop. The archbishop would receive a tenth of the *portazgo* or toll levied at Calatrava la vieja, which had been given to him by the crown.

1214 Enrique I defined the boundaries of Milagro and most of the area in question fell within the western part of the province of Ciudad Real. González, vol. 3, no. 965, pp. 666–68. Years later a dispute arose concerning Corral Rubio which pertained to the district of Milagro but which the Order also claimed. Dependents of the archbishop and the Order cut wood there. An agreement of 23 February 1232 stipulated that until a definitive solution was found the archbishop's rights would not be diminished in any way nor would the Order acquire any additional rights there. *RE*, vol. 2, fol. 157. Both Gregory VIII and Innocent III included Zufera (Azuheruela) in the list of the Order's possessions in 1187 and 1199. *BC*, pp. 23, 30–35. Enrique I, however, on 7 November 1214 ceded to the archbishop mills near the castle of Alarcos and the castle of Zuerola (Azuheruela). González, vol. 3, no. 967, pp. 668–71. This apparently provided the occasion for controversy. Archbishop Sancho of Toledo gave Fuentes in the province of Guadalajara to the Order in exchange for Suferruela (Azuheruela). *Memorial Histórico Español*, 49 vols. (Madrid, 1851–1948), vol. 41, p. 335. Another dispute arose concerning the boundaries of Verta and Bel belonging to the Order and La Guardia belonging to the archbishop. These places were located to the east of Toledo. On 27 November 1238 the parties agreed to appoint six persons, three from each side to determine the boundaries. *RE*, vol. 2, fol. 200r.

Tithes and other sums were to be apportioned in the presence of the archbishop's agent so that he would receive his fair share. If any secular person were employed in collecting these amounts he was required to swear to do so faithfully until they could be apportioned. The Order retained the right to appoint chaplains to serve in the churches under its control. The archbishop or the archdeacon of Calatrava or his vicar had to determine the fitness of the priest before confirming his appointment. If the archbishop were absent from his see and his subordinates delayed confirmation through bad faith, the Order was authorized to install the priest within a week and to seek confirmation from the archbishop upon his return. This was done so that the needs of the faithful would not be neglected. Priests serving in the churches and houses of the Order were required to obey the archbishop and archdeacon as their legitimate superiors. The people also had the obligation of recognizing the archbishop's jurisdiction.

Each year the archbishop was entitled to receive from the Order a procuration for himself and for fifty or sixty animals during four days when he visited the churches. The archdeacon would receive a procuration of ten days, three beyond the Guadiana, seven to the north of the river, when he made his visitation. In every village where there were more than ten households the archbishop was owed the *cathedraticum*, but the chaplains were not required to give him first fruits or other tributes (*pedido*) other than as mentioned above.

The archbishop's possession of churches in Valaga, Pozuelo, Huerta, Nambroca and Bel, all in the Tagus valley east of Toledo was confirmed. The status of the churches in Calatrava la vieja remained unchanged. In lands acquired henceforth by the Order the archbishop would have the same rights over the churches as mentioned above. Finally, he agreed that the tenth of the tolls collected at the watermill of Calatrava la vieja would compensate him for the demands put forward in his *libellus* and he pledged not to adduce them again.

The agreement terminated the long-standing controversy between the Order and the archbishop. Though it did not deal specifically with each of his claims, it did confirm his essential rights with respect to tithes, confirmation of clergy, procurations, *cathedraticum* and temporalities ceded by Alfonso VII. A comparison of this accord with the earlier one of 1183 reveals no substantial difference. Both texts followed the guidelines proposed by Alexander III to reconcile with the archbishop's jurisdiction the exemption given to Calatrava as an integral part of the Order of Cîteaux. Thus both pacts acknowledged the archbishop's right to judge the qualifications of clergy appointed to serve in the Order's churches and to expect obedience from them. The agreement of 1183 indicated that the clergy would also have to attend archdiocesan synods, observe interdicts and give procurations to the archbishop; in 1245 mention is made only of procurations payable upon the occasion of his visitation of the Order's churches. The thorny question of the tithe was resolved in both instances by giving the archbishop one-third, the remaining two-thirds to be used by the Order for the maintenance of the clergy and the repair of churches.

In sum, there is a striking continuity of principles expressed in the papal and royal letters relating to the controversy and in the agreements of 1183 and 1245. The archbishop's rights were upheld, though his control over churches and churchmen was probably not as extensive as he would have wished. The Order's exemption was also preserved, though in limited form. Pope Innocent IV confirmed the agreement of 1245 and it served as a model for similar settlements soon after with the sees of Jaén and Seville.[56] Relations between Toledo and Calatrava seem to have been comparatively

56. The pope's bull of confirmation dated 10 July 1245 is found in *BC*, pp. 78–82. In a bull of 7 October 1248 he guaranteed the priests serving parish churches belonging to the Order the right to baptize, to hear confessions and to administer the other sacraments *sine prejudicio alieni*. *BC*, pp. 86–87. The bishop of Baeza, whose see was shortly transferred to Jaén, made an agreement with the Order in 1245. *BC*, pp. 77–78. See other agreements with Jaén, 1252, 1283 in *BC*, pp. 88–89, *RE*, vol. 4, fols. 116–19; with Seville, 1267, 1270 in *BC*, pp. 126–28, 688–89; with Zaragoza, 1276, *BC*, pp. 138–42.

peaceful thereafter and not until the late fifteenth century was a new adjustment found to be necessary.[57]

The resolution of these difficulties owed something to the Order's role in the defense of Toledo against Muslim incursions. From Cerebruno to Rodrigo the archbishops were very much aware of the exposure of their see to enemy attack and of the fact that the knights of Calatrava were primarily charged with defending the approaches to the city. The Order's aggressiveness and its apparent usurpations no doubt aggravated the archbishops and caused them to be especially insistent upon obtaining a binding settlement of their differences. Yet in spite of irritation aroused by the Order's attitudes and behavior, the archbishops still acknowledged the very great services which the knights performed for the benefit of the kingdom and of the see of Toledo. Recognizing this, Archbishop Rodrigo penned these lines in tribute to the Cistercian spirit which inspired the Order in the first century of its existence:

> Multiplicatio eorum corona principis;
> Qui laudabunt in psalmis, accincti sunt ense,
> Et qui gemebant orantes, ad defensionem patriae.
> Victus tenuit pastus eorum et asperitas lanae tegumentum eorum.
> Disciplina assidua probat eos et cultus silentii comitatur eos.
> Frequens genuflexio humiliat eos et nocturna vigilia macerat eos.
> Devota oratio erudit illos et continuus labor exercet eos.
> Alter alterius observat semitas et frater fratrem ad disciplinam.[58]

Joseph F. O'Callaghan

Fordham University

---

57. Archbishop Alfonso Carrillo and Rodrigo Téllez Girón, master of Calatrava, concluded an agreement concerning tithes on 13 January 1482. *BC*, pp. 278–83.

58. *De rebus Hispaniae,* 7.27, vol. 2, p. 125.

APPENDICES

I

1174? 29 January Anagni.

Alexander III exhorts the master of Calatrava to obey the archbishop of Toledo.

(Madrid, Biblioteca Nacional, Sign. 13042–Dd–61: *Cartas y bulas para Toledo*, fol. 88r–88v).

Alexander episcopus, servus servorum Dei, dilecto filio . . . magistro militie de Calatrava, salutem et apostolicam benedictionem.

Cum sis ordinem Cisterciensem professus et artius satagas omnipotenti Domino famulari, decet te sollicite providere ne videaris quicquam efficere in quo tibi vel eidem ordini derogetur. Inde est quod discretioni tue per apostolica scripta precipiendo mandamus quatenus venerabili fratri nostro . . . Toletano archiepiscopo, contradictione et appellatione cessante, eum obedientiam et reverentiam promitas et exhibeas, quam abbates prescripti ordinis episcopis illis in quorum (fol. 88v) episcopatibus sunt eorum monasteria promitere et exhibere noscuntur. Si vero precepto nostro parere contempseris grave nobis erit omnimodis et molestum, nec id quantumcumque predictum ordinem diligamus, relinquere poterimus incorrectum.

Datum Anagnie IIII kals. Februarii.

II

1175? 10 October Ferentino.

Alexander III exhorts the Order of Calatrava to obey the archbishop of Toledo.

(Madrid, Biblioteca Nacional, Sign. 13040–Dd–61: *Cartas y bulas para Toledo*, fol. 90r–91v).

Alexander episcopus, servus servorum Dei, dilectis filiis militibus et fratribus de Calatrava per Toletanam provinciam constitutis, salutem et apostolicam benedictionem.

Licet vos sicut religiosos viros et devotos ecclesie filios diligamus obtentu tamen dilectionis quam ad vos et ad vestras domos habemus, fratribus et coepiscopis nostris sua non debemus iura subtrahere vel auferre. Unde quia cum vos in provincia Toletana quasdam ecclesias (fol. 90v) habeatis, diocesanis episcopis sua dicimini iura subtrahere que in eisdem ecclesiis antequam vobis concesse fuissent habere solebant, nos id sustinere nolentes, discretioni vestre per apostolica scripta precipiendo, mandamus quatenus venerabili fratri nostro Toletano archiepiscopo et suffraganeis eius in ecclesiis quas in eorum episcopatibus habetis ea iura et potestatem tam in solvendis decimis quam in clericis instituendis et in aliis, contradictione et appellatione postposita, conservetis quam ipsi vel predecessores eorum in eis antequam vobis concesse fuissent habere consueverant, nec eis quidquam exinde subtrahatis, nisi quantum de auctoritate apostolice sedis vel de ipsorum concessione vobis esse constat indultum. De cetero quia sicut accepimus vos decimas colonorum de villis quas acquiritis (fol. 91r) sine auctoritate et concessione diocesanorum episcoporum presumetis detinere, nos id indignum et sanctorum patrum institutioni contrarium reputantes, presentium vobis auctoritate precipimus ut decimas colonorum de villis acquisitis vel in posterum acquirendis de quibus episcopi decimas consueverant habere sine concessione diocesani archiepiscopi vel episcopi non presumetis aliquatenus detinere, sed eas eidem archiepiscopo vel episcopo integre permitatis et faciatis exolvi, scituri quod si contra preceptum nostrum veneritis sententiam quam diocesanus archiepiscopus vel episcopus in colonos ipsos vel ecclesias vestras in quibus non est vobis ius episcopale concessum ubi coloni ad audienda divina officia conveniunt propter hoc (fol. 91v) rationabiliter tulerit, nos, auctore Domino, ratum et firmum habebimus eamque faciemus usque ad dignam satisfactionem inviolabiliter observari. Nihilominus etiam vobis precipimus ut archiepiscopo vel episcopo in cuius episcopatu habetis ecclesias debitam obedientiam et reverentiam exhibere curetis, scituri quod si secus quod non arbitramur feceritis grave nobis erit et molestum et vos ad executionem precepti nostri artius, auctore Domino, compellemus.

Datum Ferentini VI idus Octobris.

III

1181–1182.

The Chapter of Toledo addresses a protest concerning the Order of Calatrava to the Archbishop-elect, Pedro de Cardona.

(Madrid, Archivo Histórico Nacional, Sign. 996 B: *Becerro de Toledo*, fol. 82v–83v).

De quibusdam litteris missis domino archiepiscopo a capitulo Toleti.

Venerabili patri et domino P. Dei prouidencia Toletanensis sedis archiepiscopo et Hyspaniarum primati, W. prior eiusdem sedis totiusque conuentus, salutem et debitam obedienciam.

Noscat uestre discretissima paternitas nostram lacrimabilem querimoniam de fratribus de Calatraua, qui hereditates nostras eiusdem uille et decimas parrochianorum nostrorum ibidem commorancium et uillarum adiacencium sua auctoritate et superbia nobis abstulerunt, rege eis inhibente, immo his litteris subscriptis precipiente, quatenus hereditates nostre et decime in eodem statu essent quo fuerent in morte predecessoris uestri C. archiepiscopi bone memorie.

(Alfonso VIII's letter of 12 July to Martín Pérez de Siones, master of Calatrava, follows and is published by Julio González, *El reino de Castilla en la epoca de Alfonso VIII*, vol. 3, no. 928, p. 622).

Quod ipsi facere contempserunt. Uerumtamen magister et fratres capitulum nostrum uocati, coram multis laicis et clericis litteras domini pape audierunt, magistro M. legente, qui eas attulerat. Qui tandem moti uerecundia populi Calatrauensis et ciuim nostrorum qui aderant in fraude et dolo nobiscum composuerunt, panem tamen retinentes, et compositionem non attendentes. Preterea populus suburbii de Calatraua rogauerat archidiaconem ut eis

G

ecclesiam in cimiterio fabricaret, quod fratres facere non permiserit, dicentes terram cimiterii suam esse, cum ipse archidiaconus olim dedisse eis ecclesiam unam que fuerat meskita et terram suam circa circumadiacentem quam ipse laboraverat, ad faciendum sibi cimiterium. Post factam compositionem tamen mentitam has litteras subscriptas a rege impetraverunt ad capitulum (fol. 83r).

(Alfonso VIII's letter of 29 September to the prior and chapter of Toledo follows and is published by González, vol. 3, no. 932, pp. 624–25).

Nos uero rescripsimus domino regi quod nichil poteramus nec debebamus nisi in uestri presencia de rebus ecclesiasticis deliberare. Ad hoc etiam nituntur fratres iacobitani et iam presumpserunt clericos uestros de ecclesiis uestris excipere et suos sua auctoritate intrudere. Unde sanctitati uestre unanimiter supplicamus quatenus utrorumque excessus domino pape insinuetis et eius litteris et priuilegiis roboratus et munitus tam iacobitanorum quam Calatrauensium enormitates possitis radicitus extirpare. Iactant etenim iacobitani se habere priuilegium a domino pape fundandi ecclesias in quibuscumque locis [ubi?] non apparuerint uestigia christianorum et ponendi et deponendi clericos in eisdem et accipiendi sanctum crisma a quolibet episcopo. Unde roborati suo priuilegio mutant antiquiores uillas ubi fuerunt ecclesie et cogunt homines populare alias ubi faciant ecclesias et mittant capellanos suos et sic occupant omnia iura ecclesiastica.

(Alfonso VII's donation of the mosque of Calatrava to Archbishop Raimundo of Toledo, dated 13 February, 1147, follows and is published by Fidel Fita, "Bula inédita de Honorio II," *Boletín de la Real Academia de la Historia*, 7 (1882) pp. 344–47 (fol. 83v).

Fratres uero Calatrauenses inhibuerunt toti concilio eiusdem uille ne darent in testamentis suis ecclesie baptismali ubi sepeliunt aliquam hereditatem nec uenderent archidiacono. Et ipsi etiam archidiacono presenti inhibuerunt ne compararet uel reciperet quod est mirabile dictu. Preterea nos credimus cimiteria christianorum esse ecclesiarum et fossaria sarracenorum esse mesquitarum. Quod si uerum est fossarium sarracenorum quod fuit mesquite facte ecclesie in Calatraua, secundum tenorem nostri priuilegii nostrum debet esse quod denuo populatum est, abiectis ossibus sarracenorum, cuius fossarii populatio nostra debet esse. Et si hoc totum quod datum est ecclesie Toletane in Calatraua potestis impetrare a domino papa, Fredericus archidiaconus dicit et promittit quod faciet uos habere quingentos aureos annuatim. Has litteras subscriptas impetra-uerunt fratres de Calatraua a rege ad concilium Calatrauense ut hac freti astucia omnia iura ecclesiastica possint occupare.

(Alfonso VIII's letter of 29 September to the *concejo* of Calatrava follows and is published by González, vol. 3, no. 933, p. 625.)

Licet itaque mineruam instruere non possumus, nichil omnium consulimus si pro bono uideritis, quatenus litteras ad regem a domino papa impetrare dignemini, ne instinctu et suggestione alicuius Toletane ecclesie iura a fratribus uel ab aliis permittat diminui. Tanta est enim presumptio fratrum Calatrauensium quod de litteris regis predictis roborati, quasi priuilegiatis de decimis quas nobis occupauerunt, nolunt nobis reddere nisi terciam partem et illam non totam; quia totam decimam uille sue Malagun ubi arant parrochiani nostri totam sibi retinent in diminutionem beneficii ecclesie nostre et contemptu persone uestre. Et nisi dominus papa de tanta sepissima presumptione eis penam infligerit littere preceptorie nichil nobis ualebunt.

" PRO DEFENDENDIS ORDINIS"

THE FRENCH CISTERCIANS AND THEIR ENEMIES

T HAT THE CISTERCIAN ORDER suffered a decline in both reputation and influence in the thirteenth century is an indisputable fact accepted by all commentators on its historical past. The cause of this deterioration, as one recent commentator has written, was that its "prestige advanced or declined with the degree to which its ideal was honored."[1] Two recent studies have focused attention on the major literary critics of the Cistercians in England.[2] The reaction of the Cistercians to their critics and enemies and to the problems which beset them in the thirteenth century still needs a thorough study, especially as these important questions relate to the important French ecclesiastical scene.

An institution which sets for itself the very high ideals which motivated the Founders of the Cistercian Order invites for itself in any age an extraordinary amount of criticism and attack. Even the slightest evidence of betrayal of that ideal is considered sufficient justification for exploitation. Indeed, the simple clarity of their ideal—rejection of the luxury, wealth, superfluity of the world as a

1. Coburn V. Graves, "The Economic Activities of the Cistercians in Medieval England (1128–1307)," *Analecta Sacri Ordinis Cisterciensis*, 13 (1957), p. 45.

2. *Ibid.*, pp. 45–54; David Knowles, *The Monastic Order in England, A History of Its Development from the Times of Saint Dunstan to the Fourth Lateran Council, 943–1216*, (Cambridge, 1949), pp. 662–78.

hindrance to their primary spiritual aim of personal sanctification—was difficult to misunderstand. In institutions with such ideals, the admiring world refuses to tolerate human frailty.

The admiration of the Cistercian life in the first period of the Order's existence, to the death of Saint Bernard, is proverbial. In order to remove themselves from contact with the world around them which might prove debilitating to their spiritual aim, the early Cistercians went so far as to insist that their contacts with the local bishop and his clergy be kept to a minimum. The founding fathers of the Order were careful to maintain proper and respectful relations with the local ordinary.[3] The *Carta Caritatis,* for instance, prescribed that "under no circumstances should abbeys be founded in the diocese of any bishop before the bishop himself has confirmed and ratified the written decree."[4] Yet such marks of deference to episcopal honor and authority were made with frequent qualifications which effectively removed the Cistercian Order from the direct jurisdiction of the bishop.[5] There is no doubt that the Order's exemption from episcopal control was one of the most important reasons for the exacerbation of their relations, but other factors also contributed to this deterioration. The unfortunate inability of the Order to maintain the ideals of its Founders became the justification for an attack on it in the last two decades of the twelfth century, and this escalated throughout the thirteenth century. Between the pontificate of Innocent III and the reforming bull, *Parvus fons,* in 1265, the Cistercian statutes revealed a heightened attention to the possibility of scandal in the Order. Indeed, long before Innocent III's pontificate, the ugly specter of scandal threatened. Pope Innocent II, apparently responding to a Cistercian

3. Several Cistercian monasteries in France could boast of their episcopal foundations, thus: Vaucelles (Reims); Ourscamp (Noyon); Longpont (Soissons); Igny (Reims); Loroy (Bourges); Bonnevaux (Poitiers); Loc Dieu (Rodez); Eunes (Auch); and La Clarté-Dieu (Tours).

4. *Les monuments primitifs de la règle cistercienne* ed. Philippe Guignard (Dijon, 1878), p. 79.

5. An adequate treatment of the juridical side of Cistercian–episcopal relations is in Jean-Berthold Mahn, *L'Ordre cistercienne et son gouvernement, des origines au milieu du XIIIe siècle (1098–1265),* (Paris, 1951), pp. 88–101.

request for a ruling, "lest the tranquillity of your Order be shaken by storms of contention." gave the abbots of the Order the power to settle any differences within their monasteries.[6] The first test of such a procedure did not augur well for the future of the Order. In 1165 Abbot Godfrey of Clairvaux was deposed by the abbot of Cîteaux for leading a reprehensible life, whereupon Godfrey appealed for judgment, first to the general chapter, then to the Roman curia which apparently reversed the adverse judgment of the abbots of the Order.[7]

What disturbed the abbots more than individual transgressions of the spirit of the Order was the charge of cupidity levelled at them with increasing frequency at the end of the twelfth century. The Order's involvement in the grange economy after 1150 and the success of this new capitalist venture excited a "general anger against the Cistercians," which was reflected in the concern of Pope Alexander III who wrote them in 1159 of his animadversions concerning their economic activities.[8] Ten years later, in a sharply worded reminder, Alexander III threatened a removal of their privileges unless they proceeded to remove the causes of scandal.[9] The Order was still impressing contemporaries with its charity to the poor, according to the chronicler Guillaume de Nangis,[10] but the gauntlet had formed and the general chapter had to respond. It admonished the monasteries "to impose a bridle on our cupidities and the manner in which we acquire goods," and fearing grave

6. The bull *Ne tranquilitatis,* in *Codex Dunensis, sive diplomatum et chartarum Medii Aevi amplissima collectio* ed. J.B.M.C. Kervyn de Lettenhove (Bruxelles, 1879), no. 56: 25 November, 1132 [hereafter cited as *Codex Dunensis.*]

7. *Statuta,* vol. 1, pp. 75–76.

8. Mahn, p. 110; Jean Leclercq, "Épitres d'Alexandre III sur les Cisterciens," *Revue Bénédictine,* 69 (1954), pp. 68–72. See also the letter of Archbishop Richard of Canterbury to the general chapter accusing them of cupidity, PL 207:252.

9. The bull *Inter universas* was so sharp that the Order apparently excised the more critical parts, according to Jean Leclercq, "Passage supprimé dans une épitre d'Alexandre III," *Revue Bénédictine,* 62 (1952), pp. 149–51.

10. *Chronique latine de Guillaume de Nangis, de 1113 à 1300* ed. H. Geraud, 2 vols., (Paris, 1843), vol. 1, p. 66.

scandal, the general chapter attempted to impose that bridle by urging monasteries not to acquire fields and vineyards from which other churches and monasteries were accustomed to collect tithes.[11] The inference here is clear: other churches and monasteries objected to having their fields, vineyards and tithes taken from them by the Cistercians. Numerous instances can be cited to indicate the conflict between the Cistercian abbeys and the neighborhood around them. Discord was raised on the subject of the possession of tithes and the limits of property holdings between the Cistercian abbey of Clairmarais and its neighbor, the abbey of Saint Bertin, a situation which, according to the chronicler of Clairmarais, was due to the jealousy of her neighbors over the prosperity of the Cistercian community.[12] And the monks of the Cistercian abbey of Foigny, in 1180, sent an appeal to Rome for adjudication of their quarrel with the neighboring monks of Saint Michel on the subject of the boundaries of the forest of Watigny. When a papal commission composed of the bishops of Laon, Soissons, Tournai, Amiens, and Arras, and sixteen abbots of the area decided in favor of Foigny, the monks of Saint Michel refused to accept the decision and attempted to destroy the boundary markers established by the papal commission.[13]

Apparently the admonition of the general chapter of 1180 fell on deaf ears, for in 1191, the general chapter made a stronger effort at attacking and repelling what seemed to the abbots to have been a cancerous growth in their body: the uncontrolled and excessive acquisition of goods. It ordered the monasteries, *firmiter*, to abstain altogether from the purchase of lands and movable goods, but made an exception for pasture lands if they were to be

11. *Statuta*, vol. 1, pp. 86–87, (1180:1).

12. Henri de Laplane, *Les abbés de Clairmarais. Memoires de la Société des antiquaires de la Morinie*, tome XIII, (Saint Omer, 1868), p. 92.

13. *Analyse du cartulaire de Foigny* ed. Edouard de Barthélemy, (Vervins, 1879), p. 6. The abbey of Fontenay was attacked earlier, in 1166, but the reason for the attack is not known. See *Gallia Christiana in provincias ecclesiasticas distributa* . . . eds. Denis de Saint-Marthe et P. Piolin, 16 vols., (Paris, 1856–1899) vol. 4, p. 396.

given as "free alms" by the donor.[14] In the following year, we learn
from the proceedings of the general chapter that the abbots of
Cîteaux and Clairvaux were to petition the archbishop of Reims
for protection as the abbeys of Morimond and Foigny were laid
waste by attack.[15] And when the monastery of Ourscamp, in the
diocese of Noyon, bitterly complained to the Holy See that it was
suffering attack and injury almost daily, and that ecclesiastical
sentences were being softened and then disregarded, Pope Innocent
III, in his inimitable style, sent the encyclical letter *Non absque
dolore* to the prelates of France ordering them to take immediate
steps to grant protection to any monastery being attacked under
threat of suspension from office and benefice.[16] The implication
behind the Cistercian monastery's complaint to the Roman curia
was unmistakable: the French episcopate simply watched the
monasteries being attacked without lifting a finger.

There is no need to speculate on the reasons for such lack of
concern on the part of the French episcopate. For some time in the
last two decades of the twelfth century, the power of order over
Cistercian monasteries was effectively being removed from the
local bishop by apostolic letters.[17] That such a diminution of
function, confirmed by a succession of popes, withdrew an
important source of revenue for the local bishop is beyond question.
We possess no direct evidence that the bishops reacted in any
positive manner against this, but there is every reason to suspect
that their unconcern at the plight of beleaguered Cistercian abbeys
was the reaction typical of a wounded body.

Nevertheless, it may be asked what the local bishop could have
done to protect the Cistercian monasteries from attack. This is not
an easy question to answer with respect to an age where violence

14. *Statuta,* vol. 3, p. 142, (1191:42, 43).

15. *Ibid.,* vol. 2, p. 155, (1192:47).

16. *Cartulaire de l'abbaye de Notre-Dame d'Ourscamp* ed. M. Peigne-
Delacourt, (Amiens, 1865), pp. 297–98, no. 476: 21 June, 1200.

17. Mahn, pp. 73–87 has adequately studied the ecclesiological aspect of
the power of order as it relates to the Cistercian Order.

and the moral suasion of ecclesiastical authority were both powerful stimulants to action and non-action.

Indeed, whereas Innocent III had ordered the French episcopate to intervene to protect the Cistercian monasteries from attack, the abbots of the Order acted as if episcopal intervention was more a danger than an aid. The general chapter of 1203 was faced with the awkward situation of listening to a succession of monks bringing in petitions from lay lords for redress, in the presence of Innocent III, and warning the abbots, some of whom had apparently carried their sorrows to the local ordinaries, that such action invited the danger of servitude, and deposition awaited them.[18] The general chapter preferred to deal directly with the lord in question, rather than through episcopal intermediaries, and if such negotiation became fruitless, a complaint would have to be made to the Roman curia, a time consuming procedure.[19]

The monastery of Ourscamp found no respite in its struggle against its enemies. It complained to the curia directly that it was being molested by lords and bailiffs,[20] in spite of the fact that Philip II Augustus had ordered his bailiffs to protect the goods of Ourscamp,[21] and implored the curia for a proper remedy. Innocent III responded almost a year later by asking the bishops of Beauvais, Soissons, and Noyon to curb the incursions on the monastery by ecclesiastical discipline.[22] The abbots of the Order showed their independence of episcopal interference again by sending direct representation to Rome through the abbots of Ourscamp, Vaucelles Neubourg, and Auberive to argue "the grave affairs of their houses in the Roman curia."[23]

The affair of Ourscamp which apparently lasted beyond the year 1206 showed how ineffective the procedure of appealing for

18. *Statuta*, vol. 2, pp. 284–85 (1203:2, 3).

19. *Ibid.*, vol. 2, p. 286 (1203:12).

20. *Cartulaire d'Ourscamp*, p. 305, no. 489: 4 December 1203.

21. *Catalogue des actes de Philippe Auguste* ed. Leopold Delisle, (Paris, 1856), p. 311, no. 435: March 1195.

22. *Cartulaire d'Ourscamp*, p. 310, no. 501: 27 November 1204.

23. *Statuta*, vol. 1, p. 305, (1204:48).

protection to Rome was.[24] A papacy, willing to defend, but too distant to be effective, an episcopate, smarting over the exempt status of the Cistercian monasteries, and a French crown, also willing but too absorbed in its struggle with the English, left the monasteries to their own defenses. Cupidity and excess had invaded and weakened the life and reputation of the Order, by its own admission. In recognition of this reality, the general chapter of 1194 had called upon the five senior abbots of the Order to lead their co-abbots in a special convocation to discuss remedies for "the excessively sumptuous hospitality" and the excessive number of persons who took advantage of that hospitality.[25] This convocation initiated a discussion on the malaise of the Order which ultimately led to the codification of 1202.[26]

That codification, collating the decisions of past general chapters, focused its attention on the invasion of the *mundus* into the life of the monastery and also the Order's relations with the local bishop. Ironically, the Order consistently argued that the bishop's interference in the life of the monastery left the door open to the entrance of the *mundus* into the monastery. In this struggle to maintain its independence of episcopal interference, the Order was largely successful. Yet, it was a more insidious factor, the very success of the Order itself in captivating the religious sentiments of several generations of Christian laymen, which drove the wedge by which the *mundus* entered the Cistercian monasteries. Pious gifts in the twelfth century, together with successful labor and management brought affluence. This affluence, bringing in its wake a relaxed life-style, had undoubtedly tempted a considerable number of abbeys, blurring the distinction between luxury and necessity. As a consequence, some abbeys may have been guilty of a medieval form of "conspicuous consumption." Excessive debts were con-

24. Complaints of attacks on monasteries that year came from Ourscamp as well as Boquen, in Brittany. See Potthast, nos. 2899, 2914: 24, 26 November 1206.

25. *Statuta*, vol. 2, p. 174 (1194:21).

26. *La codification de 1202 et son evolution ulterieure,* ed. B. Lucet (Rome 1964).

tracted for the purchase of lands or the construction of sumptuous buildings. This situation alarmed the abbots who empowered father-visitors to sell the movable and even the immovable goods of that abbey in order to bring its financial affairs toward solvency.[27]

The inexorable encroachment of the *mundus* on the sheltered, contemplative life of the Cistercian monasteries brought with it a decline in membership, and a decline in material donations.[28] Both situations, according to the general chapters, led to scandal. The remedy, and perhaps defense, chosen by the abbots of the Order was retrenchment. If an abbey had less than the traditional twelve monks, they should be dispersed to other abbeys because of the poverty therein. This in itself is a commentary on the state of the Order in the thirteenth century when one recalls the earlier reputation for austerity gained by it,[29] but, under the circumstances, this regulation would seem sensible and practical.

As for the possession of material goods, as always, these were mixed blessings, and under the conditions the Order then faced, more a problem than a blessing. Donations to the Order meant a wedge by which the *mundus* gained entrance into the monastery. It was as if the *mundus* were demanding an accounting for the privilege of participating in its life. Even when a pious grant was made without conditions, in "free alms," frequently the heirs of

27. *Ibid.*, dist. 7.3, 8. This legislation collected previous decisions of chapters in 1182, 1184 and 1189. See *Statuta*, vol. 1, pp. 90 (1182:9), 97, (1184:13), 115 (1189:115).

28. On the decrease in numbers, see *Statuta*, vol. 2, p. 295 (1204:1.2). The older study of M. H. d'Arbois de Jubainville and M. L. Pigeotte, *Etudes sur l'état interieure des abbayes cisterciennes, et principalement de Clairvaux, au XIIe et au XIIIe siècle*, (Paris, 1858), p. 286, provides the only statistic on the numbers of donations to one Cistercian abbey. Thus, their figures for Clairvaux show a considerable decrease, from 964 donations in the period 1164–1201, to 522 donations in the period 1202–1241.

29. Archdale A. King, *Cîteaux and Her Elder Daughters*, (London, 1954), p. 10 wrote that "the austerity of the house [of Cîteaux seems] to have frightened more than it attracted, resulting in a dearth of recruits," but his claim, based on the *Exordium parvum*, certainly applies only to the difficult years before the entrance of Saint Bernard.

the donor refused to accept either the donation itself or the conditions of the grant and attacked the monastery in question.[30] This fact places in perspective not only the increasing violence visited upon the monasteries, but also the unusually large number of papal bulls and royal decrees guaranteeing and confirming the possession of goods of monasteries. The cartularies of Cistercian monasteries contain frequent and seemingly insignificant papal bulls and royal letters confirming and protecting the possessions of these monasteries.[31] Unfortunately, they do not betray the reasons for their issuance, but we may infer that the number of monasteries to enter into a litigious and even violent relationship with the neighborhood around them was more frequent than is generally imagined.[32]

It must be said that the Order made a valiant attempt to separate itself from the snares of the *mundus* before the Fourth Lateran Council. However, the prohibition against the acquisition of possessions and revenues in other than "free alms" was obviously violated since the general chapter several times returned to the subject,[33] but the prohibition was always issued with the qualification, "if a most serious emergency threatens," providing a sufficiently inviting loophole.[34] It is apparent from the decrees of the general chapter that contact with secular men was deemed the more dangerous activity. Monks and lay brothers were forbidden to engage in secular justice; they could not enter into financial

30. This must have been the reason for the admonition of the general chapter, *Statuta*, vol. 2, p. 306 (1205:1): ". . . ne ullo iudicio sanguinis se intermisceant." On this subject, see H. de Laplane, p. 111.

31. The number of such protection bulls and royal letters is too long to be cited here. A perusal of any important Cistercian cartulary or collection of royal letters will confirm this conclusion.

32. Perhaps, we may add, disputes which ended litigiously were handled locally, hence the paucity of evidence concerning them; disputes which entered into open violence were reported to the general chapter and to the Roman curia. These are fewer in number but more fully reported.

33. *Statuta*, vol. 1, pp. 305-306 (1205:5), 321 (1206:9), 427–28 (1214:54), 448 (1215:65).

34. *Ibid.*, vol. 1, p. 321 (1206:9).

transactions with laymen, nor cultivate land and feed animals together with secular men.[35]

It is a moot question as to how effective the authority of the general chapter in these years was. The number of rebellious monks and lay brothers was large enough to concern the general chapter,[36] and the number of abbots who were less than concerned about the condition of the Order was such that the recital of the *diffinitiones* was made mandatory in all abbeys.[37]

The years immediately following the Fourth Lateran Council were particularly disturbing to the tranquillity of the monasteries. Indeed, a turmoil which seemed to have escalated in the middle decades of the thirteenth century pitted the episcopate against the crown, the episcopate against the lay lords, and the episcopate against the monasteries. The churches of Rouen, Beauvais, Reims and Paris were involved in jurisdictional disputes with the French crown. The deteriorating relations between the Cistercian Order and the secular clergy of France forms part of the unhappy history of the ecclesiastical life of France in the thirteenth century.

The attack against the monasteries, reported to the Roman curia, occurred mainly in the northern ecclesiastical provinces. The abbeys of Cambron, Dunes, Foigny, Morimond, Clairvaux, and Landais reported attacks on them to the Holy See.[38] Of these, all but Clairvaux were located in the ecclesiastical province of Reims where a bitter jurisdictional struggle between the arch-

35. *Ibid.*, vol. 1, pp. 321 (1206:8), 357 (1209:3), 428–29 (1214:58), 448 (1215:65, 66).

36. *Ibid.*, vol. 1, p. 357 (1209:1).

37. *Ibid.*, vol. 1, pp. 390–91 (1212:6, 7).

38. For Cambron, see Potthast, nos. 4623, 5331: 26 November 1212 and 15 September 1216; for Dunes see *Cronica et cartularium monasterii de Dunis*, ed. A. de But, (Bruges, 1862), p. 357, no. 288: 21 October, 1216; for Foigny, see *Regesta Honorii papae III* ed. P. Pressutti, 2 vols., (Rome, 1895), no. 135: 1 December 1216; for Morimond, see *Honorii III, Romani pontificis, opera omnia* ed. C. A. Horoy, 4 vols., (Paris, 1879) vol. 2, pp. 157–58, no. 125: 7 January 1217; for Clairvaux, see Pressutti, nos. 266, 347: 20 January, 15 February 1217; for Landais, see Horoy, vol. 2, pp. 265–66, no. 216: 12 February 1217.

bishop of Reims and the church of Amiens had involved the Cistercian monasteries there.³⁹ Pope Honorius III had nominated the Cistercian abbots of Ourscamp and Longpont, dioceses of Noyon and Soissons, to carry out the necessary papal censures against the protagonists.⁴⁰ Unfortunately, the available evidence does not suggest a relationship between the attacks on these monasteries and Cistercian involvement in the jurisdictional struggle. The attacks, however, became so serious that the general chapter of 1217 decreed that abbeys which were "frequently being disturbed by secular men" should station sentries at the doors of the abbey in order to forbid secular men from entering.⁴¹

In their effort to defend themselves against the encroachment of the secular world, the Cistercian abbeys ran the risk of causing bloodshed, "of placing violent hands" on both laymen and secular clergy who attacked them. The general chapter of the Order, in 1219, had sent an embassy to the curia with letters asking for discussions on this vital matter.⁴² Honorius had earlier granted to the general chapter the faculty of dispensing with serious irregularities within the Order.⁴³ From the discussions at Rome the following "irregularities" were to be given to the general chapter for adjudication: simony, homicide, bigamy, forgeries of letters to the pope, violence against the person of a bishop, abbot or secular cleric, and mutilation of limbs.⁴⁴ The seriousness of the Order's plight was further underscored by the stationing of two permanent representatives at the papal curia *pro defendendis Ordinis.*⁴⁵

39. See Horoy, vol. 2, pp. 93–94, no. 67: 22 November 1216; pp. 103–104, no. 76: 3 December 1216; Pressutti, no. 570: 10 May 1216.

40. Horoy, vol. 2, pp. 93–94, no. 67: 22 November 1216. The Premonstratensian Order was also absorbed into this vortex. See Horoy, vol. 2, p. 366, no. 272: 17 March 1217.

41. *Statuta,* vol. 1, p. 466 (1219:7).

42. *Ibid.,* vol. 1, pp. 507 (1219:22), 516 (1220:3).

43. A. Manrique, *Cistercium seu verius ecclesiastici Annales a condito Cistercio,* 4 vols., (Lyons, 1659), vol. 4, p. 101.

44. *Statuta,* vol. 1, pp. 522–23, (1220:29).

45. *Statuta,* vol. 1, p. 527, (1220:49).

It would be difficult not to conclude that the Cistercian Order, in the years following the Fourth Lateran Council, was passing through an extremely critical stage in its relationship with its neighbors. In its decision to defend itself by physical means, the Order had committed itself to a policy that could only lead to increasing polarization. And whereas both the papacy and the French crown continued to treat the Order with a deference reminiscent of the more tranquil days of the twelfth century, papal legates, probably reflecting attitudes among the French secular clergy, insisted on the payment of procurations from the monasteries they visited,[46] in spite of frequent papal bulls exempting the entire Order from such payments.[47] The bitterness aroused by this polarization is graphically illustrated by the warning of Pope Honorius III who deplored the insolence shown by Cistercian abbeys whenever the legates attempted to collect procurations from them.[48]

The growing ill-feeling between the Cistercian abbeys and the French episcopate is reflected in several ways. The abbey of Vauclair, for instance, was ordered to be obedient to the bishop of Laon unless it could produce documents exempting it from that obedience.[49] And the general chapter of the Order complained that bishops and clerics were introducing new, unheard-of procedures such as demanding payment from funeral processions of those buried in the confines of the monastery or placing priest-monks performing priestly duties within their dioceses under direct episcopal jurisdiction.[50] The papal reply to this complaint came

46. Pressutti, no. 2946: 4 January 1221.

47. The bull *Cum preter pauperem* was frequently reissued to the entire Order. See Pressutti, no. 1754; Potthast, nos. 6170, 6397.

48. Pressutti, no. 2946: 4 January 1221. Honorius, setting aside his own bull of exemption, ordered payment of procurations to Gregory de Crescentio, cardinal-deacon of Saint Theodore, the papal legate who has "special esteem for you."

49. Horoy, vol. 3, pp. 750–51, no. 301: 20 March, 1221.

50. *Statuta,* vol. 2, p. 7, (1221:37). The abbey of Cercamp was the subject of a jurisdictional dispute between the bishops of Amiens and Théruanne. See Pressutti, nos. 3952, 3953: 17 May, 1222; no. 4767: 10 February, 1224.

rapidly. Honorius III ordered the episcopate to desist from molesting the abbots of the Order against the privileges granted to them by the Holy See.[51]

There is no question but that the French episcopate had re-opened the question of their power of jurisdiction over Cistercian monasteries. The bishops asked the Cistercian Order to contribute through payment of tithes to the support of poor parish churches.[52] They re-opened the long dormant issue of profession of obedience to the local ordinary.[53] They maintained that as long as an abbey possessed granges or other goods in a diocese, not only should the abbey be liable to monetary demands by the bishop, but should also be required to appear at diocesan synods in order to represent its holdings. The bishops at this point had apparently introduced a new form of oath of profession, expanding the instances in which the abbot could be called to appear at a diocesan synod.[54] The reply of Honorius III to the complaint of the general chapter was swift and clear: no new form of profession to a bishop is valid, nor may bishops extort payments from the abbots for any new reasons, such as the blessing and installation of an abbot.[55]

In spite of the unwavering papal attitude in favor of the Cistercian Order, the general chapter felt that the bishops' challenge required

51. Pressutti, no. 3561: 29 October 1221. The French king also lent a helping hand, placing all the monasteries of the filiations of Cîteaux, Pontigny and Clairvaux under his protection. See *Les actes des souverains anterieurs au XV siècle conservés dans les archives departementales du Cher,* ed. J. Soyer, 2 vols. (Bourges, 1905), II, 43–46, no. XVI: 1 November 1221 to 2 April 1222 [hereafter cited as Soyer].

52. Pressutti, no. 4586: 4 December 1223. It was foreshadowed earlier when the general chapter punished the abbot of Cercamp for having professed obedience to the bishops of Amiens and Théruanne, apparently beginning the jurisdictional dispute between them over that abbey. See *Statuta,* vol. I, p. 525, (1220:40).

53. Horoy, vol. 4, p. 662, no. 234: 27 May 1224.

54. *Statuta,* vol. 2, p. 33, (1224:18). The codification of 1202 had provided that bishops could summon abbots to synods *pro fide.* See *Cod. de 1202,* dist. 4, 17.

55. Pressutti, no. 5195: 4 December 1224; no. 5206: 7 December 1224; *Statuta,* vol. 2, p. 43, (1225: 40).

greater vigilance. At the suggestion of the papal legate in France, the Order sent the abbots of La Ferté-sur-Grôsne, Clairvaux, Trois Fontaines, and Landais to the curia to discuss the affairs of the Order.[56] Attacks on the monasteries had continued;[57] demands that abbots appear at diocesan synods continued in spite of continued papal letters of exemption,[58] and, for the first time, the general chapter began to complain of burdensome debts on some monasteries.[59]

Judging by the character of papal rhetoric, the attack of the bishop of Soissons on the Cistercian monastery of Longpont was especially vehement and serious. Pope Gregory IX was "grieved" by the "grave complaint" of the abbot of Longpont that the bishop had invented new reasons for interfering in the life of the monastery.[60] According to the papal bull, the bishop of Soissons claimed the right to examine an abbot-elect for the purity of his life and his learning, to confirm his election, and finally to present and install him. Now, this is nothing less than a claim of episcopal jurisdiction over a monastery. This claim was accompanied by determined and serious physical attacks on the monks and possessions of the monastery.[61] Only when Gregory IX enlisted the bishop of Meaux to protect the monks of Longpont did the attacks by henchmen of the bishop of Soissons cease.[62]

Several other monasteries also felt the wrath of the episcopate in the decade of the 1230's. Notable among them was the mother abbey of Cîteaux. It was pressed both by the bishops and the lay lords. The bishops were warned against claiming the revenues of

56. *Statuta*, vol. 2, p. 60, (1227:21).

57. Soyer, vol. 2 pp. 47–49, no. 17: 19 December 1226 for the abbey of Fontmorigny: *Cartulaire de l'abbaye de Vaux-des-Cernay* eds. L. Merlet et A. Moutie, 2 vols., (Paris, 1857), vol. 1, pp. 305–306, no. 331: 15 December 1232 for the abbey of Vaux-des-Cernay.

58. *Les Registres de Gregoire IX,* ed. L. Auvray, 3 vols., Paris, 1898–1908, no. 169: 11 January 1228 and reissued frequently thereafter.

59. *Statuta*, vol. 2, pp. 56–57, (1227:6).

60. *Registre de Grégoire IX,* no. 1226: 10 April 1233.

61. *Ibid.*, no. 1295: 11 May 1233. The bull speaks of "evildoers" who "many times molested" the monastery.

62. *Ibid.*, no. 1566: 26 October 1233.

H

the abbey of Cîteaux for the purpose of supporting parish priests, in accordance with a decree of the Fourth Lateran Council.[63] Princes and nobles, on the other hand, were forbidden to use their rights of patronage, advocacy and custodianship over the monasteries and granges of the Order as an excuse for extorting *tailles* and other exactions from the monasteries, or eating meat and bringing their women into the confines of the abbey.[64] The seriousness of the attack against the *chef d'ordre* is reflected in the complaint lodged by the Cistercian Order with the curia. The Order complained, as it had in the past, that no one, presumably meaning the bishops, was protecting it against persecutors who were attacking goods granted to it from the very beginning of the abbey. The Order further claimed that unjust sentences of excommunication, suspension and interdict were being laid against abbots and monasteries by the French episcopate especially in the provinces of Lyon, Besançon, Bourges and Sens.[65] The abbot and prior of Cluny, designated as protectors of the abbey of Cîteaux,[66] were commanded by Gregory IX to relax the sentences should they find that the Order had been clearly maltreated.[67] These protectors-designate, according to the further complaint of the Order, had merely aggravated the situation by hurling censures against the powerful neighbors in the vicinity of the abbey and its granges, for the sound of bells and the sight of lighted candles announcing the censure had aroused the hatred and fury of the enemies of the monastery or grange.[68]

Similar difficulties were experienced by the abbeys of Long-villiers in Flanders,[69] and Preuilly in the diocese of Sens.[70] Un-

63. Manrique, vol. 4, p. 473: 4 December 1233. Canon of the Fourth Lateran Council is referred to here.
64. *Registres de Grégoire IX*, no. 1729: 23 January 1234.
65. *Ibid.*, no. 1741: 23 January 1234. See also Soyer, vol. 2, p. 72, no. 24: 15 February 1234.
66. *Registres de Grégoire IX*, no. 1273: 20 January 1234.
67. *Ibid.*, no. 1741.
68. Manrique, vol. 4, p. 471: 3 February 1234.
69. *Registres de Grégoire IX*, no. 1588; 21 November 1233.
70. *Ibid.*, no. 1745: 31 January 1234; *Chartes et documents de l'abbaye cistercienne de Preuilly* eds. A. Catel and M. Lecomte, (Montereau, 1927), pp. 230–31, nos. 367–69: June 1234; no. 375: July 1235.

doubtedly, such evidence of attack on Cistercian monasteries as we possess is fragmentary, but the evidence itself is clear enough to frame a panorama of a beleaguered Order desperately trying to hold on to what it regarded as legitimately its own, and at the same time to defend itself against encroachment on its interior life.

Besides ordering both a *retractatio* and a *compilatio* of the *diffinitiones* in 1234,[71] the general chapter legislated a tighter discipline over the Order. Even professed Cistercians who had become bishops were warned that they faced correction for their "detestable life and abominable food and dress" which "denigrates the reputation of the entire Order."[72] For the abbots of the Cistercian Order the solution in the 1230's was the same as it had been earlier: attacks on the monasteries of the Order were related to a declining reputation. There was no disposition to dispute this fact. The statutes of the general chapter deal with numerous instances of irregularity and turmoil: slander and infamy within monasteries,[73] heresy,[74] attacks by *conversi* on abbots, conspiracy and robbery.[75] Again, as in the past, no irregularity vexed the fathers of the Order more than the continued violation of the prohibition against the acquisition of men and property and consequently greater debts. Even here, the impossibility of returning to the pristine ideals of the Order's primitive period was recognized, for the general chapter of 1239 decreed that an exception to the acquisition of men and immovable goods could be made on the basis of feudal right, not just in free alms. Borrowing money for the purchase of more property, hence the risk of accumulating greater debts was still to be forbidden, and

---

71. *Statuta*, vol. 2, pp. 131–32, (1234:27) 141–42, (1235: 19). See Mahn, p. 200.

72. *Statuta*, vol. 2, p. 133, (1234:32). The warning was repeated in the following year. See *Statuta*, vol. 2, p. 143, (1235:22).

73. *Ibid.*, vol. 2, p. 141, (1235:4). A dramatic example of this was the deposition of Gilbert, abbot of Preuilly for his unjust denunciation of Dom Jacques, former abbot of Cîteaux. See *Thesaurus novus anecdotorum* eds. E. Martène et U. Durand, 5 vols., (Paris, 1717), vol. 4, p. 1367: ann. 1238.

74. *Statuta*, vol. 2, p. 143, (1235:21).

75. *Ibid.*, vol. 2, p. 181, (1237:66).

father-visitors were urged to be especially vigilant in this regard.[76] The irregular acquisition of property by various houses was the cause of grave dissensions and schisms in the Order, as the general chapter of 1239 had confessed, but it is doubtful whether the leadership found any effective solution to the problem. As long as wealth and property were incompatible in the public mind with the ideals of the Order, no solutions except perhaps outright legal and physical defenses of the monasteries were possible.

Indeed, a test of the Order's ability to defend its monasteries appeared in the decade of the 1230's when Cîteaux herself, for reasons only partially visible, fell into financial difficulties. These coincided with the growing resentment of the Order's "first fathers" against the overweening powers of the abbot of Cîteaux over the entire Order.[77] The general chapter in 1235 appealed to the Order, "for the honor of God and for prolonging charity in the Order" to support the abbey of Cîteaux in its hour of need, touched, as it was, by the hand of the Lord, i.e. by storms which destroyed its fruits and animals, and "by other afflictions."[78]

These "other afflictions" could only mean the attacks of bishops and lay lords. Aside from the fact that the "first abbots" of the Order had found in the financial plight of Cîteaux an excuse to intervene directly in its internal affairs, the significance of this call to defend the mother house of the Order is obvious. It was, in fact, a direct test of the power of charity which animated the Order from its very foundation. If the Cistercian Order was to maintain its image of charity to the poor, even if not its image of poverty, then that image of charity would have to begin at home. Indeed, the general chapter of 1236 reminded the Order that the work of charity, which is the grace of the Holy Spirit, meant that payment of the subvention to aid the financially weakened mother house must be "in the hearts of the abbots," that payment was a voluntary act, not one of necessity.[79]

We have no evidence as to the extent to which the call to save

76. *Ibid.*, vol. 2, p. 202, (1239:4).   77. Mahn, pp. 231–32; King, p. 38.
78. *Statuta,* vol. 2, p. 143, (1235:20).   79. *Ibid.*, vol. 2, p. 160, (1236:35).

Cîteaux was heeded. The general chapter, however, on two occasions, in 1241 and again in 1246, reminded the abbots of the Order that payment of the subvention for Cîteaux must be fulfilled under threat of suspension from saying the mass.[80] Compulsion, not charity, would bring the mother house out of financial difficulties. Indeed, the abbey of Cîteaux itself was placed by the general chapter under a strict regimen with certain restrictions the violation of which, we may infer, brought the mother house toward financial crisis. Prominent among these restrictions was the proviso that no new buildings be built, nor old ones remodelled, nor might the abbey increase its debts, but should, in fact, decrease its indebtedness.[81]

For the next century, the focus of the Order's attention would shift from charity toward a defense of its privileged position. Since that position had originally been won by its reputation for charity, poverty and its faithfulness to the ascetic ideal of its founders, one wonders how, toward the middle of the thirteenth century, it could be defended when these ideals were visibly compromised. Without a doubt, the papacy was enlisted in this struggle of defense against the enemies of the Order. Cistercian representatives at the Roman curia had successfully extracted from Gregory IX a wide-ranging bull, *Religiosam vitam*, which specifically mentioned every possible area of conflict between the Order and its enemies, and which protected it in each instance.[82]

Recurring scandals continued to bedevil the Order in the two decades between the First Council of Lyons and the reforming bull *Parvus fons*.[83] In this same period, attacks on the monasteries

---

80. *Ibid.*, vol. 2, pp. 231, (1241:7); 302–303, (1246:6); *Ibid.*, vol. 2, pp. 290–91 speaks of "compelling the abbots, priors, cellarers and other officials, if they had not paid their portion at the prefixed time and place, by interdict and excommunication . . ."

81. *Ibid.*, vol. 2, p. 143, (1235:20).

82. *Cartulaire de l'abbaye de Flines* ed. E. Hautcoeur, 2 vols., (Lille, 1872), vol. 1, pp. 19–22, no. 22: 13 April 1237. This bull was frequently reissued.

83. Many evidences of scandal exist in the statutes. See, for instance, *Statuta*, vol. 2, pp. 299–303, (1245:54, 57); 306–307, (1246:30); 308, (1246:37); 313–14, (1246:62); 326–27, (1247:61); 374, (1251:73); 386–87, (1252:49);

continued, and from available evidence, one can deduce that many more monasteries reported themselves under attack than in the previous three decades since the Fourth Lateran Council.[84] Of these instances, the monastery of Leoncel, diocese of Die, reported its difficulties directly to the papal curia.[85] The complaint of Leoncel was not new: that ecclesiastical censures were less severe, that canonical sentences for attacking monasteries were lighter than in the past, making the monasteries subject more frequently to attack by evil men. The monastery of Leoncel, under constant attack, sought the aid of bishops to protect it but without success, and was therefore forced to defend itself as best it could. The reply of the Holy See was characteristic: those clerics, regular and secular, who invade the monastery of Leoncel or who force the monks to pay tithes on lands held by them since before the Fourth Lateran Council, or on lands which were given to Leoncel by will of a deceased person, will suffer suspension from office and benefice; laymen guilty of the same offenses will suffer excommunication. The general chapter of 1248, receiving reports of the rising tide of attack on Cistercian monasteries—"troubled by the rising evil of the times"—counselled monasteries in a given region to form a citadel, as it were, in order to defend themselves.[86]

Not only did the Cistercian Order choose the "citadel" approach in its relations with its neighbors, the outside world, but in the decade of the 1250's it showed no disposition to find a remedy for

---

398, (1253:39); 399, (1254:4); 409–411, (1255:3, 5, 6); 425, 428, (1257:2, 12); 439, 440, 445, (1258:10, 13, 37); 454, (1259:34); 478, (1261:13); vol. 3, p. 18, (1264:2).

84. We have evidence at least of attacks reported against the following monasteries: Barbeaux, Preuilly, La Prée, Cercanceaux, Olivet, Cambron, Leoncel, Cîteaux, Morimond, Trois Fontaines, Paris, Vaux-des-Cernay, Landais, Barzelles. For these attacks, see *Statuta,* vol. 2, pp. 305, 308, (1246:35, 36); 334, (1249:1, 2); 332, (1249:1, 2); 341, (1250:26); 369, (1251, 22, 23); Potthast, no. 12677; *Les Registres d'Innocent IV* ed. E. Langlois, (Paris, 1886), no. 3610; *Chartes de Preuilly,* p. 325, no. 534.

85. *Chartularium monasterii Beatae Mariae de Leoncello ordinis Cisterciensis* ed. U. Chevalier, (Montélimar, 1869), pp. 158–59, no. 153: 28 October 1247.

86. *Statuta,* vol. 2, p. 328, (1248:5).

the evils which afflicted it and affected its reputation. Having earlier defined the basic evil as the inordinate acquisition of goods and properties, the general chapters of that decade, perhaps in resignation or frustration, turned their attention primarily toward keeping peace within the Order, and toward an increased vigilance over their traditional privileges and exemptions. To be sure, attacks on the Order by the bishops and local clergy continued unabated, and the Cistercian defense was an appeal to a papal exemption bull.[87] Old arguments of another era were used against prelates and papal legates who tried to encroach on their economic resources: since their goods were being used for taking care of the poor and for other pious works, they should be exempt from any monetary demands on them.[88] However, such arguments were, in the middle of the thirteenth century, without much effect, and the general chapter, in 1261, decreed a new approach to the problem of their relations with bishops who made claims on the monasteries.[89] Three abbots, who were once priors in a monastery of the ecclesiastical province in question, would investigate the charges against the bishop in order to determine their accuracy, then would call all the abbots of the province for consultation, in order to arrive at a common front in dealing with the bishop. Such a procedure was implicit recognition that papal bulls of privilege and exemption were insufficient, that, in fact, Rome was simply too distant to appeal to, and that adequate defense against bishops could come effectively only through the unified action of the Order. Indeed, recognition of this fact also came from the curia which had earlier allowed the Order to adjudicate cases involving irregularities of its

87. See, for instance, *Thesaurus novus*, vol. 3, p. 1253: 1 June 1251; *Chartes . . . de Preuilly*, no. 556: March 1253; *Cartulaire d'Ourscamp*, p. 304, no. 488: 5 March 1254.

88. The bull *Cum propter pauperem*, in *Les Registres d'Alexandre IV* eds. C. Bourel de la Roncière, J. de Loye and A. Coulon, (Paris, 1902–1917), no. 86: 9 January 1255. The key argument is: "Cum propter pauperem victum vestrum omnis bona vestra hospitalitati et aliis piis operibus officiossime sint exposita . . ." This bull was frequently reissued by Alexander's successors.

89. *Statuta*, vol. 2, p. 476, (1261:5).

subjects by itself without the necessity of appealing to the curia or to the local bishop.[90]

However much the Cistercian Order fretted over its relations with local bishops and magnates, its main concern seemed to have been the maintenance of peace and spiritual calm within the monasteries in the last decade before the bull *Parvus fons*. Abbots were urged to terminate complaints within their monasteries by themselves within a year, and if unable to do so, to appeal for aid to the general chapter.[91]

Complaints, most of which seem quite superficial, were handled by the general chapter. For instance, immoderate expenses of father-visitors with their large retinue occupied the attention of the general chapter of 1256.[92] Banishment from an abbey of monks and *conversi* for actions detrimental to the reputation of the Order was another issue discussed by the general chapter of 1257.[93] "Discord and very dangerous dissension by which the Order seems totally imperilled . . ." was the leading question on the minds of the Order's ruling hierarchy,[94] but the statutes of the general chapter give evidence of confusion and floundering. It is doubtful whether another attempt at a new compilation of the *diffinitiones*, commissioned in 1256, clarified the malaise which forced the Order into its "citadel." Suggestions that the *mundus* had moved into too close a proximity to the monastery were made,[95] as also the dangers to spiritual well-being of monks who traveled outside their monastery.[96] And not only did the *mundus* dare to move on the periphery of the monastery, but the charge was made in the general chapter of 1258, that princes and secular prelates and magnates were influencing the elections of abbots.[97] Introduction of new customs opposed to those of the Order and the Benedictine Rule was alleged as well as the actual interference of secular men in the operation of the granges.[98]

90. *Ibid.*, vol. 2, p. 409, (1255:1).   91. *Ibid.*, vol. 2, p. 410, (1255:5).
92. *Ibid.*, vol. 2, p. 422, (1256:3).   93. *Ibid.*, vol. 2, p. 425, (1257:2).
94. *Ibid.*, vol. 2, p. 426, (1257:7).   95. *Ibid.*, vol. 2, p. 428, (1257:12).
96. *Ibid.*, vol. 2, pp. 436, 440, (1258:3, 13).
97. *Ibid.*, vol. 2, p. 439, (1258:10).
98. *Ibid.*, vol. 2, pp. 462, (1260:5); 477, (1261:10).

The remedy was as superficial as the diagnosis. The general chapter of 1261, "in order to remove scandal from the Order and deter reckless individuals from their rashness," deposed and excommunicated Gerard, abbot of Fontaine-Jean for intolerably injuring his abbey by introducing a "foreign person of secular mien" into his abbey.[99]

Yet, in defense of the Cistercian Order, it must be said that, on the eve of the reforming bull *Parvus fons*, the general chapter had finally defined the malaise of the Order in bold and striking terms: the Order is disturbed by "spiritual laziness."[100] Such an honest appraisal of itself was the harbinger of reform. And although the bull *Parvus fons* dealt with a specific aspect of Cistercian life, the governance of the Order, it was at least a step in the right direction. Perhaps, because not much more was accomplished by Urban IV and Clement IV in the direction of reform of the Cistercian Order, we may agree with M. Mahn's observation that "in 1265, the Cistercian Order is still far from decadence; however, it shows some signs of division. It still has no need of reform, properly speaking."[101] Their enemies did exaggerate, as enemies are wont to do. But enemies do serve a necessary function, even in their exaggeration: they aid in the effort toward self-knowledge. They help to clarify the issues. And we may confidently conclude that the ruling hierarchy of the Cistercian Order, on the eve of *Parvus fons,* had succeeded in understanding the difficulties which were besetting it. Unfortunately, self-knowledge is not often followed by the will to reform.

Daniel S. Buczek

Fairfield University

99. *Ibid.,* vol. 2, p. 478, (1261:13). Pope Urban IV intervened, and commissioned the bishop of Paris to apply remedies for burdensome debts of the abbey of Fontaine-Jean. See *Les Registres d'Urbain IV* ed. J. Guiraud, 4 vols., (Paris, 1892–1929), no. 7: 22 September 1261.

100. *Statuta,* vol. 3, p. 18, (1264:2): ". . . per invisibilem spiritalis nequitiae astutiam Ordo noster concutitur et turbatur . . . ."

101. Mahn, p. 260.

THE WELSH MONASTERIES
AND THE EDWARDIAN CONQUEST

ALTHOUGH IRELAND TOOK OVER LEADERSHIP, Wales initiated and continued to participate in the Celtic monastic movement of the fifth, sixth, and seventh centuries. Welsh monks in that period, both those living regularly in monasteries and ascetics of the anchorite type, enjoyed great prestige and exercised to a large extent what would ordinarily be thought of as functions of the secular priesthood. In the period immediately preceding the Norman conquest, however, Welsh monasticism lost most of its vigor, and the Normans hastened its demise by transforming the monasteries into cathedral chapters or parish churches, or by founding new Benedictine monasteries on them. These Norman Benedictine foundations were identified with, and their membership derived from the conquerors and oppressors of the Welsh people, and so revived no Welsh enthusiasm for monasticism.[1]

A few ancient Celtic monasteries survived, mostly in remote locations: Bardsey Abbey, on an island off the west coast of Caernarvonshire; Beddgelert Priory (Caernarvonshire), more centrally located; Penmon Priory (Anglesey), which in the later middle ages acquired the dependency of Priestholm Priory, situated on a smaller

1. On these subjects, see Sir John Edward Lloyd, *A History of Wales from the Earliest Times to the Edwardian Conquest* (3rd ed.; London: Longmans, Green and Co., 1939), vol. 1, chap. v, sec. 3; chap. vi, sec. 2; chap. vii, secs. 2 and 3; vol. 2, chap. xii, sec. 4, and pp. 443–46.

island, now a reserve for puffins, off the northeast coast of Anglesey; Ynys Tudwal, off the south coast of Caernarvonshire, a settlement of which little is known, although some excavation has recently taken place there.[2] These monasteries apparently continued to be identified with Welsh culture and the causes of Welsh nationalism and independence. Welsh princes frequently used monks of Bardsey as advisers and emissaries,[3] and, among others, Llywelyn ap Gruffydd, the last independent prince of Wales, manifested friendship toward Beddgelert.[4]

In the course of the later middle ages, all these Celtic foundations adopted the rule of the Augustinian canons.[5] Another Augustinian house in Wales was Llanthony (Monmouthshire), sometimes called Llanthony Prima to distinguish it from its Gloucestershire dependency of the same name. Llanthony Prima was an Anglo-Norman foundation, dissociated from the Welsh cause, although policy played no part in its origin, which came about, as Gerald of Wales

---

2. Arthur Ivor Pryce (comp.), *The Diocese of Bangor in the Sixteenth Century: Being a Digest of the Registers of the Bishops, A.D. 1512–1646* (Bangor: Jarvis and Foster, 1923), barely mentions Ynys Tudwal in his discussion of the dissolution of the monasteries. When, in another connection, I was looking through the class of documents in the Public Record Office, London, called Clerical Subsidies, I noticed references to this monastery. On recent excavation (1962–1963) on "St Tudwal's East Island," see David M. Wilson and D. Gillian Hurst in *Medieval Archaeology*, 8 (1964), pp. 246–48. The Welsh shires did not, of course, exist at the time these monasteries were founded, but it seems simplest to indicate locations by means of present-day boundaries. On the shiring of Wales, see T. F. Tout, "The Welsh Shires," *Y Cymmrodor*, 9 (1888), pp. 201–226.

3. See e.g., Lloyd, *History of Wales*, vol. 2, p. 629, n. 89; *Littere Wallie Preserved in Liber A in the Public Record Office*, ed. J. Goronwy Edwards ("Board of Celtic Studies, University of Wales: History and Law Series," No. 5; Cardiff: University of Wales Press Board, 1940), pp. 85, 169.

4. *Littere Wallie*, pp. 58–59; Great Britain, Public Record Office, *Calendar of Charter Rolls, 1257–1300* (London: H.M. Stationery Office, 1906), p. 337.

5. See David Knowles and R. Neville Hadcock, *Medieval Religious Houses: England and Wales* (London: Longmans, Green and Co., 1953), pp. 126, 127, 149, 150, 152; on Bardsey, see also C.N. Johns in *Caernarvonshire Historical Society Transactions*, 23 (1962), pp. 129–31, and T. Jones Pierce, *ibid.*, 24 (1963), pp. 60–72.

movingly relates, from motives of pure piety.[6] Carmarthen Priory, also Augustinian, was a more typical Anglo-Norman foundation. Dr Lawrence A. S. Butler has shown that St Kinemark's Priory (Monmouthshire) was Augustinian, but so little is known of this house that it is impossible to ascertain whether its sympathies were pro-Welsh or pro-English.[7]

The introduction of the Cistercians into Wales was a different matter from that of the Benedictines. The Cistercians came from France and had for the most part no connection with the English oppressors. Furthermore, the Cistercians in many respects resembled the ancient Celtic monks, whose memory had continued to be revered even in parts of Wales where their monasteries no longer existed. Pope Gregory IX in 1232 granted a licence to the Cistercian abbot and convent of Cwmhir (Radnorshire), "who are in a mountainous district remote from parish churches," to hear the confessions of, and administer sacraments to, their servants and household, an indication that the Cistercians to some degree, at least, emulated the Celtic monks in fulfilling secular functions.[8] Many hermits, among the few ascetics who continued to earn the respect of the Welsh people, still lived in Wales, and to these also the Cistercians, with their custom of establishing monastic foundations in remote mountain fastnesses, bore considerable similarity. The Cistercians' strict asceticism, their poverty, and above all their love of solitude and remoteness, were bound to appeal to the Welsh temperament. The Cistercian system of mother and daughter houses had been a feature of Celtic monasticism, and so was also calculated to appeal to the Welsh. The Cistercians easily became the principal monastic order of Wales, drawing many Welsh recruits to their ranks and identifying themselves with the Welsh political

6. See David Knowles, *The Monastic Order in England* (Cambridge: University Press, 1950), p. 175 and n.

7. Lloyd, *History of Wales,* vol. 2, p. 432; Butler, "The Augustinian Priory of St Kinemark, Monmouthshire," *Journal of the Historical Society of the Church in Wales,* 15 (1965), pp. 9–19.

8. Great Britain, Public Record Office, *Calendar of Entries in the Papal Registers Relating to Great Britain and Ireland: Papal Letters, 1198–1304* (London: H.M. Stationery Office, 1894), p. 131 (wrongly indexed under Cymmer).

cause—although, as has been indicated, they were not the only monks to do so.[9]

There were thirteen Cistercian monasteries in Wales. In the framework of the order, two were of the family of L'Aumône: Tintern (Monmouthshire), founded directly from L'Aumône in 1131, and Grace Dieu (Monmouthshire), founded in 1226 from Waverley (Surrey), a daughter of L'Aumône. Two more were originally of the Order of Savigny: Neath (Glamorgan) and Basingwerk (Flint), founded from Savigny in 1130 and 1131, respectively, became Cistercian, with the rest of the Savigniac order, in 1147. The remaining nine were of the family of Clairvaux. Whitland (Carmarthenshire) and Margam (Glamorgan) were founded from Clairvaux in 1140 and 1147, respectively. Margam produced no daughter houses, but from Whitland, in 1143, came Cwmhir, refounded in 1176; Strata Florida (Cardiganshire), Wales's most important monastery, in 1164; Strata Marcella (Montgomeryshire), in 1170, and two outside Wales, to be mentioned later. Strata Florida produced Caerleon, *alias* Llantarnam (Monmouthshire), in 1179, and Aberconway (Caernarvonshire) in 1186; Cwmhir produced Cymmer (Merionethshire) in 1199; and from Strata Marcella, in 1201, came Valle Crucis (Denbighshire).[10] Of

9. On the introduction of the Cistercians into Wales, see Lloyd, *History of Wales*, vol. 2, chap. xvi, sec. 3. The most comprehensive study of the Welsh Cistercians is Jeremiah F. O'Sullivan, *Cistercian Settlements in Wales and Monmouthshire, 1140–1540* ("Fordham University Studies, History Series," No. 2; New York: Declan X. McMullen Co., 1947).

10. See genealogies in Knowles, *Monastic Order,* pp. 724–25. Some recent studies of more limited scope than O'Sullivan's (see n. 9, above) may be mentioned here. The only book since O'Sullivan's to deal fully with one Welsh Cistercian monastery is Rhŷs W. Hays, *History of the Abbey of Aberconway* (Cardiff: University of Wales Press, 1963). To the information given there should be added that in reviews by C. H. Talbot in *Journal of the British Archaeological Association,* 3rd ser., 27 (1964), pp. 129–130; F. G. Cowley in *Welsh History Review,* 2 (1965), pp. 283–84; and W. Ogwen Williams in *Transactions of the Honourable Society of Cymmrodorion,* 1965, Pt. 1, pp. 156–58. Dr Talbot's corrections of my supposed errors of judgment are mere blunders on his part; in particular, he makes the mistake of supposing that the abbeys of Buildwas (Shropshire), Dore (Herefordshire), and Croxden (Staffordshire) were nearer to Cymmer than to Cwmhir. The additional details that he gives,

these, Whitland, Cwmhir, Strata Florida, Strata Marcella, Caerleon, Aberconway, Cymmer, and Valle Crucis were strongly Welsh in outlook, sympathy, and membership. The other five had fundamentally Anglo-Norman sympathies, although they too attracted some Welshmen to their ranks, as witness the name of Cynan, the holy abbot of Margam, praised by Gerald.[11] Cistercian abbeys in England will not be treated here, but three may be mentioned that had strong Welsh connections and probably a considerable number

however, are valuable, based as they are on his own research, published in *Letters from the English Abbots to the Chapter at Cîteaux, 1442–1521* ("Camden Fourth Series," vol. 4; London: Royal Historical Society, 1967). A. Leslie Evans, *Margam Abbey* (Port Talbot: Privately published, 1958) is of much value for the local knowledge it displays, but suffers from the author's ignorance of previous scholarship, in particular from his failure to use O'Sullivan's *Cistercian Settlements;* see the review by T. J. Pierce in *Welsh Hist. Rev.,* 1 (1960–63) 98–99. E. T. Davies, *Ecclesiastical History of Monmouthshire,* Pt. 1 (Risca, Mon.: Starsons, 1953), pp. 60–87, makes some good use of sources and provides a map (pp. 72–73), but also fails to use O'Sullivan's work. The only serious objection to F. G. Cowley, "The Monastic Order in South Wales" (Ph.D. thesis, University of Wales, 1965) is its inaccessibility. David H. Williams has expanded his valuable article, "The Cistercians in Wales: Some Aspects of Their Economy, *Archaeologia Cambrensis,* 114 (1965) pp. 2–47, into a small book, *The Welsh Cistercians: Aspects of Their Economic History* (Pontypool: Hughes and Son, 1969). The same author has also written "Grace Dieu Abbey," *Monmouthshire Antiquary,* 1 (1964), pt. 4, pp. 85–106, and "The Cistercian Abbots of Medieval Gwent," *ibid.,* pp. 107–111, which may be described as an annotated list of abbots of Tintern and Caerleon. Robert Richards gives an account of the Welsh Cistercians and Cymmer Abbey in *Journal of the Merioneth Historical and Record Society,* 3 (1957–60), pp. 223–49. See also *Bibliography of the History of Wales,* Prepared by the History and Law Committee of the Board of Celtic Studies of the University of Wales (2nd ed.; Cardiff: University of Wales Press, 1962), pp. 59–66; Glanmor Williams, *The Welsh Church from Conquest to Reformation* (Cardiff: University of Wales Press, 1962), a monumental, classic work; and Rhys W. Hays, "The Welsh Cistercians: Recent Research and Future Prospects," *Studies in Medieval Culture,* 3 (1970), pp. 70–80.

11. See Knowles, *Monastic Order,* pp. 659–60, 671n. Caerleon was of Welsh foundation, but in its later years seems to have had monks with English names and associations; H. D. Emanuel, "A Document Relating to the Monastery of Caerleon *alias* Llantarnam," *National Library of Wales Journal,* 5 (1947–48) pp. 222–23, presents a document of 1465 in which Abbot William Nunam asks the bishop of Llandaff to ordain an acolyte named Matthew Hardyng.

of Welsh monks: Buildwas (Shropshire), founded in 1135 as a Savigniac house; Dore (Herefordshire), a daughter of Morimond, founded in 1147; and Vale Royal (Cheshire), founded from Dore in 1274.[12]

Talley Abbey (Carmarthenshire), Wales' only house of Premonstratensian canons, was also strongly identified with the Welsh cause, the most important of the new foundations in this respect, other than those of the Cistercians.[13] The Welsh friaries were few and have been studied little, largely because of paucity of sources, but it appears that the Franciscans of Llanfaes (Anglesey) and the Dominicans of Bangor (Caernarvonshire) and Rhuddlan (Flint) were largely Welsh in nationality and sympathy. William de Merton, warden of Llanfaes, was employed extensively on missions for Llywelyn ap Gruffydd in the years immediately preceding the conquest. Other friars with more distinctively Welsh names were also associated with Llywelyn.[14]

Welsh Cistercians played an important role in the struggle for Welsh independence from England. Cistercian abbots were trusted advisers of Welsh princes, for whom they often acted as emis-

---

12. Knowles, *Monastic Order,* pp. 249, 648n, 667, 725–26; Williams, "Cistercians in Wales," *loc. cit.,* pp. 6–7, 10; *Calendar of Ancient Correspondence Concerning Wales,* ed. J. Goronwy Edwards ("Board of Celtic Studies, University of Wales: History and Law Series," No. 2; Cardiff: University of Wales Press Board, 1935), pp. 8, 177; on Dore, see also David H. Williams in *Monmouthshire Antiquary,* 2 (1965) pp. 65–104, and on Buildwas, O'Sullivan, pp. 89–90.

13. See *Bibliography of the History of Wales,* pp. 65–66.

14. *Calendar of Ancient Correspondence,* pp. 62, 89, 96, 99–100. An agreement of 18 August 1261, regarding boundaries of land, between Llywelyn and Richard, bishop of Bangor, mentions among those charged with seeing that the agreement is kept, Adam, prior of Bangor; J., lector of Bangor; Jervasius (=Iorwerth) and "Trahaern" (*sic; recte* Trahaearn), friars of Llanfaes; a letter of 12 December 1963, recording Gruffydd ap Gwenwynwyn's homage to Llywelyn, names among the judges in the event that certain problems arise; the abbots of Aberconway and Strata Marcella; the prior of the Dominicans of Bangor; Friar Iouaf (*sic*) of the same order; and Friars Ieuaf Goch and Iorwerth ap Cadwgan, Franciscans of Llanfaes (*Littere Wallie,* pp. 77–80, 97–98). Other examples of friars with Welsh names appear later in the present article.

saries.[15] The Cistercians' preoccupation with the Welsh nationalist cause resulted, indeed, in a lack of diversified interests, evidence of which is seen in their almost complete failure to produce daughter houses outside Wales. There was in principle no reason why the Welsh communities should not have sent monks to establish new houses, for example, in Scotland or Norway, but they did not. Outside Wales, they produced only three daughter houses in Ireland and one in England. From Tintern came Kingswood (Gloucestershire) in 1139 and Tintern Parva in 1200; from Whitland, Cumber in 1200 and Tracton (Albus-Tractus, the "White Strand") in 1225. David H. Williams points out, in addition, that monks from Margam were sent to Ireland in 1227 to help reform the Cistercian order there, that Monasteranenagh and Holy Cross Abbeys were affiliated to Margam in 1227 and 1228, respectively and that as late as 1445, Margam was still the visitor of Abbeydorney.[16] Even with these additions, the list is not long, and its brevity testifies to the Welsh Cistercians' absorption in Welsh politics.

The monasteries' position was bound to undergo considerable change as a result of the Edwardian conquest and settlement of the late thirteenth century. Professor James Conway Davies, writing in 1940, observed, "The purely political side of the Edwardian Conquest can be briefly told. . . . The military story of the Conquest has been exhaustively, if not finally, recounted. There still remain to be dealt with certain major problems of the history of the period which has so far been barely glossed. There still remain sources of information which have not yet been even scratched. These problems include the economic, social, and administrative aspects, not to mention the legal side, which have hitherto been almost

15. *Littere Wallie*, pp. lv, 138; Hays, *Aberconway*, pp. 50–51, 53–54; and other examples.

16. Knowles, *Monastic Order*, p. 724; Williams, "Cistercians in Wales," *loc. cit.*, p. 3; *Brut y Tywysogion or the Chronicle of the Princes: Peniarth MS. 20 Version*, trans. with Introduction and Notes by Thomas Jones ("Board of Celtic Studies, University of Wales: History and Law Series," No. 11; Cardiff: University of Wales Press, 1952), pp. 100, 202.

completely ignored."[17] While additional research has, of course, been undertaken since these words were written, it remains necessary to inquire into the extent to which the Welsh monasteries, especially the Cistercian houses, were affected by these various aspects of the settlement.

It is recognized that much deterioration in monastic life had taken place by the time of the monasteries' dissolution by King Henry VIII in 1536–1540. Professor Glanmor Williams, assessing the extent of Welsh monastic decline as even greater than some other writers have, sums up, "There is still a tendency to think of medieval monasteries in too static a way; to suppose them to have been much the same sort of places in Henry VIII's reign as they had been in their golden age in the twelfth and thirteenth centuries. They were not, of course. They had in fact been subjected to some desperate crises during the intervening centuries: economic depression; pestilence among men and beasts; spiritual and intellectual decline; long wars and crippling taxation; broken contacts and relaxed discipline; the Glyndŵr Rebellion and prolonged devastation."[18]

Granting the seriousness of the decay, how much of it is to be ascribed to the Edwardian conquest and settlement? Edward I can hardly be blamed for such hardships as "pestilence among men and beasts." Yet some historians consider the conquest fundamentally responsible for most of the monks' major problems. In the following quotation, W. Ogwen Williams refers directly only to Aberconway, but there is reason to believe that he meant his words to have more general application. "After the Edwardian Conquest," he writes, "it is only too clear, the Cistercians of Aberconway had lost heart. Harassed [sic], too, by the royal officials of the principality and bewildered by economic changes with which it was

17. *The Welsh Assize Roll, 1277–1284: Assize Roll No. 1147 (Public Record Office)*, ed. James Conway Davies ("Board of Celtic Studies, University of Wales: History and Law Series," No. 7; Cardiff: University of Wales Press Board, 1940), p.v.

18. "The Dissolution of the Monasteries in Glamorgan," *Welsh Hist. Rev.*, 3 (1966–67), p. 24.

I

unable to cope, the abbey after 1284 seems to have become an institution merely lingering on, sustained only by the inert force of its existence."[19]

Let us try to summarize and assess the various developments that took place as a result of the conquest. A number of routine documents testify to the necessity of protecting the Welsh monks from possible harm resulting from military operations. Letters of protection were common for the "abbot and convent," and are occasionally recorded for individual monks of various houses, during and between the campaigns of 1277 and 1282–1284.[20] Edward used some monasteries as military and administrative headquarters during this period. A letter from Payn de Cadurcis to Edward, written between 22 March and 28 March 1277, reported that Payn had arranged to meet with others on Easter Monday at Whitland Abbey to decide on operations against the king's enemies.[21] Edward used Aberconway Abbey as headquarters for a long time in 1283, and initiated the building of Conway Castle at the same location before completing arrangements for the transfer of the monks to their new location at Maenan.[22] Chancery enrolments during the periods of war are also dated from the camp near Basingwerk, from Valle Crucis Abbey, from Bardsey, from

19. Review, Hays, *Aberconway, loc. cit.,* p. 158.

20. For examples, relating to Aberconway, Basingwerk, Cymmer, Neath, Strata Florida, Valle Crucis, Bardsey, Carmarthen, Llanthony, Bangor, Llanfaes, and Brecon (on which monastery see the later discussion in the present article), see Great Britain, *Calendar of Patent Rolls, 1272–1281* (London: H.M. Stationery Office, 1901), pp. 129, 223, 224, 232, 249, 363, 405; *ibid., 1281–1292* (London: H.M. Stationery Office, 1893), pp. 27, 68, 71, 73, 123, 338; *Calendar of Chancery Warrants, 1244–1326* (London: H.M. Stationery Office, 1927), p. 45; Hays, *Aberconway,* pp. 58–59. These letters are sometimes for the abbot or prior alone, sometimes for the convent as well, or, in addition, for their proctors or servants. Sometimes phrases are added such as "buying victuals for the maintenance of their house." One enrolment, dated 27 May 1277, records a safe-conduct for John de Cadeweyn (*sic*), monk of Strata Marcella, going to his house (*C. Pat. R., 1272–1281,* p. 211). For Talley Abbey, see later in the present article.

21. *Calendar of Ancient Correspondence,* pp. 71–72.

22. Hays, *Aberconway,* pp. 57–59.

Llanfaes, and from the camp at Rhuddlan.[23] Edward used Rhuddlan Friary as a base for administrative operations and took steps to see that the friars there should not suffer as a result of the conquest: on 1 October 1278, he instructed Master Thomas Bek and John de Kirkeby to "make letters to the prior and convent of the Friars Preachers of Rhuddlan that they shall have their estovers in the forest of Pervethald [*sic: recte* Perfeddwlad] by Rhuddlan and free fishery in the river of Rhuddlan and that they may grind freely at the king's mills there at the king's will; also to let [Ifor] their prior have letters directed to Bogo de Knovill, sheriff of Salop, to put David de Rydemayn in any competent service in his baili-wick."[24]

The personnel of the Welsh monasteries and friaries were often employed on the king's business. Edward used Robert de Henley, prior of the Benedictine house of Cardigan, as financial agent in the building of the castle of Llanbadarn Fawr.[25] In connection with the post-conquest rebellion of Rhys ap Maredudd, Edward made use of the abbot of Cwmhir. An enrolment dated 16 July 1287, reads, "To the abbot of Cwmhir and Walter de Pedwardyn. Notification that the king has granted to them power to admit to his peace and will the men of Straudeuwy [*sic*] adherents of [Rhys ap Maredudd], the king's rebel, in his attempt [*imprisa*] who may wish to come to the king's peace. These letters patent shall last from Friday before St Margaret for the six following days."[26] Other

23. Great Britain, Public Record Office, *Calendar of Close Rolls, 1279–1288* (London: H.M. Stationery Office, 1902), pp. 214–15, 231; *C. Pat. R., 1272–1281*, p. 242; ibid., *1281–1292*, pp. 72–73, 127; *C. Chancery Warrants, 1244–1326*, p. 3. A memorandum by the sheriff of Shropshire and Staffordshire is dated at Cymmer Abbey, 20 May 1283 (*Littere Wallie*, pp. 192–93); see also *ibid.*, p. 180.

24. *C. Chancery Warrants, 1244–1326*, p. 4; see also *ibid.*, p. 9; *Littere Wallie*, p. 149.

25. *Ibid.*, p. 131.

26. Great Britain, Public Record Office, *Calendar of Welsh Rolls*, in *Calendar of Chancery Rolls, Various* (London: H.M. Stationery Office, 1912), p. 307; on this rebellion, see Ralph A. Griffiths, "The Revolt of Rhys ap Maredudd, 1287–1288," *Welsh Hist. Rev.*, 3 (1966–67), pp. 121–44.

examples, dealing less directly with military affairs, will be given below.

A number of monasteries suffered damage to houses and lands. Effects of such damage seem, however, to have been largely temporary, chiefly because of Edward's statesmanship, demonstrated by generous reimbursement. Commissioners appointed 25 June 1284, to examine, rule on, and meet claims for war damages were Robert de Chester, warden of Llanfaes—a new man in the position, since William de Merton, Llywelyn's aide, had been warden shortly before the outbreak of war in 1282; Nicholas de Rademere, prior of Rhuddlan Friary, also a new man, since the prior's name in 1278 had been Ifor, as noted above; and Ralph de Brocton, king's clerk. Payments to the Cistercians included £160 to Valle Crucis, represented by Madog, abbot; £100 each to Aberconway, represented by Adam, subprior, and Madog, monk, and to Basingwerk; £80 to Anian, prior, Cynfrig, chanter, and Madog, *magister conversorum*, representing Cadwgan, abbot of Cymmer, and the monks thereof; £78 to Strata Florida; and £43 to Strata Marcella. In addition, the abbot of Valle Crucis quit-claimed Edward for £4 for damages to the appropriated church of Bryneglwys, and John, monk of Basingwerk, proctor of the appropriated church of Holywell, similarly quit-claimed him for one mark. Of the Celtic foundations, Beddgelert, burned in the war, received £50, Priestholm £46, and Bardsey 10 marks. Llanllyr (Cardiganshire), an establishment of Cistercian nuns, received 40 marks through its proctor John "*dictus* Kaeau" (or Kaean), monk of Strata Florida. The friars of Bangor were awarded £100, those of Rhuddlan £17 10s., and those of Llanfaes £8. The commissioners also awarded sums to various ecclesiastical officers and to many churches. A grant of three marks to the church of "Hœnemere" (Hanmer?) *ad opus anacorite loci* shows the persistence of the hermit life in Wales.[27]

27. *Littere Wallie*, pp. 60–65, 71, 73,.76, 80–82, 84, 89, 93, 95–97, 107–108, 132–33, 174; for Beddgelert, see also *C. Charter R., 1257–1300*, p. 337. In 1281, Cynfrig had been prior of Cymmer, and Cadwgan had been *magister conversorum* (*Littere Wallie*, pp. 45–46).

Certain later claims by Strata Marcella, Basingwerk, and Whitland Abbeys were found to be correct; the last, amounting to £260 was never paid, since the monks gave up their rights in return for other considerations.[28] Aberconway Abbey was especially and permanently affected by the conquest: required to change its location and to make other adjustments in its land-holdings, it received a number of grants of land and sums of money in settlement of its affairs.[29] As the construction of Conway Castle affected Aberconway, so did that of the castle of Llanbadarn Fawr affect Strata Florida, but to a much smaller degree: a document of 1 December 1278, reads, "Whereas William de [Valencia], the king's uncle, lately caused a parcel of his land of [Llanbadarn Fawr] to be assigned to the abbot and convent of Strata Florida in recompense for a parcel of land of the abbot and convent that they remitted and quit-claimed to the king for his castle of [Llanbadarn Fawr], as is more fully contained in the deed made between William in the king's name and them: the king, ratifying and accepting the transaction, grants and confirms it as the deed aforesaid testifies."[30] Basingwerk was also involved in a minor transaction: from "the camp near Basingwerk," on 22 August 1277, Edward issued a mandate to Guncelin de Badlesmere, justice of Chester, to "pay out of the issues of his bailiwick to the abbot and convent of Basingwerk, 55 marks for a house bought of them."[31]

The Premonstratensian abbey of Talley had close relations with the South Wales prince Rhys ap Maredudd, and numbered among its canons men with such obviously Welsh names as Gruffydd, prior in 1281, and Elidyr.[32] Talley, too, was affected by Edward's military operations. On 6 January 1278, letters of protection were issued for two years to the abbot and convent of "Talilaghau," an English clerk's attempt to spell the abbey's Welsh name, Tal-y-llychau, "now in the king's hands by reason of its impoverishment through the Welsh war and by divers inconveniences it has sus-

---

28. O'Sullivan, pp. 74–75, 81.   29. See Hays, *Aberconway*, chap. iv.

30. *C. Welsh R.*, p. 177.   31. *C. Pat. R.*, *1272–1281*, p. 242.

32. *Littere Wallie*, pp. 59–60, 83, 106, 160. A Philip, cellarer in 1281, is also named.

tained because of that war, and no one is to be lodged in the abbey
or any of its granges."[33] The mention of granges constitutes a
reminder of the similarity of Premonstratensian organization to
Cistercian. On 6 August 1278, a safe-conduct, until Michaelmas,
was issued to the Cistercian abbot of Hayles (Gloucestershire),
visiting the abbey of Talley; this routine bit of paper-work is of
some interest because of Hayles's special connection with Aberconway Abbey.[34] On 7 July 1279, the canons of Talley again
received letters of protection,[35] and on 2 January 1285, after the
completion of the conquest, Edward issued the following statement: "Inasmuch as the land of Wales, which since no short time
was subject by feudal law to the Kings of England, is now united
to the King's dominion not only by power but by the way of
justice, and forasmuch as the King has found that the abbey of
[Talley] of the order of Prémontré in the diocese of St David's has
fallen from opulence to poverty: Grant, as far as the King can, to
the abbot and convent of [Welbeck] of the same order of the
fatherhood (*paternitam*) of the said abbey of [Talley], so that the
said abbot and monks of [Welbeck] may, as often as needs, exercise
in the said abbey the jurisdiction belonging to such fatherhood, and
do all else according to the requirements of the order."[36] No
mention is found, however, of direct reimbursement to Talley.

The confusion engendered by the Welsh wars seems to have
caused at least one Cistercian abbey to have problems with its
conversi. David H. Williams calls attention to the imprisonment in
Montgomery castle, in 1277, of three *conversi* of Strata Marcella.
He cites as authority an entry in the Close Rolls, dated 27 September
1277: "To the constable of the castle of Montgomery. Order
to cause brothers [Anian], Adam, and John, lay-brethren (*conversos*)
of the house of [Strata Marcella], imprisoned at Montgomery by
reason of a dispute between [Anian] bishop of St Asaph and the

33. *C. Pat. R., 1272–1281*, p. 251.

34. *Ibid.*, p. 275; see Hays, *Aberconway*, pp. 135–36, 145.

35. *C. Pat. R., 1272–1281*, p. 320.

36. *C. Charter R., 1257–1300*, p. 284; cf. Knowles and Hadcock, *Medieval
Religious Houses*, p. 168. Welbeck Abbey was in Nottinghamshire.

prior of [Chirbury], to be delivered from prison, as the bishop has mainprised to have them before the king at Shrewsbury in three weeks from Michaelmas next to stand to right concerning the things that the king or others will speak against them."[37] On 26 October 1280, Anian, bishop of St Asaph, wrote to Edward, praying him "to deliver brother William, *conversus* of the Cistercian order, of Anian's diocese, who is imprisoned in Montgomery castle by the bailiff of that place." It appears likely that a fourth lay brother of Strata Marcella had managed to get himself in trouble.[38] A friar of Bangor also suffered arrest. On 5 December 1278, an order was issued to the constable of Montgomery Castle to deliver to Llywelyn, prior of Bangor, a friar "who was arrested lately at Bangor while going from that house to the said town with certain goods, together with two grooms following him by reason of the goods aforesaid, which the constable is ordered to deliver to the prior." The bailiffs of Montgomery were given similar notification.[39]

The Edwardian conquest and settlement necessitated the performance of many routine administrative tasks. Many monasteries received confirmation of their charters, usually by *inspeximus*. Beddgelert was granted charters to replace some that had been destroyed when the house was burned. The term "free warren" appears twice. Basingwerk Abbey was granted free warren in its demesne lands in Flint, and the prior of Llanthony was confirmed free warren in all his lands in South Wales.[40]

37. *C. Close R., 1272–1279* (London: H.M. Stationery Office, 1900), p. 404; cf. Williams, "Cistercians in Wales," *loc. cit.,* pp. 24, 26. Williams refers to the provision of beer for the *conversi,* another Cistercian practice that accorded with ancient Celtic custom.

38. *Calendar of Ancient Correspondence,* p. 105.

39. *C. Welsh R.,* p. 180.

40. For confirmation of charters and liberties to Aberconway, Basingwerk, Grace Dieu, Strata Florida, Valle Crucis, Beddgelert, Llanthony, Priestholm, St. Dogmael's Abbey, and Pill Priory (the last two in Pembrokeshire, of the Order of Tiron), see *C. Charter R., 1257–1300,* pp. 273, 289–91, 337, 355, 423, 457–60, 468–69 (on pp. 457–59 Strata Marcella and Valle Crucis are confused); *C. Pat R., 1281–1292,* p. 451; *C. Welsh R.,* pp. 298–301; Hays, *Aberconway,* pp. 70–75.

The king made attempts at first to use Cistercian abbots and other Welsh religious in positions of authority. Professor O'Sullivan observes that "the immediate effect of the Edwardian Conquest and Settlement was to enhance the position and prestige of the Welsh Cistercians, who, from the first, were chosen to occupy posts of authority and influence. . . . The Crown could not afford to antagonize such an influential body of men by spoliation or injustice, and acted accordingly."[41] He calls attention to the use of the abbots of Whitland and Tintern, noting that in the latter case the practice was not new.[42] Before the conquest, however, the Cistercian abbots and other Welsh religious had been the trusted advisers of independent princes; afterwards, they could rarely be of more than local importance, except under special circumstances—for example, during the rebellion of Owain Glyndŵr in the early part of the fifteenth century. O'Sullivan further observes, "This policy of utilizing Cistercian influence was continued under Edward's successors, and Cistercians were employed on local boards of investigation, as envoys, arbiters, and judges, and especially as collectors and sub-collectors of the aids granted by Convocation."[43] These positions soon deteriorated, however, into little more than this last type of appointment, and the influence of a tax-collector, during the time that Welsh Cistercians held the position, was slight at best.[44] The abbots of Basingwerk, Strata Florida, and Whitland were on occasion summoned to Parliament as tenants-in-chief by military tenure, but there seems to be no indication of any particular influence there.[45] In addition to the Cistercians, Edward I made some use of other monks and friars from Welsh houses. He appointed the prior of Carmarthen to the position of treasurer for South and West Wales and employed Ifor, prior of Rhuddlan, and

41. *Cistercian Settlements*, p. 75.

42. *Ibid.*, pp. 71–72; *C. Welsh R.*, p. 324; *C. Close R.*, *1272–1279*, pp. 392–93 (among many other examples).

43. *Cistercian Settlements*, pp. 71–72.

44. *Ibid.*, p. 72; Hays, *Aberconway*, pp. 84–86.

45. O'Sullivan, pp. 72, 77, n. 52.

Llywelyn, prior of Bangor, in many connections.[46] The conclusion must be, nevertheless, that in the long run the conquest of necessity greatly diminished the importance of such Welshmen.

It is true, as W. Ogwen Williams says, that there is evidence of harassment by English government officials. This was an inevitable result of the nuisance of changing the details of legal and administrative procedures, and was probably quite temporary. Such harassment was not limited to monasteries with Welsh sympathies: besides Aberconway, Cymmer, and Whitland, similar difficulties are reported from Carmarthen.[47]

Among the most complex effects of the conquest, and those that must have most confused the monks, were the legal changes. These doubtless affected some monasteries less than others; thus those that held lands in England would already have had some experience with English law. Tintern had its lands in Hewelsfield, Gloucestershire, temporarily taken into the king's hands.[48] Basingwerk held lands in Derbyshire, which it was able to extend greatly after the conquest. Some of these were in one of the royal forests, so that adjustments were necessary to ensure exemption from forest law.[49] Cwmhir owned a water mill in Clun, Shropshire, for which the abbot had to render 6s. 8d. yearly to the lord. Since the title to the lordship was in dispute, this holding occasioned some legal difficulties.[50]

Routine matters, arising from the king's introduction of feudal law into Wales, necessarily affected the Welsh monks. On 2 Novem

46. Great Britain, Public Record Office, *Calendar of Fine Rolls, 1272–1307* (London: H.M. Stationery Office, 1911), p. 411; *C. Welsh R.*, pp. 162, 167, 169, 177. The prior of Carmarthen also served in a judicial capacity (*ibid.*, p. 268); see also *Calendar of Ancient Correspondence*, pp. 181, 183. An earlier prior, William, had been chaplain to Eleanor, the king's mother (*ibid.*, p. 116; *C. Pat R., 1272–1281*, p. 430).

47. Hays, *Aberconway*, pp. 87–91; O'Sullivan, pp. 82–83, 88–89; *C. Pat. R., 1272–1281*, p. 182; see n. 19, above.

48. *C. Close R., 1279–1288*, p. 17; *C. Fine R., 1272–1307*, p. 136; *Calendar of Ancient Correspondence*, p. 148; Williams, "Cistercians in Wales," *loc. cit.*, p. 18.

49. *Ibid.*, p. 13; *C. Charter R., 1257–1300*, p. 373.

50. *C. Close R., 1279–1288*, pp. 260–61; see map in Williams, "Cistercians in Wales," *loc. cit.*, p. 30.

ber 1281, Geoffrey de Brug', monk of Basingwerk, being duly sworn, said that he had seen no plea between any men and did not know the laws and customs of the Welsh. In the same year, the abbots of Whitland and Strata Florida made statements concerning Welsh laws and customs, the former showing slightly greater knowledge. Other routine provisions represented no change. The abbot of Basingwerk was granted quittance of the common summons before the justices in eyre in Derbyshire, and the abbot of Tintern similar quittance in Gloucestershire.[51]

Basingwerk was in a complicated position, evidenced by a letter of 14 July 1278, from Edward I to Llywelyn ap Gruffydd: "The king is not displeased because Llywelyn exacts from the abbot of Basingwerk those things that he and his predecessors have always been wont to receive heretofore, but it was the king's intention when he wrote to him for the bishop to induce him to do those things that are known to pertain to his honor rather than to cause any immunity to be extended to the abbot to do what he and his predecessors have been wont to do to Llywelyn and his progenitors, but the king requests him not to demand from the abbot other things than he ought justly to demand and than he has been wont to receive heretofore, and to treat the abbot so kindly that it may not behoove the king to send thither his justices at the just complaint of the abbot, whom the king cannot fail any more than others of his realm in doing justice, in order to hear his complaint and do justice to him. . . ."[52] Basingwerk's traditional English sympathies evidently played a part in this situation, in which it owed a complex dual allegiance resulting from the legal settlement after the military campaign of 1277.

The Welsh Assize Roll of 1277–1284 consists of cases extracted by the king's clerks from the Curia Regis Rolls of the same period. Some cases relating to Wales were not so extracted; for example, Professor Davies mentions the case of "Margaret de la Pole against Gregory, abbot of Welshpool [*i.e.*, Strata Marcella], why he pur-

---

51. *C. Welsh R.*, pp. 197, 207; *C. Close R., 1279–1288*, pp. 117, 177.
52. *C. Welsh R.*, pp. 174–75; see *Welsh Assize Roll*, p. 48.

sued a plea in Court Christian of her lay fee in Byttington."[53] A number of cases relating to Welsh monks were extracted, however, and contribute to our knowledge of their problems at this difficult time. In 1279–1280, Roger de Molis, bailiff of Llanbadarn Fawr, and Hywel ap Meurig were assigned to hear and determine the complaints and trespasses that Cynan ap Maredudd ab Owain had committed upon the abbot and convent of Strata Florida. If reasons existed why Roger and Hywel could not proceed in the matter, the parties were to come before the king in his next Parliament and there receive judgment. There had been trouble for some time between Strata Florida and Cynan. An agreement, enrolled at the Builth court, refers to extended litigation and disputes concerning the boundaries of the two parties' lands. The matter was referred to Llywelyn, abbot of Whitland, Anian, abbot of Caerleon, and Gruffydd ap Maredudd ab Owain, Cynan's brother; in default of acceptance of their arbitration, the offender was to pay twenty marks to the king and eighty marks to the other party, besides defraying the expenses of justice. The arbitrators' decision, generally overlooked by scholars interested in establishing the extents of Welsh monastic lands, was drawn up with great care and detail and duly submitted.[54]

Welsh abbots often proved inefficient litigants. Prolonged litigation took place between the abbot of Cwmhir and Peter Corbet concerning six acres of land at Hopton, of which the abbot claimed that his predecessor, Cadwgan, had been wrongfully disseised. On 6 October, 1279, the abbot was non-suited for failure to appear. He reopened the suit, but at the next court, on 2 December 1279, he was again non-suited because, being newly created abbot, he had never been in seisin of the land. Subsequently, Corbet claimed to hold the land as appurtenant to his barony of Caus and asked judgment whether he should answer without a

53. *Ibid.*, pp. 26–27. On 1 March 1270 or 1271, the abbot of Strata Marcella had been named James; together with Goronwy Puffing, prior, and Anian Ddu, monk, he witnessed a document of that date (*Littere Wallie*, p. 132; *C. Welsh R.*, pp. 171–73). On 21 July 1278, Dafydd ab Anian was prior (*Littere Wallie*, pp. 108–110).

54. *Welsh Assize Roll*, pp. 197–98, 300–301.

writ. The abbot was instructed to sue out his writ if he wished, and Corbet was *sine die*. The case came before the court again on 25 April 1281, when the abbot was amerced for failure to appear.[55]

In another example, the abbot of Basingwerk, in October 1279, brought a writ in a plea of trespass against Hywel ap Gruffydd and then failed to appear; the same happened in a plea of trespass by the abbot of Valle Crucis against Robert Crevequer on 14 January 1280, and in another by the abbot of Strata Marcella against Peter Corbet on 26 July 1281.[56] Professor Davies concludes that such non-appearance was a "favorite device" of the Welsh abbots, but surely it is more reasonable to suppose that changes to English law and to court procedure that had no parallel under Welsh law had bewildered the monks more than the economic changes that W. Ogwen Williams accuses of so doing.[57]

In a plea at Oswestry in 6 Edward I (1277–1278), Geoffrey ap Hwfa successfully claimed, against Adam ab Ithenard, Madog, his brother, and the abbot of Valle Crucis, certain lands and tenements in Nanheudwy. Llywelyn Fychan, "lord of that fee," was ordered to give seisin of the land, "whereof he [Geoffrey] says that a Hwfa ab Ithenard was seised on the day of his death," to Geoffrey. The plaintiff seems to have made up matters with his uncles, for on 14 January 1280, Adam de [*sic*] Ithenard and Madog, his brother, with Geoffrey, son of Hugh [*sic*] and Philip, his brother, brought a writ on lands in Aberceiriog against the abbot of Valle Crucis. On this occasion the plaintiffs failed to appear.[58] The same thing,

55. *Ibid.*, pp. 183–84, 281, 285, 288, 292, 294, 302, 304, 306, 312, 317, 320.

56. *Ibid.*, pp. 183–84, 284, 285, 306, 326, 330. Professor Davies incorrectly cites the abbot of Strata Marcella as plaintiff against Crevequer. On the latter case, see also O'Sullivan, p. 89; Williams, "Cistercians in Wales," *loc. cit.*, pp. 7, 42.

57. *Welsh Assize Roll*, pp. 183–84; see n. 19, above. On the general subject, see also O'Sullivan, chap. vii, especially p. 81, where it is shown that the abbot of Whitland suffered from the change to English law and its requirement that both parties to a suit appear in person in court. No date is given.

58. *Welsh Assize Roll*, pp. 183–84, 238, 284, 289. Professor Davies again makes the mistake of citing Strata Marcella instead of Valle Crucis (see n. 56, above). For further incidental reference to Valle Crucis, see *ibid.*, pp. 202–203, 246–48.

failure of the plaintiff to appear, happened when Robert Pigot proceeded in pleas of trespass and taking of cattle against Edeneweyn, abbot of Strata Marcella, on 6 October 1281, and when Cadwgan ap Cadwgan ap Herbert brought a writ on land in "Bromrochpol" against the abbot of Strata Marcella on 31 May 1282; in the former case Peter Corbet, on 8 December 1281, successfully claimed his court.[59] It appears that the Welsh abbots were more successful as defendants than as plaintiffs.

The counties of Cardigan and Carmarthen were more independent of Edward than were the areas in North Wales where he had established his English feudal law. "Not even the justice of West Wales would have presumed to discipline the abbots of Whitland and Strata Florida."[60] A case involving Strata Florida as plaintiff, dating from shortly after the conquest, is mentioned below. The abbot of Talley, with other landholders in West Wales, was required to furnish jurors when necessary.[61] The prior of Carmarthen in 1276 became engaged in lawsuits involving the bailiffs of Edmund, the king's brother, and requirements not previously made of the priory. At the time of the election of a new prior, John Edrich, on 26 May 1281, the temporalities of Carmarthen Priory were in the hands of the justice of West Wales.[62]

Elsewhere in South Wales, the abbot of Neath was involved in a case in which the earl of Gloucester and his bailiff brought a plea of trespass against him,[63] and the prior of Llanthony brought a serious complaint to the king's attention, in response to which Edward, on 12 October 1279, issued a commission of oyer and terminer to Walter de Hopton "and his fellows, justices for plaints, trespasses, and excesses committed in the parts of the march and of Wales, touching the trespasses of Theobald de Verdun, in causing beasts, as well of the plough as others, of Nicholas, prior of Llanthony Prima in Wales, at the prior's manors of Oldcastle (*de Veteri*

59. *Ibid.*, pp. 183–84, 295–96, 323, 331, 334, 336, 344.
60. *Ibid.*, p. 71. 61. *Ibid.*, p. 87n.
62. *C. Pat. R., 1272–1281*, pp. 182, 430, 437, 440.
63. *Welsh Assize Roll*, p. 32; see n. 88. below.

Castro) and Redcastle (*de Rubeo Castro*) to be taken by certain of his men and driven to his castle of Ewyas, and impounded and detained there, the said prior not being permitted to replevy them until some had perished of hunger, and until he had agreed with the said Theobald as to certain undue exactions; and other trespasses committed against the said prior; and touching the persons who came by night to the prior's manor of Newenton, broke his houses there, beat and wounded the prior and his men and certain of his fraternity and canons, and killed two of the said canons: the jury to be provided by the sheriff of Hereford, the king's bailiffs of [Abergavenny], and the bailiff of Edmund, count of Champagne, the king's brother, of the Three Castles." A later stage of the proceeding, dated 2 November 1281, associated Thomas Bek, bishop of St David's, and Robert de Tybotot with Walter de Hopton for the purpose of hearing this case.[64]

Some time after the conquest, on 12 June 1290, the king issued a commission of oyer and terminer to two judges on complaint of the prior of Brecon, a Benedictine priory dependent on Battle Abbey (Sussex), "that he is greatly wronged, touching tithes belonging to him and his church of Brecon, and his free court and prises of ale which he claims from his men and tenants in [Builth], and also by a toll exacted from him, his men, and tenants when coming to the land and town of [Builth] to trade, by John Giffard, keeper of the king's castle of [Builth], and his ministers, who assert that the king has the right to the foregoing."[65] Shortly afterwards, on 24 October 1291, the abbot and convent of Strata Florida had a similar complaint, for which a similar commission was issued, "that whereas [Maredudd] ap Robert, sometime lord of [Cydewain], by charter granted them in frank almoin his land of Aberunhull [*sic*] in [Cydewain], Edmund [Mortimer], to whom certain lands of the said [Maredudd] fell, asserting that they are bound to find for him and his household or in his absence for his bailiff all necessary victuals every Friday in the year, distrains them

64. *C. Pat. R., 1272–1281*, p. 350; *C. Welsh R.*, p. 190.
65. *C. Pat. R., 1281–1292*, p. 402.

and by their oxen and beasts at their grange of Aberunhull, situated in the said land."[66]

Professor O'Sullivan has stressed that the conquest did not entail the economic destruction, or even oppression, of the Welsh Cistercians. The king did not despoil or impoverish the Welsh houses, as older writers, such as George Roberts, supposed. A requirement was made that woods be cut down at Basingwerk, Strata Florida, Whitland, and Talley, but this requirement was for the protection of travelers, including the monks and those with whom they did business, and was not an oppressive measure.[67]

There is evidence, indeed, that the Cistercian houses were in financial difficulties immediately before the conquest, and that Edward I took some action to relieve these difficulties. On 1 August 1275, Llywelyn ap Gruffydd lent £12 to Cymmer Abbey for expenses of a trip to Cîteaux by the abbot, also named Llywelyn, and on 7 November 1281, he lent another £10 on security of the grange of Cyfeiliog. To Cadwgan, abbot of Cwmhir, Prince Llywelyn lent 40 marks on 13 May 1276, also on a pledge of land. He lent £20 to the abbot of Valle Crucis on 25 May 1275; £8 to Tudur, prior of Valle Crucis, on 9 August 1275; £12 to the prior on 17 May 1276; and £33 to Madog, the abbot, on 1 August 1280.[68] He also extended generosity to Aberconway, although the details are obscure.[69] These loans may to some extent have compensated for the extraordinary taxation to which Llywelyn subjected the monasteries in the period 1277–1282.[70] Edward's

66. *Ibid.*, p. 459.

67. *Cistercian Settlements*, pp. 72–73; cf. Roberts, "Strata Florida Abbey," *Archaeologia Cambrensis*, 3 (1848), 110–36. See also *C. Pat. R., 1272–1281*, p. 256; *C. Welsh R.*, pp. 171, 184–85, 186–87, 293, 301–302; Williams, "Cistercians in Wales," *loc. cit.*, pp. 12–18. A *conversus* named Madog was in charge of the program at Strata Florida.

68. *Littere Wallie*, pp. 32–33, 36, 40, 45–46. For further references to Cadwgan of Cwmhir, see *ibid.*, p. 44, where he and two others are recorded to have stood surety for one John ap Hywel, whom they petitioned Prince Llywelyn to release from prison, and n. 55, above.

69. Hays, *Aberconway*, pp. 55–56.

70. On this subject, see W. H. Waters, *The Edwardian Settlement of North Wales in Its Administrative and Legal Aspects, 1284–1343* (Cardiff: University of Wales Press Board, 1935), pp. 26–29.

compensation to the monasteries for war damages has already been mentioned. In addition, he showed much generosity to Aberconway in connection with the transfer of its location to Maenan; remitted payments called putures that Aberconway, Basingwerk, and the Knights Hospitallers had been accustomed to make to Llywelyn; and granted further remissions to Basingwerk.[71]

Basingwerk also received, on 7 November 1290, a grant of a weekly market on Wednesday at the manor of Glossop, Derbyshire, and of a yearly fair there on the vigil, the feast, and the morrow of St Barnabas. This charter was afterwards cancelled, and the market granted on Monday and the fair on the vigil, the feast, and the morrow of St Mary Magdalen. On 20 August 1292 another grant was made to Basingwerk of a weekly market on Friday at the manor of Holywell, Flint, and of a yearly fair there on the vigil, the feast, and the morrow of Holy Trinity.[72]

A large number of economic changes, fundamentally affecting the Welsh Cistercians, took place in the later middle ages—loss of the *conversi*, entry into competition in the wool trade, switch from economy of agriculture to one of rents;[73] but it is difficult to see that the Edwardian conquest was particularly responsible for any of these developments, although in the case of Aberconway, the transfer to Maenan, resulting from the conquest, and the acquisition of rental income there, hastened the process of conversion to rent economy.[74] In the long run, there is no doubt that payments claimed and services requested by the King were hardships to the monks, but it is doubtful whether they would have been felt as such had they not come on top of other troubles like those mentioned by Glanmor Williams. Thus, Aberconway cited (c. 1316),

71. See Hays, *Aberconway*, chap. iv; *C. Welsh R.*, pp. 301–302, 304; *C. Pat. R., 1292–1301* (London: H.M. Stationery Office, 1895), p. 143.

72. *C. Charter R., 1257–1300*, pp. 372, 423; Williams, "Cistercians in Wales," *loc. cit.*, pp. 21, 39.

73. *Ibid.*, pp. 2–47; O'Sullivan, chap. v. An additional valuable contribution to the economic history of the Welsh Cistercians is Geraint Dyfnallt Owen, "Some Agrarian Conditions and Changes in Southwest Wales in the Sixteenth Century" (Ph.D. dissertation, University of Wales, 1935).

74. See Hays, *Aberconway*, chaps, iv, vi.

as a reason for refusal to grant a corrody, a recent pestilence among the animals.[75] Basingwerk, probably in 1346 or 1347, cited various reasons for failure to grant a subsidy: "The abbot has recently received from the King a letter which asked him to help the King with a loan of twenty pounds in view of the great business of the realm, and the dangers threatening the English church. The abbot replies that he and his twenty fellow monks living in the said monastery among the Welsh near the road have a heavy burden of hospitality; and that it is notorious that they have in Wales and Cheshire rents which are very small and possessions which are incredibly sterile . . . yet they have contributed a gift towards the thousand marks granted to their lord the Prince of Wales in the county of Chester . . . the abbot therefore prays the king . . . with which they cannot comply without utterly ruining themselves. Dated: *in predicto monasterii de consensu totius capituli ix. kal. Octobr.*"[76]

The history of Tintern will illustrate more effectively the point at issue here. On 15 July 1400, the English provincial chapter issued an order for yearly taxation of nearly all English and Welsh Cistercian abbeys for the purpose of supporting Cistercian scholars at Oxford University. Amounts were presumably assigned in accordance with the various houses' degree of prosperity. In a list of seventy-four, Tintern was bracketed with Whalley (Lancashire), Beaulieu (Hampshire), and Vale Royal at 53s. 4d., behind only the great houses of Furness (Lancashire), Rievaulx (Yorkshire), and Fountains (Yorkshire) at 66s. 8d.[77] In 3 Henry IV (1401–1402) the abbot of Tintern submitted a petition, which was granted, to the king in Parliament, asking that he be excused payment of a tenth granted by the clergy, for which he was collector in the diocese of Llandaff, on the ground that he could not collect it from others, some of whom had flatly refused to pay, and that his monastery

75. *Ibid.*, pp. 91–93; see n. 18, above, and Henry S. Lucas, "The Great European Famine of 1315, 1316, and 1317," *Speculum*, 5 (1930), pp. 343–77.

76. *Calendar of Ancient Correspondence*, p. 185. The document is partly illegible.

77. R. C. Fowler, "Cistercian Scholars at Oxford," *English Historical Review*, 23 (1908), pp. 84–87.

K

would be ruined if required to make up the deficit.[78] David H.
Williams points out that the year 1405 was an especially bad one
for the monasteries of South Wales, including Tintern, whose lands
sustained considerable damage from the Glyndŵr rebellion.[79] Later
in the century, a casual reference rated Tintern as the poorest abbey
in the land, contrasting it with Westminster, the richest.[80]

In all of this, there is little indication that the Edwardian conquest
had much effect on the monasteries' economic activities or prosperity. In their later centuries, the Welsh monasteries became more
concerned with economic affairs, but similar developments were
taking place all over Europe. The Welsh monasteries had had their
economic difficulties before the conquest. The subsequent exactions
of the King and the Prince of Wales were not welcomed, but if
economic activities in general had prospered, these exactions would
probably have been of little moment. David H. Williams cites few
economic changes resulting from the conquest; he and other writers
cite much evidence of the extreme economic problems resulting
from Glyndŵr's rebellion.[81]

Dr C. H. Talbot observes that the economic and political preoccupations of the Welsh Cistercians may have accounted to a great
extent for the slight impact they made in the cultural and spiritual
spheres. He contends that "not one work of spiritual or literary
merit (if we except the prayers of Cadogan [sic] of Bangor) emerged
from the Cistercians of Wales during the 400 years they were in

78. Great Britain, Parliament, *Rotuli Parliamentorum* (London: House of
Lords, 1767–77), vol. 3, p. 481.

79. "Cistercians in Wales," *loc. cit.*, p. 6.

80. John Russell, *Boke of Nurture,* in *Early English Meals and Manners,* ed.
Frederick J. Furnivall ("Early English Text Society," London: Oxford
University Press, 1868), pp. 76–77:

"Also the abbote of Westminster, the hiest of this lande
The abbote of Tynterne the poorest, y vndirstande,
They ar bothe abbotes of name, and not lyke of fame to faude;
Yet Tynterne with Westminster shalle nowther sitte ne stande."

Russell, who was usher and marshal to Humphrey, duke of Gloucester
(d. 1447), is here discussing order of precedence.

81. "Cistercians in Wales," *loc. cit.;* Williams, *Welsh Church,* chap. vi.

existence."[82] Here he ignores the patronage accorded by the monasteries in their later years to Welsh bards, a subject that is only now receiving the attention it deserves;[83] more important for present purposes is his failure to mention the chronicle-writing that took place in the Welsh abbeys. The following discussion does not deal with the provenance of particular manuscripts,[84] but of the writing itself.

The *Brut y Tywysogion*, earlier parts of which were composed at St David's and Llanbadarn Fawr, comes in its present form from Strata Florida, as does the *Annales Cambriae*, ultimately the same chronicle. The *Brut* is the basis for present-day knowledge of Welsh history up to the Edwardian conquest. The *Brut* ends with 1282, the *Annales* with 1288, circumstances that help to account for the comparative darkness of the period from the conquest to 1485. A continuation of the *Brut* to 1332 is thought by Professor J. Goronwy Edwards to have come from Valle Crucis, while Thomas Jones thinks it a conflation from various places; it is so meager that certainty seems impossible. Jones suggests that another version, the *Cronica de Wallia*, which ends with 1285, also comes from Strata Florida, but J. Beverley Smith has presented strong reasons for believing that its place of origin was Whitland.[85] Some entries in the *Brut* reflect other documents, probably deriving from such

82. Review, Hays, *Aberconway, loc. cit.,* pp. 129–30.

83. See Williams, *Welsh Church,* chap. xi; article by G. J. Williams on abbots of Margam as patrons of Welsh literature in *Transactions of the Port Talbot Historical Society,* 1 (1965), no. 2, p. 69–81.

84. Thomas Jones suggests, for example, that the Peniarth MS. 20 version of the *Brut y Tywysogion* was written at Valle Crucis (*Brut y Tywysogion: Peniarth MS. 20 version,* pp. xlvii–xlix).

85. For reference to one text of the Brut, see n. 16, above; in this version, see especially the introduction, pp. xxxix–xli, lxi–lxiii. See also review by J. G. Edwards, *EHR,* 5 (1942), pp. 370–77. Another text, lacking the continuation to 1332, is in *Brut y Tywysogyon or The Chronicle of the Princes: Red Book of Hergest Version; Critical Text and Translation with Introduction and Notes* by Thomas Jones ("Board of Celtic Studies, University of Wales: History and Law Series," No. 16; Cardiff: University of Wales Press, 1955); here, see especially the introduction, pp. lii–lv. The only edition of the *Annales Cambriae* is that of J. Williams ab Ithel ("Rolls Series," No. 20; London: Longman, Green, Longman and Roberts, 1860); it is to be hoped that some

monasteries as Aberconway, Basingwerk, Caerleon, Cwmhir, Strata Marcella, Whitland, and Talley.[86]

Another chronicle, composed at Aberconway, is much slighter than the *Brut*, and ends with 1283. One sentence in it was evidently written considerably later, and significantly reveals the monks' viewpoint: "And after many years, it happened that . . . the prince of North Wales reassumed the entire name of the whole principality of Wales, which he enjoyed, with his successors, until the time of Prince Llywelyn ap Gruffydd ap Llywelyn ab Iorwerth Drwyndwn, since whose death they have had, to the present time, no prince of their own race, as will plainly appear in what follows."[87]

The *Annales de Margam* and the little-used *Chronicle of the Thirteenth Century*, which refers to events involving Margam, Neath, and Tintern, are written from the Anglo-Norman rather than the Welsh point of view, but they too end early—with 1232 and 1294, respectively. Hitherto unpublished manuscripts may carry the story further; Jones refers, for example, to a "Book of Basingwerk" that ends with 1461.[88] The general cessation of the chronicling of Welsh history is, however, highly significant and, with the narratives them-

competent scholar will undertake to edit this chronicle, but, so far, plans in this direction have not borne fruit. Thomas Jones has edited " 'Cronica de Wallia' and Other Documents from Exeter Cathedral Library MS. 3514," *Bulletin of the Board of Celtic Studies,* 12 (1946–48), pp. 27–44; on this, see also J. Beverley Smith, "The 'Cronica de Wallia' and the Dynasty of Dinefwr," *BBCS,* 20 (1962–64), pp. 261–82.

86. See Sir John Edward Lloyd, *The Welsh Chronicles* ("The Sir John Rhys Memorial Lecture, British Academy, 1928; from the Proceedings of the British Academy, Vol. XIV;" Oxford: University Press, n.d.), pp. 16–20; *Brut y Tywysogyon: Peniarth MS. 20 Version,* p. xxxiv n.

87. *Register and Chronicle of the Abbey of Aberconway,* ed. Sir Henry Ellis ("Camden Society," No. 39; vol. 1 of *Camden Miscellany;* London: Camden Society, 1843); translation and discussion in Hays, *Aberconway,* pp. 143–53.

88. *Annales de Margam,* in *Annales monastici,* ed. Henry Richards Luard ("Rolls Series," No. 36), vol. 1 (London: Longman, Green, Longman, Roberts and Green, 1864); see the introduction, pp. xiii–xv, where the editor notes that one or two leaves are lost at the end. "Chronicle of the Thirteenth Century: MS. Exchequer Domesday," *Arch. Camb.,* 3rd ser., 8 (whole number 29) (1862), 272–83; this records, among other details, that in 1284, Edward I "in Abbatia de [Neath] intravit et dedit Abbati Adae unum

selves, tells much about the preoccupations and outlook of the monks. Constant interest in Welsh political and military history is evident in the chronicles. "With the Edwardian conquest, the curtain descends," wrote Dr Frank R. Lewis.[89] Professor O'Sullivan adds, "[The Welsh Cistercians'] loss of the sense of the spiritual is a phenomenon for which it is extremely difficult to account. A possible explanation may be that, in view of their nationalistic outlook, retrogression set in with the loss of Welsh independence . . . Aberconway, Margam, and Strata Florida ceased to chronicle Welsh history after the Edwardian Conquest."[90] The monasteries' subsequent preoccupation with economic affairs, "getting and spending," as G. G. Coulton, using Wordsworth's phrase, described it, is typical of the later middle ages. Their concern for patronage of bards shows that even after the conquest they did not limit their interests exclusively to economic matters. In general, though, the conclusion may be drawn that the conquest did indeed contribute to the decline of the Welsh monasteries,[91] and that the monks themselves were to blame for this situation, since they had failed before the conquest to establish any significant interest or activity, except the economic, that was unconnected with Welsh political nationalism.

Rhŷs W. Hays

Wisconsin State University
Stevens Point

Baudekyn pulcherrimum" (p. 281). It mentions, too, that the dispute between Adam, abbot of Neath, and the earl of Gloucester (see n. 63, above), was settled in 1289 (*ibid.*). For the "Book of Basingwerk," see *Brut y Tywysogyon: Peniarth MS. 20 Version*, p. xii.

89. "The Racial Sympathies of the Welsh Cistercians," *Cymmr. Trans.*, (1938), pp. 111–12.

90. *Cistercian Settlements*, p. 129.

91. One effect of the conquest, its influence on Welsh attendance at the chapter-general at Cîteaux, has not been discussed here; on this, see *ibid.*, p. 71; Hays, *Aberconway*, pp. 81–82. On 27 June 1284, Edward issued a letter for the abbot of Basingwerk, "going beyond seas, nominating Simon de Sancto Edmundo, his monk," his attorney for one year (*C. Pat. R., 1281–1292*, p. 124).

THE STATUTE OF CARLISLE AND THE
CISTERCIANS 1298-1369

FROM ONE POINT OF VIEW the Statute of Carlisle represents both the capstone of Edward I's legislation in respect to the regular clergy, and the pediment of all the anti-papal enactments of the two reigns which followed. The law begins by observing that the ends for which religious houses were established by the crown, the lords and their antecedents were being frustrated by the "divers, heavy and importable tallages, payments and impositions upon all of the said monasteries and houses" by their foreign superiors. These charges, it is averred, were made without the consent of the king and the nobles and were contrary to the laws and customs of the realm. It is therefore enjoined that no rent, tax or levy of any kind, whether by guise of mutual sale, loan, exchange or other contract, be carried out in the king's dominions by any person of religion under royal jurisdiction. A similar prohibition is directed against foreign superiors from imposing such tributes. A further clause concerns itself with the abbatial seal. Should any presume against the statute and be convicted "he shall be grievously punished according to the quality of his offence and according to his contempt of the king's prohibition."[1]

The statute was born at a time of considerable stress; its enactor was old, weary and ailing, with but a few months until dissolution;

1. *Statutes of the Realm*, 9 vols. in 10 pts. (London, 1810-1822), vol. 1 pp. 150-52; *Rotuli Parliamentorum*, 6 vols. (London, 1832), vol. 1, p. 217.

its supporters were resentful of papal taxation and provisions; its political and ecclesiastical background was unsettled; the Bruce was at large in Scotland, prolonged wrangling with Philip IV was increasing tension with France, the papal court under Clement V had recently begun to live in its "Babylonian Captivity" and, Archbishop Winchelsey, that "spiteful and perverse" man had only just departed for Rome in disgrace and in suspension.

That Edward was convinced of the necessity for the law there is no doubt. His reasons were threefold. In the first place, from 1276 onward the debasement of the coinage by Jews and merchants had been a constant irritant. In the search for a solution a variety of measures were tested. Justices were appointed to try those accused of coin clipping but as this proved inadequate a complete reminting of the currency was decided upon three years later.[2] By 1284 defective monies were still sufficiently numerous to force the formulation of a statute of money. In turn this was supplemented seven years later by a "little" statute of the same name which instructed sheriffs and customs officers to publish the penalties reserved for those who might be tempted to transgress the law.[3] Yet the evil endured and even flourished for in June of 1294 commissions were again issued for the examination of the coins on deposit in various repositories throughout the kingdom in order that the true might be sifted from the base.[4] Concurrently, a survey of the goods and revenues of alien religious houses was made lest they be shipped abroad, while the crusading tenths were sequestered before they could be forwarded to Rome. Although the laws against bad money provided the pretext for all this activity it is clear that the

2. *Calendar of Patent Rolls* (1272–1281), pp. 236, 238. Hereafter cited CPR. *Red Book of the Exchequer,* 3 pts., ed. H. Hall, *Rolls Series,* No. 99 (London, 1896), vol. 3, pp. 980–82.

3. *CPR* (1281–1290), pp. 129–30; *Calendar of Close Rolls* (1288–1296), pp. 9, 203. Cited CCR. *Statutes of the Realm,* vol. 1, pp. 219–20.

4. M. Powicke, *The Thirteenth Century,* (Oxford, Clarendon Press, 1962), p. 670. See also *CPR* (1281–1292), p. 86. The abbot of Bruern was implicated in a case involving Guy Bertaldi and his colleagues, charged with contravening the money laws. *CCR* (1296–1302), p. 264.

financing of the expedition to Gascony was as much in mind as the rehabilitation of the coinage.[5]

It is undeniable, moreover, that Edward's attitude to *apportum* was deeply influenced by the course affairs were taking in France. His cousin at Paris was pursuing a fiscal policy toward the church that was hardly one whit different from his own although implemented with much more finesse and unscrupulousness. From a tenth in aid of a new venture to the Holy Land, to a tenth for a Capetian crusade to Aragon, to a tenth "for the urgent need of the kingdom" against England was not so long or so difficult a step as it appeared. All the while the view of what constituted the *temporalia*, the goods subject to the tax, was increasingly broadened until the *spiritualia*—the *bona immuna*—came to embrace only "the offerings of the altar and the sanctuary." Finally all properties, movable or immovable, clerical as well as lay, were ordered taxed. Since 1284 Philip's demands were unremitting, fluctuating from a tenth to a hundredth and leading, by 1295, to large and widespread arrears.[6] To the Order of Cîteaux, unrivalled in wealth and connections, the levies had become unsupportable. At a general chapter the imposts were deplored and strongly worded protests were drafted first to the curialist prelate, Pierre Barbet, and then to Pope Boniface in the name of "all the clergy of the realm." The gist of these was that the fathers were willing "to contribute from the goods conferred upon us, according to natural equity and legitimate sanctions," but, *nova vectigalia instituti non posse*.[7]

Clericis laicos, the pontiff's answer to Cistercian complaints, absolutely forbade any secular power to raise money from its clergy except with the express permission of the Holy See. The conse-

5. *Bartholomaei de Cotton, Historia Anglicana,* ed. H. R. Luard, *Rolls Series,* No. 16 (London; 1859), pp. 299–302; *The Chronicle of Walter of Guisborough,* ed. H. Rothwell, *Camden Series,* 89 (1957), pp. 249–50.

6. E. Lavisse, *Histoire de France,* 9 vols. in 18 pts., (Paris, 1911), vol. 4, pt. 2, pp. 109–111, 113–17, 240–42.

7. Kervyn de Lettenhove, "Études sur l'histoire du XIIIème siècle," *Mémoires de l'Academie Royale des Sciences des Lettres et Beaux Arts de Belgique,* 28 (1854), pp. 10, 14–15.

quences of this inhibition on Franco-Papal relations need not divert us here. It is enough to say that peace was only restored after a papal retreat, culminating in the canonization of Philip's grandfather.[8] The peace lasted little more than a year. By 1298 Philip was committed to an invasion and occupation of Flanders, a venture which necessitated further taxation. News of this tax may have been bruited in England by the envoys charged with negotiating Edward's marriage to Princess Margaret Capet. It is also possible that the English White Monks were asked to render material assistance to the mother house in its great need and that word of that request reached the Plantagenet court.[9] Notwithstanding the nuptial alliance Edward had every reason to suspect King Philip of double dealing. With seeming ease the Capetian had wrecked the chain of alliances which English money and concessions had effected among the dynasts of Flanders and the Empire, and checkmated the great force led by Edward himself to rescue Guy Dampierre. There was, besides, the French agitation of the Scots.[10]

On his return from Flanders in 1298 Edward was faced with a new Scottish campaign and little with which to finance it. "In his most urgent necessity" he ordered Robert Burghesse, Warden of the Cinque Ports, to notify all his assistants to prevent the departure of the Cistercian abbots and monks to their general chapter unless they had the king's special licence. On the same day he despatched a letter to Abbot Rufinus of Cîteaux (1294–1299) informing him of the prohibition and requesting that the monks be held excused.[11] There were of course several precedents for this sort of action; none

8. For a translation of the texts of the bulls issued during this contest see B. Tierney, *The Crisis of Church and State,* (Englewood Cliffs, N.J.: 1964), pp. 175, 178.

9. This at least occurred in 1302. See below p. 145, Philip, it must be noted, agreed to the marriage arrangements in the abbey of l'Aumône.

10. Powicke, pp. 695–698.

11. *CCR* (1296–1302), pp. 215-16. Sixteen other bailiffs received these orders. Shortly before this order was sent out the abbot of Rievaulx had obtained a letter of protection in anticipation of his journey to the chapter and had nominated attorneys to act in his absence. *CPR* (1292–1301), p. 354. A special letter was drafted and sent to Cîteaux explaining the abbot of Stanlaw's absence. *CCR* (1296–1302), p. 217.

of them however was inspired by quite the same degree of shrewdness as was presented on this occasion.[12] Forty-six abbots received a directive and request in the days that followed to the effect that they "aid him with all the *apportum* that [they] would carry to the coming general chapter." The money was to be turned over to the treasurer and chamberlain of the exchequer at York. Remuneration was promised *non sine condignis premiis suo tempore rependendis*.[13] During the third week of August writs were sent out to all sheriffs directing that inquisitions be held to ascertain what members of the Order had sent contributions out of the kingdom as a subsidy to Cîteaux or whether they had sent wool instead.[14] No returns to these have been discovered, an absence which tempts one to conclude that the prohibition was meticulously obeyed. Likewise, no acknowledgments of the monies delivered, if delivered they were, to the exchequer have come to light.

The ban was continued into the next year, mainly as a reaction to new events in France. In February of 1299 King Philip had made two further demands on Cîteaux threatening dire consequences unless they submitted.[15] Edward therefore addressed the abbot

12. The earliest example occurs in King John's time, the occasion being a Cistercian refusal to grant an aid. Gervase of Canterbury, *Gesta Regum*, 2 vols., ed. W. Stubbs, *Rolls Series*, No. 73 (London: 1880), vol. 2, p. 105; *Chronica Johannis de Oxenedes*, ed. H. Ellis, *Rolls Series*, No. 13 (London, 1859), pp. 125–26. Henry III debarred them also from attending for a similar reason and, as well, prevented them from selling their wool abroad. *Annales Monastici*, 5 vols., ed. H. R. Luard, *Rolls Series*, No. 36 (London, 1865), vol. 3, pp. 163–64. Licences were frequently issued to those going abroad: *CPR* (1232–1247) p. 481, to the abbot of Boxley; *Ibid.* (1258–1266), p. 340, to the abbot of Fountains. The king placed a similar ban earlier on Cluniac *apportum*. Cf. R. Graham, *English Ecclesiastical Studies*, (London, S.P.C.K. 1929), p. 106.

13. *CCR* (1296–1302), p. 216. Despite his need of a war chest Edward did not cut back on the charities in which he had a personal interest. In April of this year, for instance, he gave over to his foundation at Vale Royal 1,000 marks for the building fund. *Ibid.*, p. 158.

14. *CCR* (1296–1302), p. 218. A statute enacted at the general chapter of that year provided that all affiliates of the Order were to pay specified sums to Cîteaux and laid it down that those who failed to do so would be excommunicated. *Statuta*, vol. 3 (1298:4,8).

15. Lettenhove, *op. cit.*, p. 23. In this year also the *Ordinatio de libertatibus perquirendis* was published. *Statutes of the Realm*, vol. 1, p. 131.

general anew asking that all the Cistercian superiors in his kingdom be once more absolved from attending except John, Abbot of Garendon (c. 1299–1330), who had his permission to attend. In the interim the English fathers who had foregathered at London prior to crossing the channel received a message from the king stipulating that only those of them who had royal permission would be allowed to depart. A memorandum was the next day sent to the Warden of Cinque Ports apprising him of this decision. By the next April the king decided to repeal the ban on overseas travel but the injunction against the transport of *apportum* remained in effect. It is possible that this relaxation was the outcome of Abbot Robert of Holm Cultram's pleas or possibly it was a reaction to the general suspicion of the prelates and barons to royal equivocation in the matter of the charters. At all events, letters allowing the nomination of attorneys, charters of protection, with and without clause *volumus*, were issued to abbots intent on attending the general chapter that autumn.[16]

A revival of the strife between King Philip and Pope Boniface in the latter half of 1301 let loose a new rash of troubles for Cîteaux and her daughters. The apprehension of Bishop Bernard Saisset prompted the publication of the bull, *Salvator Mundi*, and, the summoning of the French clergy to a meeting at Rome, to which the abbot of Cîteaux was invited.[17] Materially, the lot of the Order was, at this point, a sad one. Every attempt by the *pater abbas*, John Pontoise (1299–1304) to improve it with the help of his English subordinates was frustrated by Edward's vigilance. Thus in February of 1302 letters were despatched to a dozen abbots asserting that it

---

16. *CPR* (1292–1301), p. 431. *CCR* (1296–1302), p. 314. Licences allowing overseas travel in 1299 were granted to Brother Henry Radelegh of Hayles in the service of Earl Edmond of Cornwall, *CCR* (1296–1302), p. 265 and to the abbot of Sawtry, the nature of whose business is not disclosed. *CPR* (1292–1301), pp. 479–80. Edward spent a fortnight at Holm Cultram in the autumn of the previous year and was indebted to its abbot. *CPR* (1292–1301), p. 514 *seq.*; *CCR* (1296–1302), pp. 348–49.

17. *Les Registres de Boniface VIII*, 4 vols., ed. G. Digard, (Paris, 1884–1939), Nos. 4422–4423.

had come to his ears that the abbot general had sent special emissaries to their communities with instructions to collect a subsidy for Cîteaux's use. They were warned not to act counter to the ordinances against exportation by contributing money or other negotiables with royal licence for "it might otherwise redound to the king's prejudice."[18]

In the meanwhile *Asculta fili* had made its way to Paris only to be supplanted by a *bâtise* of Capetian composition, *Scire te volumus*. Shortly also, a series of royal prohibitions were published, one of which made illegal any unauthorized departures from France. Nevertheless, when the Roman council assembled that November Abbot Pontoise was among the almost two score French prelates present. His defiance resulted in a royal threat to seize Cistercian properties but even this failed to shake his loyalty to the pontiff.[19] Thus, at the indictment of the pope and the most recent bull, *Unam Sanctam*, by the French court in June of 1303 only the voice of Cîteaux vehemently rejected the proposal to call a General Council to depose him. For this new act of defiance Pontoise was incarcerated and the properties of the Order taken into the king's hands.[20] Philip was not content only with the removal of his enemy from view. So long as John was confined in a royal cell he stood as a martyr for his Order and a symbol of resistance to royal tyranny. By 1304 the pressures on him became so great that he resigned. His replacement, Abbot Henry of Jouy, was of less heroic stuff, amenable to royal wishes and desirous of peace without dignity if need be. With his accession all real opposition to Capetian oppression passed away.[21] It is not surprising therefore that the Plantagenet, busy now on his last campaign against the Scots, was so receptive to

18. *CCR* (1296–1302), p. 576.

19. *Registres de Boniface VIII*, No. 4424. For the forgeries see P. Dupuy, *Histoire du différend d'entre le Pape Boniface VIII et Philippe le Bel, Roy de France*, (Paris, 1655), p. 42 *seq.*

20. Word of Abbot John's imprisonment and the confiscation of property is implied in the bull *Super Petri Solio* which excommunicated Philip. *Registres de Boniface III*, No. 4428.

21. A. King, *Cîteaux and her elder Daughters*, (London: Burns & Oates, 1954), pp. 49–50.

the petition of those wishing to put an end to foreign levies on English foundations.

Some time before Pontoise's resignation, in December of 1303, a second attempt was made to collect the English *apportum*. Proctors were sent over from the mother-house to aid the abbot of Dore, the executor of the collection. Again the crown was notified of what was afoot and again a warning was issued.[22] This second failure evoked a protest from Abbot Henry of Cîteaux (1304–1315) which, in turn, spurred the remonstrance of the nobles against the carriage of *apportum* in the Lent Parliament of 1305. Within days of his election as abbot general, in the autumn of 1304, Henry found the Order and especially Cîteaux smothering under a welter of debts, most of them originating from the accumulated impositions of the previous twenty years. He believed, moreover, that the situation was to a great extent aggravated by the continued opposition of King Edward to the payment of tribute by his insular affiliations. The principal theme of his letter to the English was, however, that the money was indispensable if the common privileges were to be preserved inviolate and that, if it continued to be detained, the unity of the Order would be destroyed. The plea fell on deaf ears, nobles and clerics being unanimous in opposition.[23]

Even though the baronial petition and the statute which was formulated to meet it emphasize the role of the magnates it is not at all clear how far they were the direct outcome of baronial fears and dissatisfaction. It is certain of course that a few patrons early devised dampers against excessive demands made upon clients by foreign religious superiors.[24] But the evidence of such directed against Cîteaux appears to be wanting. By any measure this is indeed a revealing fact inasmuch as the law was intended to inhibit the passage of money to that alien authority in particular. Either

22. *CCR* (1302–1307), pp. 68–69.
23. *Memoranda de Parliamento*, ed. F. W. Maitland, *Rolls Series*, No. 98 (London, 1893), pp. 312–14; *Rot. Parl.* vol. I, p. 178b.
24. S. Wood, *English Monasteries and their Patrons*, (Oxford: Clarendon Press, 1955), pp. 148–50; Graham, pp. 106, 230–32. It should be noted that patronal interests in Cistercian foundations were originally held in "pure, free and perpetual alms."

patrons had only just become aware of the injunctions of the *Carta Caritatis* respecting tribute or Cîteaux's exactions had only just become oppressive. My belief is that baronial concern was a more comprehensive matter, *apportum* being merely the ankus to settle the more ancient, prevalent and provoking abuses of provisions and taxation.[25] This is not to say that the English White Monks and their benefactors were unaffected by either. For some time before the turn of the century the Cistercians were very much involved in the phenomena of appropriations and this insinuates that patrons could be affected directly whenever one of the livings they had bestowed on the monks was provided for by the papacy.[26] Similarly, their interests could be impugned by papal taxation if their clients held any land of them by secular service, a condition in which not a few of Cîteaux's affiliates found themselves by the middle of the thirteenth century.[27] Generally, however, the discontent of the baronial patrons of religious institutions was deeper on the side of those who endowed and supported non-Cistercian establishments. This may well account for the remarkable assertion in the plea that

25. Cf. especially W. A. Pantin, *The English Church in the Fourteenth Century,* (Cambridge: University Press, 1955), pp. 47–75; A. H. Sweet, "The Apostolic See and the Heads of the English Religious Houses," *Speculum,* 28 (1953), pp. 468–84; A. Deeley, "Papal Provisions and rights of royal patronage in the early fourteenth century," *English Historical Review,* 73 (1928), pp. 497–527.

26. Sweet, p. 475 cites the instance of Clement VI's provision of a Fr William to the conventual priory of Castleacre in 1344. For instances of papal provisions to Cistercian livings note *Calendar of Papal Letters* (1198–1304), p. 182; (1305–1342), p. 158; (1342–1362), p. 279. Hereafter cited *CPL.* There is also the case of William Marcel, a monk of Tintern, accused of forging papal letters "by which he was able to obtain a dignity or office together with his accomplices." *Ibid.* (1305–1352), p. 350.

27. A glance through the knight's fees in *Kirkby's Inquest,* ed. R. H. Skaife, *Surtees Society Publications,* 49, (1866), pp. 190–385, shows that eight of the northern cloisters held fees immediately of the king or of others who held of the king in chief. Twenty-seven houses were ordered to despatch knights for the king's service in the years from 1297 to 1300. *Parliamentary Writs and Writs of Military Summons,* 2 vols. in 4 pts., ed. F. Palgrave, (London, 1827–1834), vol. 1, pp. 269:45, 286: 15, 16, 289:17, 291:19, 293:20, 21, 333:17, 335:19, 337:20, 338:20. These lands were subject to all secular service and other encumbrances.

action was taken "on behalf of the Cistercians," when it should, more properly, have said that it was taken at their behest.

Perhaps the most telling argument favoring the notion that the White Monks inspired the debate of 1305 on *apportum* is the fact that some forty heads of houses or their proctors were present and the rolls record not a single protest against it either then or when it was enacted.

Several factors appear to have conspired to create English Cistercian opposition to these payments. In the first place there were the levies paid to Cîteaux to meet the general taxes imposed by the papacy on the Order even in the face of their exemptions. Two imposts were collected for the crusades. In 1200 Innocent III commuted the fortieth on all ecclesiastical goods to a fiftieth in the case of the Cistercians and then allowed it to be compounded for in the sum of 2,000 marks. Later, the Second Council of Lyons (1274) approved a tenth for six years leaving it to the pontiff to decide how it was to be gathered and how disposed. Initially Gregory X proposed to reserve the tenth of the Cistercians to defray his expenses; he later resolved to recognize their exemption but finally compromised by requesting £100,000 Tours to be collected by the chapter for a confirmation of their exemptions. By the last quarter of the century, however, the popes were regularly requesting "loans" from Cîteaux for all manner of projects. Sometimes these had to be written off or deferred because of the increasing commitments of the Apostolic See and a shrinkage of its fiscal resources. Consequently, while the papacy received the proceeds the abbot of Cîteaux was left with the onerous task of collecting and incurred the odium of the taxation.[28]

---

28. *Radulphi de Coggesnall Chronicon Anglicanum*, ed. J. Stevenson, *Rolls Series*, No. 135, (London, 1875), pp. 113–16, 130–31; *Roger de Hovedene, Chronica*, 4 vols., ed. W. Stubbs, *Rolls Series*, No. 51, (London, 1871), vol. 4, pp. 108–110; *Annales Monastici*, vol. 2, p. 253. Cf. *Calendar* of *Papal Letters* (1198–1305), pp. 555–56. Note too the several entries in Cistercian records with respect to the collectors. *Statuta*, vol. 3, (1277:31), (1279:40), (1281:21). Only recently Boniface VIII had requested a loan from the White Monks and had received 6,000 florins. The money was used to carry on the struggle with the Colonna. *Les Reglsíres de Boniface VIII*, No. 2617.

Hardly less exasperating were the sums raised in aid of distressed brethren. These were usually administered by the general chapter through Cîteaux. A clause in the *Carta Caritatis* provided for such contingencies and expected that contributors would be "animated by a lively charity."[29] By the last half of the thirteenth century hard-nosed business practice rather than charity seems to have been the rule, a fact to which Abbot Adam of Meaux (1310–1339) could attest.[30] Prominent among the indigent was the mother-house at Cîteaux. Apparently in the period immediately preceding the internal struggle over the constitution at mid-century the financial plight of the community was grave. When, for instance, Pope Urban IV sent out a commission headed up by Bishop Nicholas of Troyes to undertake a reform, among the measures he proposed was that the financial crises be avoided and that affiliates should not be expected to make excessive contributions.[31] Additional burdens were imposed in the last quarter of the century as a result of King Philip's exactions. From a letter addressed to the most prominent abbots of the Order by Abbot Theobald in January of 1286 we learn of a protest personally lodged with Philip by the abbots of Cîteaux and Pontigny against the first of them. A compromise resulted "not without great labor and with no little difficulty" because otherwise "future dangers, loss of souls and shipwreck of conscience might ensue."[32] To the English monks the language of blackmail was readily comprehended.

29. *Les Monuments primitifs de la Règle Cistercienne,* ed. Ph. Guignard, *Analecta Divionensia,* (Dijon, 1878), p. 79.

30. *Chronica Monasterii de Melsa,* 3 vols., ed. E. A. Bond, *Rolls Series,* No. 43, (London, 1868), vol. 2, pp. 184, 308–311.

31. Cîteaux's distress dates from the last year of Abbot Walter's reign (c. 1219–1235) and continued through that of his successor James I, whose resignation was forced by the abbots of the first four daughters. The papal commission was set up at the request of Philip, Abbot of Clairvaux, who entered a protest against the regular election of Abbot James II in 1262. *Statuta,* vol. 2, (1238:9); *The Chronicle of Melrose,* facsimile edition, ed. P. L. Humphries, (London, 1936), p. 129; *AM,* vol. 2, p. 316; *Annales Furnesiensis,* ed. T. A. Beck, (London, 1844), pp. 220–21.

32. ". . . ad vitandum futura pericula, animarum dispendia, conscientiarum naufragia . . . non sine magnis laboribus et difficultate non modica. . . ." Lettenhove, p. 8.

Another significant determinant in the attitude toward *apportum* was the financial standing of many of the English houses. From the outset of Edward's reign royal custodians were frequently appointed to Cistercian cloisters in danger of bankruptcy and abandonment. The general chapter was also aware of conditions by virtue of the numerous requests for permission to disperse, a few of them deeming five-year closures necessary in order to set matters aright.[33] Cîteaux's impositions can have had little to do with this situation but its tallages must surely have exacerbated abbatial dispositions. The real blame it need hardly be said lay exactly where Thomas Burton was to place it. "Edward," he says, "was the first [king] who subjected Holy Church and the people to the tenth, the fifteenth and other taxes."[34] Having been drained by their own prince it is improbable that many of them were either able or willing to subsidize a foreign lord regardless of how palatable the general chapter made the pill.

Although the White Monks were not "snorting with German aggressiveness" there is no reason to doubt the assertion that the monks of England, in company with the more politically oriented elements of the day, were to some extent infected by the new and diffuse virus of nationalism. O'Dwyer and O'Sullivan have adduced ample evidence of it among the Cistercians of Ireland and Wales, while Keeney has observed that the notion of the monarch as the symbol of the community of the realm reached its pitch about this time and that all subjects, in the king's view, were obliged to assist him in protecting it.[35] Thus when Edward requested the

33. *Statuta*, vol. 3 (1280:44), Vaudey (1281:38, 63), Kirkstall and Flaxley (1291:61), Rievaulx (1292:62), Fountains. For the appointment of royal custodians see *CPR* (1281–1292), pp. 2, 49, 85, 431; (1292–1301), p. 303; (1301–1307), pp. 28, 320.

34. *Meaux*, vol. 2, p. 278.

35. B. W. O'Dwyer, "The problem of reform in the Irish Cistercian monasteries and the attempted solution of Stephen of Lexington in 1228," *Journal of Ecclesiastical History*, 15 (1964), pp. 186–91. J. F. O'Sullivan, *Cistercian Settlements in Wales and Monmouthshire*, (New York: Fordham University Press, 1947), p. 69; B. C. Keeney, "Military Service and the Development of Nationalism in England, 1272–1327," *Speculum*, 22 (1947), pp. 536–37.

L

apportum of 1298 he claimed that "the advantage and profit of the entire realm is concerned" and that as they love the advantage of the king's realm they will have it ready for him.[36] The same spirit underlay the royal seizure of those estates of "alien religious of the power of the king of France and his allies."[37]

The prohibition against travel abroad was invoked by the English fathers to explain their absence from the chapter in September of 1305. But their brethren at Cîteaux were not impressed in the least and asked Rome to intervene. In late April of the next spring Pope Clement commissioned Archbishop William Greenfield of York and Bishops Henry Woodlock of Winchester and Ralph Baldock of London to order the White Monks, under pain of excommunication, to attend general chapter meetings.[38] At this point our information is so fragmentary that it will not permit us to make any worthwhile remarks about the success of the papal intervention. Canivez' edition of the *Statuta* for example contains not a single entry relating to the English brethren from the beginning of the century to the first years of Edward III's reign. On the face of it this argues that the abbots ignored the papal injunction; otherwise it would be reasonable to find some mention of disciplinary action, matter of appeal or decision concerning one or other of them.[39] Cîteaux's silence is partly balanced by the records of the English chancery. Under the year 1308 a royal order to the Constable of Dover and Warden of the Cinque Ports, Robert Kendale, authorized the release from detention of the abbots of Buckland, Cleeve, Coggeshall, Dunkeswell, Netley, Newenham and Tilty, they having "passed the sea without the king's licence to attend the general chapter at Cîteaux."[40] It is clear therefore that (a) a royal

36. CCR (1296–1302), p. 216.

37. D. Matthew, *Norman Monasteries and their English Possessions* (Oxford: University Press, 1962), pp. 86–87.

38. CPL (1305–1342), p. 19.

39. A scrutiny of the statutes reveals that there are no entries dealing with the English foundations in the years 1221, 1242, 1256, 1264–1265, 1283–1290, 1294–1295.

40. CCR (1307–1313), p. 79, Dated 4 October.

licence to attend chapter meetings was indispensable; (b) royal officials at coastal stations had been instructed to apprehend unlicenced religious travelers; (c) Cistercian statutes cannot be used as enumerators of English attendance at the general chapter in this period.

Permits were issued to eighteen heads of houses to attend the general chapter of 1309.[41] Thereafter, until near the middle of the century, the abbots of England and Wales were represented, on the average, at every second meeting. Of those so licenced the superiors of Savigniac origin constitute about one-third while the Welsh and Marcher establishments are mentioned in another third. The southern and western monks were warranted more frequently than those from across the Welland and Teify. From whatever region they were, the fathers were continually cautioned against carrying anything that could be construed as *apportum* although enough cash was allowed each in order to defray the expense of his journey. An analysis of the sums mentioned in the licences as "pocket money" does not indicate that the crown established a regular tariff based on the status of the recipient, the distance of the journey or its duration. Prestigious and powerful abbots such as those of Fountains and Furness received allowances no greater than those permitted to the less prominent superiors of Thame and Holm Cultram. Despite the longer, more arduous and dangerous trips undertaken by the heads of Cymhir and Basingwerk, the abbots of Netley and Forde who resided by the channel were allowed the same sums. To confound even the most simple observations there are several cases in which the superiors were permitted to carry varying amounts; in 1312 the abbot of Stratford was allowed £10 while three years later his allowances amounted to £40. Similarly, Beaulieu's abbot was allocated £10 in 1309 but in 1321 his portion was raised to £20.[42] The usual figure mentioned is £10 but the larger sums, those ranging up to the apparent

---

41. *Ibid.* (1307–1313), p. 165.

42. *CCR* (1318–1323), pp. 165, 542, 351; (1313–1318), pp. 69, 305, 492; (1318–1323), pp. 379, 492; (1327–1330), pp. 205, 567; (1330–1333), p. 580.

maximum of £40, together are almost equal in incidence. There are also several licences in which the clause "saving reasonable expenses" is substituted for a definite amount but these generally date from the years following the outbreak of the Hundred Years War.[43] Presumably, the exact figure reserved depended in part upon the liberality of the customs officer, in part upon the persuasive powers of the individual religious and in part upon precedent. It is impossible to say whether these allotments worked any hardship on the religious traveler, but we do know that royal envoys and messengers in service received similar amounts thus implying that most allocations were liberal and even generous.[44]

Despite the vigilance of port officials some of the monks early discovered ways of smuggling *apportum* and of making unlicenced trips to Cîteaux. Our first intimation of non-compliance with the bans occurs shortly after the turn of the century. In February of 1301 Edward directed the Warden of the ports and all responsible reeves to make careful search of all wool sacks, hides and all other merchandise "because the king now understands that certain persons scheming together have carried such money and silver out of the realm," by those means. But the malpractice continued until in 1316 Edward II was obliged to publish anew the prohibitions of the Carlisle statute.[45] Defiance of the injunction against unauthorized travel to Cîteaux all the while continued and, if one may trust the king's assertions, was winked at and even facilitated by royal agents. On 15 August 1325 Warden Kendale of Dover received a letter in which it is noted that "the king is much perturbed at his permitting certain abbots . . . of the aforesaid order . . . to pass the sea . . . without the king's licence."[46] It is noteworthy also that royal records do

43. *CCR* (1327–1330), p. 403; (1330–1334), pp. 145, 331; (1333–1337), p. 121; (1337–1339), pp. 118–19, 567; (1346–1349), p. 500.

44. For the wages of Cistercian envoys and messengers in the royal service during the first half of the fourteenth century, see *CLR* (1226–1240), pp. 42, 114, 161; (1240–1245), pp. 141, 168, 184; (1245–1251), pp. 5, 46, 96. See especially, M. C. Hill, *The King's Messengers*, 1199–1377, (London: Edward Arnold, 1961), pp. 46–50.

45. *CCR* (1313–1318), pp. 426f.   46. *Ibid.* (1323–1327), p. 502.

not mention any further surreptitious passages to the chapter after this date. It may well be that Kendale was replaced by a series of more zealous Wardens, or that overseas travel was made more hazardous than usual by reason of the near state of war which existed with France.[47] In either case, Cîteaux took advantage of Carnarvon's deposition in 1327 to address a protest to the new monarch and the Queen Mother. Royal prohibitions against *apportum* and attendance at General Chapter, it claims, were having a debilitating effect upon the unity of the Order. Attention is also drawn to Pope Clement's admonition of 1306 which places every absentee, *ipso facto*, under the penalty of excommunication.[48] The only indication that we have of the crown's reaction to this plea is in the more liberal granting of licences to attend the chapter meeting in September 1329; the ban on *apportum* was apparently not even reconsidered.[49] Until the outbreak of war in 1337 the English, in varying numbers, attended the autumn convocations of the Order without interruption. From that time forward their presence seems to have been a rare occurrence.[50]

Regardless of the obstacles placed in the way of the travel of religious to Cîteaux the crown did nothing to prevent French superiors from carrying out visitations in the cloisters of their British affiliates. The first mention of this traffic after the prohibitions of 1298–1299 is a letter of protection issued to the Abbot of

47. Ralph Bassett occupied the post by February of 1306. Three years later he had been replaced by Bartholomew Burghersh. It is reported that the Cistercians were so afraid of the portsmen in 1293 that they dared not leave the country. *Flores Historiarum*, 3 vols., ed. H. R. Luard, *Rolls Series* No. 95 (London: 1890), vol. 3, p. 86. For the ports and the sort of men operating out of them see K. M. E. Murray, *The Constitutional History of the Cinque Ports*, (Manchester: University Press, 1935), pp. 33–41.

48. *Statuta*, vol. 3 (1328:15), p. 384. This plea was carried to England by envoys appointed by Cîteaux and the four senior houses.

49. The abbots of Stratford, Thame, Pipewell, Newminster, Salley, Whitland and Cumhir were the recipients. *CCR* (1327–1330), pp. 564, 566–67.

50. *CCR* (1330–1333), pp. 331, 580, 586; (1333–1337), pp. 88, 121, 243, 246, 323, 483, 488, 506, 523, 671, 676; (1337–1339), p. 118; *CPR* (1327–1330), pp. 132, 163, 314; (1330–1334), p. 393; (1334–1338), p. 30.

Cîteaux, John Pontoise.[51] A second mission is noted a little more than a score of years later. On that occasion the abbot of Aulnay, accompanied by three monks and eight alien grooms mounted, made the rounds. In the late fall of 1325, after Edward II refused to permit any of his abbots to attend the general chapter, two religious, one of them a monk named Nicholas, were appointed to go over to the English communities. Two further visitations are recorded prior to the outset of the great war; the one in the first half of 1330 by the abbot of l'Aumône, the other four years later by a Brother Bernard, a monk of Clairvaux. From the tone and phraseology of the royal notes it is clear that the recipient was representing the general chapter and that his commission was to all the families of the Order in the kingdom. In this connection the expressions most frequently, although not invariably, employed are, "to visit divers houses of the order," or, "houses subjected to that order," or, "houses of his order."[52]

Notwithstanding the freedom allowed to alien principals, control over the attendance of the English monks at the general chapter was inevitably bound to contribute to the general decline in the internal discipline of the English communities and to the growing fragmentation within the Order. The most striking instance of these tendencies in the years from 1306 to 1337 occurs at Bindon in Dorset. John Montecute, elected head of that community in or about 1316, proved so unsuitable a governor that he was deposed and Roger Hornhull put in his place.[53] For several years thereafter

---

51. *CPR* (1302–1307), p. 200. Dated 26 November 1303 at Dunfermline. It is difficult to see how Abbot Pontoise could have made his visitation in person for he had been jailed shortly before by Philip. It may be that he obtained permission for the visit before his detention and that Edward issued it on receipt of the request.

52. See for instance, *CCR* (1333–1337), p. 489.

53. Bindon's misfortunes did not originate with Montecute but arose out of poor relations with their neighbours and some poor business transactions. *CCR* (1296–1302), p. 120; *CPR* (1292–1301), pp. 192, 216, 260, 317–18; *Calendar of Fine Rolls* (1272–1307), pp. 368–69. There is no mention in the *statuta* of this ouster.

the community enjoyed only fitful terms of peace. From a letter of
Edward III to Abbot William IV of Cîteaux (1315–1337) and the
instructions given to royal commissioners we learn that when
Hornhull took office his predecessor and eight of the brethren
seceded and allied themselves to a gang of local hoodlums and
began attacking and harassing the properties and employees of the
house. On one occasion the rebels took physical possession of the
cloisters and proceeded to work their will. Animals valued at £700
were driven off and books, chalices, vestments and the conventual
seal were carried away. A few of the faithful religious were captured
and dragged off to Doncaster. Hornhull's position was made the
more difficult by the fact that Abbot John Chidley of Ford (1330–
1354), his immediate superior, aided and abetted Montecute's
lawlessness.[54] After the plundering incident Abbot Roger appealed
to the crown. By the latter half of May 1329 the earl of Devon,
Hugh Courtney, the abbot of Beaulieu and Hugh Peynz had been
appointed guardians of the house with explicit instructions to
recover all the goods which had been stolen. This was the first of
five similar commissions appointed by the crown in the next two
years.[55] There is no indication why so many missions were required unless there was a fair amount of support for Montecute in
the locality and that the breakdown in communications between
England and Cîteaux prevented any decisive capitular action against
Abbot Chidley. Be that as it may, at the end of April 1331 the ring-
leader and one of his aides were apprehended near London and a
royal writ of aid was given to those entrusted with the business of
returning them to Bindon for discipline. Enroute Montecute
managed to escape his guards and remain at large until late July
when he was recaptured, placed under a heavy guard, and restored
to his abbot. In the interim royal officers had rounded up the other
dissidents and clapped them into jail. In custody Montecute was as
dangerous as when free for King Edward requested Cîteaux to order
the banishment of the rebels to more distant establishments and to

54. *CCR* (1330–1333), p. 619.
55. *CPR* (1327–1330), pp. 384, 391; (1330–1334), pp. 19, 63, 131, 203.

transfer the visitation of Bindon from Abbot John of Ford to someone more discreet.[56]

The situation at Bindon reflects to some degree also Cîteaux's inability to maintain its primitive ideals. Almost everywhere the exemption privilege had given way to indirect secular control, wealth had overshadowed the spirit of poverty, good observance and discipline were replaced by malpractice and laxity, and, most distracting of all, overmuch concern with commercial transactions and litigation was substituted for holy indifference. Papal concern about the disintegration of the Cistercian spirit found expression in Benedict XII's bull, *Fulgens sicut stella*, published in 1335 after consultation with Cîteaux and the abbots of three of the first daughters. In fifty-seven clauses the pontiff dealt with every major issue and abuse then embarrassing the Order. But however well intentioned and determined Benedict may have been to restore the gleam to "the morning star in the middle of a clouded sky" his efforts had no enduring influence.[57] Resistance to reform from within, the less zealous attitude of later pontiffs and the socio-economic changes resulting from the Great Plague and the Hundred Years' War ensured the continuance of the march away from primitive commitments.[58]

Further assaults against Cistercian unity were made with the renewal of hostilities between the English and French kingdoms in the late spring of 1337. The English monarch anticipated the struggle by republishing in more stringent terms the ban on the export of money in January of that year.[59] During the summer months

56. *CPR* (1330–1334), pp. 142, 201; *CCR* (1330–1333), p. 619.
57. J. B. Mahn, *Le Pape Benôit XII et les Cisterciens,* (Paris: Bibliothèque de l'école des hautes études, 1949), p. 75 *seq.* See also, J. McNulty, "Constitutions for the Reform of the Cistercian order, 1335," *Transactions of the Lancashire and Cheshire Antiquarian Society,* 47 (1933–1944), pp. 157–67.
58. King, p. 53.
59. *CCR* (1333–1337), p. 653. Over a year later it was published anew. *Ibid.* (1337–1339), p. 414. At a much later date Cîteaux appointed certain abbots, whether English or French is not stated, to visit the abbey of Bruern, then in trouble because of its abbot. *CPR* (1338–1340), p. 169; (1350–1354), p. 62.

all alien property including the estates of the Cistercians was seized by the crown.[60] In the middle of July 1343 rumors had reached the king that envoys of the abbots of Cîteaux and Prémontré had arrived in the island intending to collect the *apportum* due from their affiliates. Letters were again despatched to all abbots and priors of these orders to deliver the *apportum* which they owed as well as the arrears of the previous six years to the Exchequer. Those who refused to comply were to be distrained.[61] Only the chronicler of Meaux provides us with any information about the execution of this directive on the local level. Abbot Hugh Leven was attached to satisfy the king in the matter but he replied that neither he nor any of his predecessors owed *apportum* to his superior in foreign parts and that he was willing to prove it. A jury was empaneled at Beverley and was given sworn testimony supporting the abbot's contention. In the next year another inquest was held at York on the same matter and again vindicated his claim. Abbot Hugh was allowed to go *sine die*; *salva regi actione alias si, etc.*[62]

Such contacts as there were between England and Cîteaux were made more tenuous by the struggle between Edward III and the Valois, and, of the twenty chapters which assembled in the period from 1344 and 1365, Englishmen seem to have been present at only seven of them.[63] On the other hand the disorder and chaos which prevailed over most of northern France prevented visitation of the English houses by continental authorities. The general chapter therefore, in the first half of 1350, delegated the powers of visitation

60. T. Rymer, *Foedera*, 10 vols. (London, 1739–1745), vol. 4, p. 778. This is clear from a royal letter to the treasurer and barons of the Exchequer. *CPR* (1340–1343), pp. 374, 441; (1354–1358), p. 132; *CCR* (1346–1349), p. 480. These estates were immediately farmed out to the proctors of the alien abbots at specified sums. See Matthew, pp. 90–91.

61. *CCR* (1343–1346), pp. 74–75.   62. *Meaux*, vol. 3, pp. 29–30.

63. This figure is based on the letters patent and close granting to the abbots of the Order permission to go overseas and/or letters of protection for their properties while they were absent. It includes those notices indicating that the abbots were abroad "on the business of his house," and those whose expressed intention was to go to the Roman court. In regard to the latter, a side trip to Dijon can be assumed.

to all Anglo-Welsh communities to the abbot of Stratford. He was to be assisted by Ralph Saint Martin, described as the Warden of the house of Benington, and Ralph le Porter. Special letters of protection were issued by the king to expedite their mission.[64] In the next year the general chapter established a new commission with powers of correction and visitation which were to last for three years. No names were contained in the Cistercian brief but this deficiency is made up in part by an entry in the chancery rolls. In mid-June of 1353 Abbot John Lindelay of Whalley (1350–1387) and Abbot Adam Stanlegh of Rewley (1351–1370) "going by command of their superiors to all places of the order in England and Wales to further business affecting the order" received royal protection during the execution of their duties.[65] Whether in fact John and Adam continued their work through to 1355 as provided for is not known. In June of 1354 the king extended protection and safe conduct for one year to the monk John Aldenardo, proctor and chaplain to Cardinal William, Bishop of Tusculum. John had come to England on business affecting "the cardinal and the said order."[66] Meaux's chronicle discloses the nature of that business. Pope Innocent VI had ordered certain of his legates to undertake a visitation of the entire Order. From the moment the task was begun the visitors extorted as much money as they were able in support of papal projects. Upon which, Cardinal William, a former Cistercian, intervened and by promising 6,000 florins paid in advance secured the recall of the papal agents.[67] To all appearances then the monk John's mission was to collect the English portion of that sum. Yet no mention is made in the chronicle about Meaux's contribution nor does the royal licence allow John to return home with anything other than "his expenses in gold and silver."

The last recorded visitation in the days of Edward III was made by the abbots of two of the first four daughters. In the year following the English victory at Poitiers, the renowned theologian Abbot Bernard II of Clairvaux (1345–1358) sent one of his subjects, John

64. *CPR* (1348–1350), pp. 490, 497.
66. *CPR* (1354–1358), p. 73.
65. *Statuta*, vol. 3 (1352:13).
67. *Meaux*, vol. 3, p. 153.

de Barra, to tour the island communities. Of his mission we know nothing. In March of 1362 Abbot Raymond of Pontigny and his escort of twenty mounted men and footmen were given protection and safe conduct so that a general visitation commanded by the general chapter could be undertaken.[68] Some details of his work have survived. On his arrival he associated with him John, Abbot of Whalley, John, Abbot of Boxley and Dom Sampson, a monk of Savigny. The party arrived at Meaux on May 26, a short while after an unscrupulous intriguer, the *quondam* abbot John Ryslay, had made terms with his community.[69] In the interval between these two missions the treaty of Bretigny-Calais ended for a time the Anglo-French conflict. As a consequence Edward III ordered the restoration of the "lands, rents, fees and advowsons" belonging to the foreign Cistercians.[70] Whether they were to remain in their hands during the next round of hostilities which began in 1369 we have no sure means of knowing. We do know, however, that in the last year of the king's life, when the war was being waged "with ineptitude and failure" John Dullemont, abbot of Clairvaux (1360–1380) and the commissary general of the general chapter, was issued with a charter of protection with clause *rogamus* prior to a general visitation of the English houses of the Order. This was the last mission of a senior alien superior to the Anglo-Welsh communities until the year 1410.[71] Miss Rose Graham has sketched out the story of the relationships between the insular and continental monks during the Great Schism. We need only remark that what occurred in that troublous period was merely the refinement and elaboration of attitudes and policies already set in motion at the beginning of the century.

68. *CPR* (1354–1358), p. 627; (1361–1364), p. 172.

69. *Meaux,* vol. 3, pp. 150–51.

70. *CPR* (1358–1361), pp. 552, 558. So, for instance, Edward ignored patronal interests in the vicarage of Roderham and presented himself on the grounds that the same was "in the king's gift by reason of the temporalities of the abbot of Clairvaux being in his hands on account of the war with France." *CPR* (1340–1343), p. 474.

71. *CPR* (1374–1377), p. 279.

One other clause of the statute of Carlisle bears consideration. Clause four establishes that in those monasteries where the seal has hitherto been in the custody of the abbot and not of the community —the Cistercians and Premonstratensians are especially cited—the convent is to have its own seal. This instrument is to be under the control of the prior and four of the most worthy and discreet men of the community. The purpose of this ordinance is stated in un-equivocal terms, "that the abbot should be able of himself to establish nothing. All future undertakings bearing only the seal of the abbot will be adjudged void and of no force in law."[72] For lack of evidence to the contrary I think it fair to assume that this facet of the statute was also inspired by the men of religion, and, because it coincided with the ternary aims of the crown, royal approbation was easily acquired.

The seal, abbatial or conventual, is of incontestable importance in the life of a religious community. In law it provided conclusive evidence of a transaction and bound its owner.[73] By itself it is a passive instrument. In the hands of a wise and discerning superior it could be transformed into a cornucopia of worldly successes. Possessed by a poor and injudicious administrator it could just as easily play the role of "snakes and scorpions." That it was more often cast in the latter piece is certain from the chronicles and chartularies of virtually every Cistercian cloister in the nation for, while the abbot was obliged to consult with his subjects before committing them to any irrevocable course he was not compelled to take their advice. Now, however, the crown was determined to

72. R. Graham, "The Great Schism and the English monasteries of the Cistercian order," *English Historical Review*, 44 (1929), pp. 373–87.

73. *Year Book*, 20 *Edward III*, 2 pts., ed. L. O. Pike, *Rolls Series*, No. 31 (London, 1908–1911), pt. 1, p. 98; *Rot. Parl.* vol. 1, p. 178b; *CPR* (1361–1364), p. 526. The importance of the seal to the Cistercian community is illustrated in a royal mandate to the sheriffs and bailiffs of the realm to arrest a vagabond monk of Beaulieu who had "with him a false seal like the seal of the chapter of the said house, on account of which the abbot and convent fear they may incur damage through fraud and malice of the said monk. *CPR* (1258–1266), p. 481. A vagabond abbot in fact used the seal to make injurious contracts. *Ibid.* (1247–1258), p. 565.

preserve not only its own right to interfere in the internal operations of the individual community but to protect the interests of baronial patrons.[74] Mismanagement, malfeasance or anything which tended to diminish the material endowment of a monastery was the business of the king. Thus by inhibiting the power of the abbot in ordering the fiscal assets of his community and by giving the *maior et sanior pars* a greater voice in the material government of their communities, the crown took a step in the direction of insulating itself and other patrons against future pleas for assistance arising out of the incompetence or unbusinesslike conduct of superiors. As well, this clause must be looked upon as constituting an integral part of the general prohibition against *apportum* and, while no evidence has come to light to demonstrate that the abbatial seals of English houses were used to contract obligations in favor of Cîteaux in lieu of *apportum*, it is clear that the crown was aware of the possibility.[75]

There is just sufficient evidence to show that the clause was obeyed. When in 1331 John Montecute laid seige to the abbey of Bindon he and his cohorts "broke open a coffer containing the seal of the abbey, and carried away the seal. . . ."[76] Significantly also when Benedict XII undertook to revamp the financial administration of the Cistercian family he followed the precedent established by the English crown of restricting the absolute power of the abbot over finances. Henceforward all alienations of lands, rents and rights must first have the consent of the community as well as the special licence of the general chapter. The latter could be acquired only after a written process of the intended transaction had been submitted and an investigation had been completed by two capitular delegates. These requirements having been satisfied, the abbot of the community concerned and the father abbot closed the busi-

74. Royal interference in the domestic matters of monasteries of the Cistercian affiliation was long standing. Edward I by taking bankrupt houses or those heavily laden with debt into a sort of receivership confirmed the royal right to direct internal matters.

75. Graham, p. 75.

76. *CPR* (1330–1334), p. 63. Dated 23 January 1331.

ness by affixing their seals to the instrument.[77] Order was introduced
into financial records by the appointment, in every community, of
a treasurer. His duty was to keep up monastic accounts and to
report annually to the general chapter. The traditional roles of
monarch and pope were therefore, completely reversed in respect
to the Order. The legal ramifications of this statute were especially
obvious to Sir Edward Coke. In the words of Maitland this law,
"should be famous, for it was one of the few illustrations that Coke
could give of his doctrine that a statute may be void for unreason-
ableness. . . ."[78]

Lawrence A. Desmond

St Paul's College
University of Manitoba

77. *Statuta,* vol. 3, (1335:4, 5).

78. F. Pollock and F. Maitland, *History of English Law,* 2 vols. (Cambridge:
University Press, 1968), vol. 1, p. 509.

THE CISTERCIAN DILEMMA AT THE CLOSE OF THE MIDDLE AGES: GALLICANISM OR ROME

THE FORTUNES OF THE ORDER OF CÎTEAUX in the fifteenth century were closely linked to papal–Gallican relations. A series of papal privileges since 1099 had placed the Cistercians under the protection of the Holy See and defined the immunities of monastic exemption. The prestigious leadership of the popes from Gregory VII (1073–1085) to Innocent III (1198–1216) had made of apostolic patronage an awesome reality. The great age of Cistercian expansion—its Golden Age—paralleled the developments that extended the jurisdiction of Rome throughout Christendom.

Resistance to papal absolutism was systematically curbed but never extinguished. In the kingdom of France it found expression in the Gallican decrees of the clergy which led up to and culminated in the Pragmatic Sanction of Bourges (1438). In effect, the king had designated himself protector of the Gallican church against the anti-conciliar and anti-canonical impositions of the bishop of Rome. And the arena for the conflict between pope and king was more often than not the sphere of ecclesiastical benefices and tithes. Since the thirteenth century, and especially after Pope Clement IV issued *Licet ecclesiarum* in 1265, the papacy has reserved to itself "plenary disposition" over certain kinds of ecclesiastical *benefices in vacancy*.[1] The "kinds" were gradually broadened by subsequent decrees to the end of the fourteenth century. Major benefices—bishoprics and

---

1. *Decretales Gregorii IX*, 3.4.2 in *Corpus Iuris Canonici*, ed. E. Friedberg, vol. 2 (Leipzig, 1881).

abbeys—and most minor benefices were numbered among papal reservations.

The monarchies inevitably resented the implied jurisdiction of Rome over the "national" churches. The king of France in particular saw the advantages of loyal prelates in sees and abbeys that were overrun by the English in the Hundred Years' War. Similarly the immediate influence of the popes at Avignon jeopardized the royal centralization that had overcome only with great difficulty and never completely the independent spirit of the south. So it was that Charles VI (1380–1422) and Charles VII (1422–1461) championed the cause of the Gallican clergy against papal pretensions.

The tension between monarchy and papacy presented a dilemma to the Cistercians. The obedience of the abbot of Cîteaux was divided between Rome and Gallicanism. A prominent ecclesiastic in the Gallican church, the abbot was the head of an Order whose privileges were guaranteed by the papacy. Commitment to either party portended harassment by the other. The most significant effect of this paradox was the decline of the jurisdiction of the abbot of Cîteaux over the Order.

Pope John XXII (1316–1334) exercised his authority with determination against his adversaries in Italy. Nomination to benefices was a prerogative that he understood and guarded. Even the "exempt" Cistercians could not escape the sweep of his decrees. The earliest commendatory abbeys in the Order can be found in Italy and date from this pontificate.[2] Before long the system of reservations began to affect the Order. In 1344, Pope Clement VI delivered a strong admonition to the monks of Clairvaux that the provision of their monastery was reserved to the Apostolic See, and their election ignored the papal position.[3] In a similar mandate,

2. G. Mollat, (ed.), *Jean XXII* (1316–1334): *Lettres communes* (Paris: A. Fontemoing, 1904–1946), vol. 4, n. 16132, p. 162; vol. 5, n. 22798, p. 418; vol. 6, n. 29630, p. 621; vol. 7, n. 41571, p. 296; vol. 10, n. 53615, p. 213; vol. 11, n. 57357, p. 204.

3. E. Deprez, (ed.), *Clément VI* (1342–1352): ·*Lettres closes, patentes et curiales se rapportant à la France publiées ou analysées d'après les registres du Vatican*, vol. 1, fasc. 1, (Paris: A. Fontemoing, 1901); n. 1259, p. 281. Clement VI attributed the reservation to Pope John XXII.

Bonport in Evreux fell under papal reservation; and the abbot of Tornet in Frejus was promoted by the same pontiff in 1345.[4] Pope Innocent VI provided a certain Peter with the monastery of Prully in Sens, and Pope Urban V reminded the monks of Vauclair in Laon that he was suspending his right to provision in recognizing the abbot-elect.[5] Inevitably the bond of charity that united the houses of the Order in monastic observance was strained to breaking. The consequences of the papal practices had a direct effect upon the religious discipline of the whole Order. Already under Pope John XXII there was a bull, issued *ad petitionem*, urging all those abbots promoted by the Holy See to attend the general chapters and to obey the abbot general.[6]

Before the end of the fourteenth century, the organization of Cîteaux betrayed its vulnerability. Single houses either escaped the jurisdiction of the Order or, worse, ignored it. And then, the crisis of the schism contributed to the disintegration and made reconstruction impossible. The Order mirrored the divisions that rent western Christendom. The Cistercians in France were identified with the Gallican obedience to Clement VII. Hence abbatial control over monasteries of the Urbanist obedience slackened. Pope Urban VI's actions were drastic. He suspended the jurisdiction of the abbot of Cîteaux Gerard de Buxières over his adherents and in 1376 he enjoined the abbots of Germany, Bohemia and Poland to hold their own general chapters.[7] Similar measures brought the Italian abbots to Rome in 1382, and the abbots of the Empire to Vienna in 1393.[8] Urban VI strove with all his powers to weaken French

4. *Ibid.,* n. 1281, pp. 289–90; vol. 2, fasc. 3, n. 2207, p. 92.

5. P. Gasnault, (ed.), *Urbain V: Lettres communes,* vol. 2, fasc. 1, (Paris: E. de Boccard, 1964), nn. 5346, 5442, pp. 48, 60.

6. C. Henriquez, (ed.), *Regula, Constitutiones et privilegia ordinis Cisterciensis: item congregationum monasticarum, et militarium quae Cisterciense institutum observant,* (Antverpiae: ex officina Plantiniana Balthasaris Moreti 1630), n. 58, p. 89.

7. Bliemetzrieder, "Der Zisterziensen-Orden in grossen abendländischen Schisma," *Studien und Mitteilungen aus dem Benediktiner und dem Zisterzienser-Orden,* 25 (1904), pp. 63, 78–80.

8. *Ibid.,* pp. 70, 80.

M

166 *William J. Telesca*

influence upon the Order and convoked general chapters for Cistercians of his obedience under "Roman" abbots. In 1384 he further innovated when he appointed Abbot Michael of Milan vicar general of the Order. King Richard II of England eagerly cooperated with these acts. He entrusted to the abbots of Rievaulx and Wardon, with apostolic power and permission, responsibility to hold a general chapter for the Cistercians in England, Wales, Scotland and Ireland.[9] Under Boniface IX this policy continued; besides the chapters mentioned, the abbots of Hungary, Dalmatia, and Croatia now convened separately. And in 1406 another chapter of anti-Gallican Cistercians was held at Heilsbronn in Nurnberg. The irreparable harm to the abbatial hierarchy in German territories was still in evidence in 1422 when special reformers were appointed for six provinces on the French border, *si securus ad ea patuerit accessus*, to undertake to reform morals, correct vices, decree and ordain, institute, abrogate, depose and elect.[10] It is improbable that all of the French abbots remained loyal to Gerard de Buxières. There is evidence that the abbot of Clairvaux was an adherent of Popes Urban VI and Boniface IX.[11] Although the Council of Pisa (1409) brought a semblance of unity in the profession of obedience to Alexander V, the once universal system of Cistercian monasticism was never fully restored.[12] Even the Council of Constance failed to do that. The prestige of the abbot of Cîteaux over the whole Order had been greatly diminished.

The centralization that took place in the papal curia paralleled a similar evolution in the monarchies. Political growth under the Capetians was a steady series of successes against opposing forces within and without the kingdom. In fact, the work of Philip Augustus, Louis IX, and Philip IV was durable enough to sustain

9. *Ibid.*, pp. 64–65 (note 4 also).

10. *Statuta*, vol. 5, n. 22, p. 244. The provinces were Mayence, Treves, Cologne, Magdeburg, Salzburg, and Bremen.

11. Bliemetzrieder, p. 63. There are two letters cited which were written to the abbot of Clairvaux by Pope Boniface IX in 1390 and 1394.

12. As the *orationes* indicate, the Cistercians rallied around the Pisan Alexander V and John XXIII; *Statuta*, vol. 4 (1409), pp. 102–103; (1410), p. 118; (1411), p. 134; (1418), p. 214.

monarchic institutions during the fourteenth-century crisis. The Cistercians were affected by these political developments. Although they were a papally exempt Order, their abbeys appeared in the records of Parlement with greater frequency after 1300.[13] The earliest royal charter of general protection for the whole Order dates from the reign of Philip IV.[14] In special instances, individual monasteries received guarantees from kings even earlier. When Charles V, in 1368, stopped at the abbey of Vaucelles, he accorded it his privileges. He referred to the traditional generosity of his predecessors to the Order of Cîteaux. The collection of documents which he confirmed cited a text of Philip Augustus which in itself acknowledged earlier royal munificence (*progenitorum nostrorum inherendo vestigiis*). There were included under special royal protection the churches of the religious of the Cistercian Order, Pontigny, Clairvaux, and their daughter-houses, Longport (in Soissons), Chaalis (in Senlis), Orcamp (in Noyon), Vaucelle (in Cambrai), Notre-Dame de Prez (in Troyes), Froimont (in Beauvais), Du Gard (in Amiens), Foulcarmont (in Rouen), Longvilliers (in Ponthieu), Cercamp (in Amiens), and two that defy identification, Buostel and Balancias.[15] This was quite an extension of royal protection, considering that Clairvaux's progeny alone numbered over sixty at St Bernard's death in 1153. Among the royal patrons mentioned by Charles V besides Philip Augustus were Louis VIII, St Louis IX, Philip II, Philip IV, and Philip V. The document itself is significant because it portends the role the Order would assume during the papal-Gallican rivalry.

More and more the Order turned to the kings for the advantages of their immediate safeguard. The once prestigious pronounce-

13. In 1301, Parlement registered a royal decision in favor of Cîteaux over Cluny regarding possession of the monastery of the Holy Savior in Navarre; see Le Comte Beugnot, *Les olim ou registres des arrêts,* vol. 3, pt. 1 (Paris: Imprimerie royale, 1844), pp. 62–63; the king also authorized an inquest into the misdeeds of the abbey of Nerlac in Bourges and reported a verdict of guilty with the resultant fine to the abbot of Cîteaux, pp. 265–66.

14. Henriquez, p. 228.

15. Laurière, Secousse, *et al.* (ed.), *Ordonnances des roys de France,* 21 vols. (Paris: Inprimerie royale et nationale, 1723–1849), vol. 5, pp. 141–44.

ments of the papacy were losing their force in a society callous from too much tribulation, probably insensitive too to the ambitious designs of the pontiffs themselves. Isolated abbeys were vulnerable to roving bands of unscrupulous soldiers who plundered and despoiled. The general chapters revealed a change in policy under King John. They continued to plead the plight of the Order before the papal chair, but more realistically individual monasteries sought the security of powerful lay patrons, certainly the king himself. The ordinances of King John reveal ten instances of royal protection of Cistercian houses at their request.[16] Charles V renewed or granted royal protection to six monasteries.[17] The struggle for their very existence aroused the monks to seek any measures, especially those practically useful. The particular monasteries that were desperate were for the most part located in the peripheral areas of France where English incursions and French counter-attacks created a destructive theater of war. Between 1350 and 1400 the truces only freed the Companies of Mercenaries to rob and plunder and perpetrate even greater desolation.

The appeals of the Order for monarchic intervention found a prompt response. The kings were eager to intrude in the affairs of a clergy that was engulfed in the sweeping jurisdiction of the papacy. Furthermore, the crown was convinced that patronage of sees and royal ecclesiastical foundations belonged to royal prerogative, and it resented papal attempts to nominate without royal consent.[18] Already under Urban V, before the schism, the king and his clergy had elicited a remarkable concession. The usual taxes, the annates

16. *Ordonnances,* vol. 3, p. 294 (Hauterive); p. 537 (Eschaalis); p. 542 (Clairvaux); p. 374 (Morimond); vol. 4, p. 343 (Eschaalis); p. 452 (Prully); p. 117 (Loroux); p. 25 (Fontfroid); p. 119 (Berdouès); p. 317 (La Prété).

17. *Ibid.,* vol. 5, p. 248 (Eschaalis and Valloire); p. 351 (Savigny): p. 400 (Valasse); p. 592 (B. Maria de Gratia Dei); vol. 6, p. 179 (N. D. de Peguy); p. 543 (Clairvaux); vol. 7, p. 166 (Chaalis and Cercamp); p. 569 (Val de Cernay).

18. In a strong Gallican statement of 6 October 1385, Charles VI attacked the pretensions of the papacy that ignored his own responsibility to his clergy and the churches of the realm, *quarum Patronus esse dignoscimur; Ordonnances,* vol. 7, pp. 133–37.

and common service, were reduced to half in the kingdom, and henceforth France was referred to as a *patria reducta* in the Apostolic Camera.[19]

After 1378, the Cistercians in France were more closely linked to the destinies of the Gallican clergy. Unfortunately, specific evidence is too often lacking, but the schism obviously prevented unity between the houses of the different nations. There is every reason to believe that reliance of the abbot of Cîteaux upon the monarchy increased. Even the Gallican popes (Clement VII and Benedict XIII) could not exercise their power effectively, and in the absence of any prestigious papal protection, the abbot of Cîteaux petitioned the king to safeguard the exemptions and privileges of the Order. There were some, apparently, who interpreted broadly the king's assertion of canonical rights of confirmation and infringed upon the Order's liberties. The king sternly rebuked the offenders in a lengthy ordinance.[20] Thereafter, the abbot and/or religious of the Order participated in the decisions of the king against Benedict XIII. The abbot of Cîteaux was present when Charles VI consulted his "most learned and upright" prelates in 1403 after which he announced the restoration of obedience to Benedict XIII,[21] and in 1407 when he reaffirmed withdrawal.[22]

The election of Martin V in 1417 at the Council of Constance (1414–1418) healed the schism. The king rejoiced and pledged his obedience and the same generosity and munificence which had been offered to Pope Gregory XI.[23] The Cistercians of course also had cause for joy. They, like the Gallican clergy, wrought im-

19. Dom Kirsch discovered and edited a 15th-century text, the *Codex Sessorianus* that noted this privilege; Kirsch, "Die Annaten und ihre Verwaltung in der zweiten Halfte des 15. Jahrhunderts," *Historisches Jahrbuch,* 9 (1888), pp. 300–312; see art. 4, p. 307; also A. Clergeac, *La Curie et les bénéficiers consistoriaux,* (Paris: Librairie Alphonse Picard et Fils, 1911), p. 15.

20. *Ordonnances,* vol. 8, pp. 306–307.

21. *Ibid.,* pp. 593–96, 28 May.

22. *Ibid.,* vol. 9, pp. 191–95, 5 April.

23. *Ibid.,* vol. 10, pp. 471–73, 9 September. France eventually negotiated its own concordat with the pope; B. Hubler, *Die Constanzer Reformation und die Concordate von* 1418, (Leipzig: 1867), pp. 194–206.

portant concessions from the new pontiff. In 1424, *Militanti ecclesiae* restored their exemption from the payment of tithes, abused since the late thirteenth century.[24] The Order necessarily derived advantages from the settlement which Charles VI and his son Charles VII honored in the lifetime of Pope Martin V (d. 1431).[25]

The crisis occurred in the pontificate of Eugenius IV (1431–1447). Upon his election, Eugenius ignored caution and recklessly undermined the status quo. On 18 December 1431, he dissolved the Council of Basel, Martin's last act to appease the conciliarists, which was already in assembly. The French delegation went to Rome to weigh the pope's intentions. Eugenius only communicated the declaration that the concordat had terminated with the death of his predecessor. This was a turning point in papal-French relations.[26] Charles VII reverted to his heroic defence of Gallican liberties. He forbade papal provisions and contested rights of presentation to episcopal sees. Then he abolished all reservations and expectative graces while the French held firm at Basel. Finally, the king convoked an assembly of clergy to Bourges for 1 May 1438. Four archbishops, twenty-five bishops, numerous abbots and priors, and delegates from collegiate chapters and universities attended. There were even envoys from Basel and nuncios from Rome. Finally after two months of bitter debate, on 7 July 1438, the victory of the Gallicanists was announced with the publication of the Pragmatic Sanction.[27]

This is a pivotal document in the history of Gallicanism. In a sense it was the application of the Councils of Constance and Basel

---

24. C. Cocquelines, *Bullarum privilegiorum ac diplomatum Romanorum pontificum amplissima collectio,* 6 vols. (Romae: typis et sumptibus Hieronymi Mainardi, 1739–1760), vol. 3, pt. 2, p. 446.

25. Although Parlement and the University of Paris resented the arrangements of the concordat, Charles VI hesitated to break relations with the papacy at a time when the threat of the English was so imminent and Anglo-papal relations were so cordial; this thesis is offered and substantiated by N. Valois, *Histoire de la Pragmatique Sanction de Bourges sous Charles VII,* (Paris: Alphonse Picard et Fils, 1906), pp. lv ff.

26. The details and the *pièces justificatives* are in Valois, pp. lxiv–lxvii.

27. The text is in *Ordonnances,* vol. 13, pp. 267ff.

to the "national" interests of the French crown and clergy. The whole procedure for collations, elections, expectatives, annates, services, and appeals that had been so favorable to Rome, was attacked. Papal jurisdiction was practically excluded from the royal domain. A complete rupture was anticipated as matters worsened in the following year when on 25 June 1439, the anti-pope, Felix V, was elected at Basel and acknowledged by the Gallican party. Once again, it was only Charles' fears of the threat of the English that averted an open schism. By the end of 1440, he renewed his obedience to Eugenius.[28]

The Order of Cîteaux was affected by the broader issues between pope and king. Its position in the controversy is somewhat interesting. Ties were never severed with Rome. The general chapters continued to petition the Holy See for bulls of protection while abbots played an active role in Gallican affairs. Pope Eugenius was compliant to the pleas of the Order. He issued three bulls in 1438, the year of the Pragmatic Sanction (perhaps, because of it) which were aimed at curbing the frequent resignations of abbeys before the Roman curia; at upholding residence of one year for the abbot-elect; at preserving obligations of the abbots-elect to the general chapters and the abbot of Cîteaux.[29] Meanwhile, the abbot Jean of Bonval in Rodez had very special responsibilities at the Council of Basel,[30] and a minor dispute which gave precedence to the abbot of Cîteaux over the abbot of Cluny at the assembly attests to the former's presence there.[31] Furthermore, the general chapter of 1433 numbered among its statutes the Baselian decree on the election of prelates.[32]

28. *Ibid., Ordonnances* of 2 September and 21 November 1440, pp. 321–24.

29. Henriquez, nos. 76–78, pp. 118ff.

30. E. Martène and U. Durand, *Thesaurus novus anecdotorum,* 5 vols., (Paris: sumptibus bibliopolarum Parisiensium, 1717), vol. 4, pp. 369–70, 375–76.

31. This preeminence was also recognized at Constance; H. Charrier, "L abbaye de Cîteaux," supplement hors abonnement du *Miroir dijonais et de Bourgogne,* no. 65, p. 1818.

32. *Statuta,* vol. 4, pp. 393–95.

Most probably, the unity of the Order prescribed in the Charter of Charity was never fully recovered after the schism. Furthermore, the involvement of the Gallican abbots in the controversy between monarchy and papacy undoubtedly damaged the ecumenical character of the Order. The schism had made the Roman popes more jealous than ever of their jurisdiction in Italy, and since Martin V, expedients employed on the peninsula gave credence to the charges that the popes were temporal princes. During the schism and throughout the fifteenth century, the general chapters appointed commissioners and reformers to visit the Italian houses, but there is no way of knowing how effective these measures were. Apparently, the bonds with the English Cistercians were also weakened by the circumstances of the times. Is the instance of 1437 when the abbots of England and Scotland excused themselves from attendance at the general chapter because of the hazards of war the only one?[33] Under the abbacy of Guy IV of Autun (1460–1462), King Edward IV (1461–1483) forbade the annual contributions of the English Cistercians to the mother-house of Cîteaux.[34] There is in the case of the Iberian peninsula sufficient evidence that the monastic ties of the French abbots to their Spanish affiliations were severed. Spain had not been spared during the schism.[35] Even afterwards, Alfonso V of Aragon remained a stubborn foe of Martin V. It would not be presumptuous to imagine deterioration in Cistercian monasticism in Spain. In fact Martín de Vargas, abbot of Mount Sion, near Toledo, obtained from Pope Eugenius a bull for the establishment of a Spanish Congregation of Cistercians outside the jurisdiction of the abbot of Cîteaux and the general

33. H. Denifle, O.P., *La désolation des églises, monasteres, hô pitaux en France vers le milieu du XVe siècle*, 2 vols. (Macôn: Protat Frères; Paris: Alphonse Picard et Fils, 1897–1899), vol. 2, pp. 578–79.

34. A. King, *Cîteaux and Her Elder Daughters*, (London: Burns and Oates, 1954), p. 61.

35. Pedro de Luna, apostolic legate of Clement VII, gave a gloomy picture of the state of ecclesiastical affairs in Castile in 1388, especially attacking the widespread abuse of the *commendes*; J. Mansi, *Sacrorum conciliorum nova et amplissima collectio*, 53 vols., (Florence: expensis Antonii Zatta Veneti, 1759–1927), vol. 26, cols. 742–43.

chapters.[36] Only a more direct and immediate supervision could repair the ruin, both temporal and spiritual, of the houses in the peninsula. The Order seemingly resented this bold maneuver and eventually succeeded in rescinding the papal bull.[37]

Whether the action of Pope Eugenius was prompted by the Pragmatic Sanction and the Gallican policies of the Order is a difficult question to resolve. Eugenius and his successors never accepted the Pragmatic Sanction and for the most part ignored it in their dealings with the French clergy. But they were never comfortable as long as it remained the law of the land. In a sense the lines were never clearly drawn between the papal and monarchic parties. The clergy, and certainly the Cistercians, were often the third party who could shift their position to their own advantage. Behind the façade of free elections lay the king's determination to place his candidates in important benefices. He even awarded his choice a royal writ, a *quod licet*, which permitted entrance past the guards who were stationed to intimidate a conventual chapter.[38] The clergy resented this infringement of their liberties. They continued to solicit apostolic confirmation of their election or presentation.[39] On the other hand, the king was just as adamant in his resolve to prevent papal nominations to benefices of persons who resided "outside the kingdom and the Dauphiné and the other domains of the king and the lord dauphin."[40] The system of

36. The constitution was reluctantly drawn up at the chapter of 1438; *Statuta*, vol. 4, pp. 454–61.

37. Jean de Cirey could not conceal his animosity over the bold action of Brother Martin who obtained the bull "per nonnullos laterales [of Eugenius IV] familiares." He then added: "Verum quia unitas ordinis per hoc multum scindebatur et ledebatur, cum multis laboribus et expensis, vigilancia domini Cisterciensis et patrum ordinis, fuit obtenta tante presumpcionis amplissima revocacio." Cirey's work, the *Defensorium pacis,* is MS II H I of the Archives générales de la Côte d'Or of Dijon; the text cited is 2. 32, fols. 126r–126v.

38. Valois, p. cx.

39. *Ibid.,* p. cxiii, esp. the note, pp. cxxv–cxxvi.

40. Such were the conditions of the royal commissioners handed to the papal legates at Poitiers in June 1443; Valois, *pièce justificative,* n. 61, pp. 112–13.

reservations was denied and the right of elections was specifically upheld in abbeys.[41]

To what extent then did the Pragmatic Sanction offer solace to the Order of Cîteaux? The Order promulgated the bulls of Eugenius in the general chapters. It published the *diffinitio* on the Congregation of Spain. And at least in one instance it yielded to the disposition of the Holy See when the pope presented his candidate against that of the abbot of Morimond to the Spanish house of Beata Maria de Oliva.[42] The answer can perhaps be found in the area of commendatory abbeys. In the papal-French negotiations since the Council of Constance, the matter of *commendes* always received primary consideration. The French sought their complete elimination or effective control. They were a prevalent abuse in the Gallican church. Yet up to the pontificate of Pope Eugenius IV, there is no mention or instance of a commendatory abbey in the Order of Cîteaux in the territories of the French king. In fact the first reference in the general chapters is in 1453, under Nicholas V, although it can probably be attributed to Eugenius IV. Also, it is surrounded by circumstances which intimate that Gallicanism motivated the action of the pope. At a time when relations between the powerful ducal house of the Bourbonnais and the crown were tense, Eugenius exploited the situation by supporting the former.[43] Duke Charles V had presented his candidate to the see of Clermont against the royal nominee, and the contested election, brought before Martin V, had not been resolved when Eugenius ascended the papal chair. After long delays, on 10 May 1445, the ducal candidate was confirmed in his episcopal promotion.[44] The pope was very generous to the Bourbons and showered them with ecclesiastical gifts and honors.[45] At the request of the duke, in 1434,

41. *Ibid.*, p. 114.   42. *Statuta,* vol. 4, n. 40, p. 572.

43. Duke Charles V of Bourbon had led two nobles' rebellions, the Wars of the Praguerie, against the king in 1440 and 1442; A. Allier, *L'ancien Bourbonnais,* vol. 2 (Moulins: Crepin-Leblond, 1934), pp. 338–47.

44. *Gallia Christiana,* 16 vols. (Paris, 1856–1899), vol. 2, p. 292; also *Instrumenta,* pp. 78–99.

45. Allier, *op. cit.,* vol. 2, pp. 306, 352–53, 356, 449.

he named Jean de Chauvin to the abbacy of Montpeiroux, a Cistercian abbey in the diocese of Clermont.[46] This was the first commendatory grant by the pope of a Cistercian abbey in French territory.

The general chapter of 1453 also initiated action against the bishop of Evreux, Pierre de Comborn, who was administrator (commendatory) of the monastery of Obazine, in the diocese of Limoges.[47] He was a member of the prominent family of the lords of Treignac who were the *vicomtes* of Comborn in the *seneschaussée* of Haut-Limousin.[48] In the Gallican assemblies of the mid-fifteenth century, Pierre de Comborn was always numbered among the ultramontanist opposition. In 1444 he was one of four partisans of the Holy See at Bourges.[49] But even earlier, Pope Eugenius IV had put him forward to contest the election of the king's physician Pierre Beschebien to the see of Chartres.[50] Royal opposition ultimately compelled Eugenius to transfer Comborn to Evreux and to revoke his anathemas against Beschebien. Throughout the controversy, Comborn continued to administer Obazine down to 1467.

Jean de Chauvin and Pierre de Comborn were both papalists, or better, ultramontanists. Both were expressions of papal jurisdiction against the Gallican pretensions of the crown. In both cases, the Cistercians in a sense became the victims of the rivalry between pope and king for control of the clergy. Obazine and Montpeiroux were the two earliest *commendes* in France, at least the earliest cited in the statutes of the Order. They occurred in territories Limoges and

46. *Gallia Christiana*, vol. 2, p. 400.

47. *Statuta*, vol. 4, pp. 684–85; also *Gallia Christiana*, vol. 2, p. 638.

48. In the protocol of the Estates-general of 1484, they were listed 17th in order of appeal to the king of 22 noble families named. A. Bernier, *Journal des États-généraux de France tenus a Iours en 1484 sous le règne de Charles VIII* in *Collection de documents inédits sur l'histoire de France*, (Paris: Inprimerie royale, 1835), pp. 714–15. On Pierre de Comborn's ties to the house of Treignac, see Valois, p. 202.

49. Valois, pp. cxliii–cxliv. There were 43 ecclesiastics present.

50. He was referred to by the pope in 1441 as bishop and abbot of Obazine; *Supplicationes Eugenii IV* of the Vatican Archives, 375, fols. 211v–212r.

Clermont, where monarchic jurisdiction was jeopardized by belligerent opposition. More *commendes* of Cistercian houses followed. Under Pope Nicholas V (1447–1455) the first of the numerous bulls to curb the practice appeared.[51] It obviously had little effect, and in 1458, the general chapter revealed its distress over the increasing *commendes* in the Order.[52]

There was every reason for alarm by the Cistercians. The *commende* was a horrible infringement of their liberties, and it had drastic consequences upon the pyramidal hierarchy provided by the *Charter of Charity* for the mutual welfare of the abbeys. Yet there is perhaps a note of exaggeration in the protests of the Order. At the end of the fifties, the statutes included Cadouin, La Colombe and Dunes among the *commendes*.[53] The records unfortunately are not too revealing. But overall, the number of *commendes* was still seemingly slight. It is not presumptuous to conclude that if Gallicanism did not exclude papal influence in France at any time, it at least impeded its free exercise. Subsequent developments bear this out.

Pope Pius II (1458–1464) ascended the papal chair with an obsessive determination to abolish the Pragmatic Sanction of Bourges. Unsuccessful in his efforts with Charles VII, he catered to the ambitions of the dauphin Louis.[54] And in the first year of the new king's reign, the pope accomplished the revocation of the Pragmatic Sanction (27 November 1461).[55] Theoretically, the constitutional basis of Gallicanism was removed and rivalry over the provision of benefices terminated. When Pope Sixtus IV (1472–1484) and Louis XI agreed to the Concordat of 1472 (31 October) at Amboise, the

---

51. Henriquez, n. 83, pp. 125–26.

52. *Statuta*, vol. 5, p. 23 (n. 43).

53. *Ibid.*, vol. 4, p. 745 (n. 91); vol. 5, p. 19 (n. 23); p. 40 (n. 84).

54. J. Combet, *Louis XI et le St.-Siège*, (Paris: Librairie Hachette, 1903), p. xviii. The author argues that Louis felt the Pragmatic Sanction added to the spiritual and temporal power of the lords and prelates, and he hoped to dispose of the goods of the church himself after its abolition which he had sworn even as dauphin.

55. *Ibid.*, p. 8; *Ordonnances*, vol. 15, p. 193.

papal regime was restored to France.[56] Once again, consider the implications for the Cistercians.

The province of Reims sprawled over the royal sees of Reims, Chalôns, Beauvais, Senlis, and Laon, and the Burgundian lands of Amiens, Cambrai, Arras, Thérouanne, and Tournai. In the period of the Pragmatic Sanction, ducal cooperation with Pius II had permitted the free exercise of papal prerogatives so that reservations and expectatives, non-existent in royal territories, were abundant in the duchy.[57] On the other hand, whereas Pius II granted only one expectative in the royal lands of Reims before May 1462, afterwards, more than two hundred were reputedly distributed by him in one day.[58] No Cistercian houses were numbered among this generous display, but consistent with the anti-Gallican policies of the pope before 1461, where royal jurisdiction was tenuous, Ourscamp in Noyon had been granted *in commendam* to the bishop of Sens, Vauclair in Laon to Roderigo Borgia, and Dunes to his kinsman, Francesco de Piccolomini.[59] Furthermore, the Burgundian bishop of Thérouanne was permitted to levy a caritative subsidy on all ecclesiastics, even Cluniacs and Cistercians, notwithstanding their exemption.

The gravity of the situation between 1461 and 1472 was reflected in the action of the general chapters. Their protests against the *commendes* grew louder and more frequent.[60] Finally in 1473 the chapter decided upon an extraordinary measure. The abbot of Cîteaux was delegated to lead a commission of the abbots of Clairvaux of France, Poblet of Spain, Altenberg (Vetusmons) of Germany, and Balerne of Burgundy to appeal directly before the Holy See for apostolic assistance. An assessment of 6,000 ducats was levied upon each house of the Order according to its ability to pay

---

56. *Ordonnances,* vol. 17, p. 548.
57. L'abbé Dubrulle, *Bullaire de la province de Reims sous le pontificat de Pie II,* (Lille: Librairie Réné Girard, 1905), pp. 9–10.
58. *Ibid.,* p. 12.   59. *Ibid.,* pp. 7–8, 67.
60. While the problems of individual commendatory abbeys were cited time and again, it is sufficient only to mention the general statutes that bemoaned commendatory evils in 1469 and 1472; *Statuta,* vol. 5, p. 253 (n. 71); pp. 308–309 (n. 33).

to support the embassy. That the abbot of Cîteaux was empowered to borrow the deficit with or without interest (*ad mutuum sive ad usuram*) betrayed the desperation of the general chapter.[61] After a long delay the delegation departed for Rome in 1475. Besides several scant references, there are only two accounts that relate the interesting details of the journey and the papal audience. They both belong to Jean de Cirey, abbot of Balerne, participant, and a valuable eyewitness.[62] The abbots persisted in their efforts for almost a year. Humbert de Losne of Cîteaux, already infirm, did not survive the ordeal and died in Rome. Jean de Cirey was elected his successor while still in Rome.[63] At last, the abbatial delegation returned home, having obtained several bulls of protection from the curia.[64]

A review of subsequent events reveals the futility of the venture. The spread of the *commende* among Cistercian abbeys was not halted. Actually, it was accelerated very definitely under the concordatory regime of Louis XI and Sixtus IV. Extant records numbered twenty-one monasteries of the Order under papal provision between 1472 and 1483, and eleven were in the kingdom of France.[65] No less than thirty-six monasteries were conferred in consistory between 1480 and 1483 in contrast to papal confirmation of two elections. Eighteen were provided after cession or resignation in compliance with royal insistence.[66] The Order was in a serious state of deterioration.

61. *Statuta*, vol. 5, pp. 317–19 (n. 7).

62. *Defensorium Pacis*, 2.34, fol. 127*v*. Canivez edited the second account, *De Legatione Ordinis ad Sixtum Papam IV*, in the Appendix to the *Statuta*, vol. 5, pp. 761 ff.

63. *Statuta*, vol. 5, p. 765. Cirey added that he refused the abbacy from Pope Sixtus who after the election hesitated to give his confirmation.

64. There are three bulls *ad petitionem Hymberti* and three *motu proprio* for 1475 in Henriquez, pp. 149 ff.

65. C. Eubel, "In commendam verliehene Abteien während die Jahre 1431–1503," *Studien und Mitteilungen aus dem Benediktiner—und dem Zister-zienser—Orden*, 21 (1900), pp. 10–15, 244–47. The author's study of the appropriation of monasteries in this period is invaluable and offers pertinent information from the Vatican Archives for almost 300 papal provisions.

66. P. Ourliac, *Le Concordat de 1472: étude sur les rapports de Louis XI et de Sixte IV*, (Paris: Librairie de Recueil Sirey, 1944), pp. 64–68.

The crisis of the seventies was certainly the result of the concordat. Jean de Cirey struggled with all his might to restore the privileges of the Order and to obtain new bulls from Rome. Sixtus IV issued thirteen bulls, Innocent VIII sixteen, on behalf of the Order, and most were directed *ad petitionem* against commendatory abuses. The juridical bond prescribed by the *Charter of Charity* between the Order in France and the Spanish and Italian houses remained weak. Commendatory abbots now began to put serious gaps in the monastic structure in France. Cirey had already admitted the failure of the Roman embassy in 1477 when he proposed new steps for the Order to pursue.[67] Perhaps the death of Louis XI in 1483 offered some hope. There was a widespread Gallican reaction among the clergy, and the abbot of Cîteaux played a prominent role in the ensuing events. Monks and clergy rebelled against royal beneficiaries and expelled them from abbeys and chapters. They implored young Charles VIII to summon an Estates-general to review their complaints. They made it very clear that they wanted the Pragmatic Sanction, *cujus, regnante Ludovico, cursus impeditus fuit.*[68] Jean de Cirey was very active. His election as deputy of Burgundy had been requested by the king himself.[69] The protocol followed at the assembly was that recommended by the abbot of Cîteaux.[70] He obtained the precedence of the Burgundian legation over all but that of Paris and he was chosen on the committee to discuss the Estates' proposals with the royal council.[71]

On 10 February 1484, the king was present to hear the grievances of the first estate, the clergy. In a lengthy discourse, Master Jean Derly spoke on the need for reform. He cited the deformity in the church, "in the Benedictine, Augustinian, and Cistercian Orders" where "nearly all the abbeys and all benefices are held *in commendam*, usually by the unworthy."[72] The repeated appeal to uphold the liberties of the Gallican church, the decrees of Constance, Basel

67. *Statuta*, vol. 5, pp. 363-64 (n. 7).   68. Bernier, p. 82.

69. *Ibid.*, p. 739 (n. 1).

70. *Ibid.*, pp. 737-41. Cirey's *procès-verbal* listed the order by which those present could address the king.

71. *Ibid.*, p. 310.   72. *Ibid.*, p. 196.

and Bourges rang out throughout the debates, and the clergy begged for the royal protection that Charles VII always proffered. In the end the Estates-general accomplished nothing. Perhaps the young king was swayed by the powerful prelates of the realm and the "bishops of the king" as Louis' appointees were derogatorily referred to.[73] Gallicanism was unable to abrogate the concordat.

The crisis in the Order was serious. The statutes of the general chapters and the papal bulls of protection revealed more the decline of Cistercian monasticism than they offered any hope of a restoration to pristine glory. The administrative government that was placed before the Fourth Lateran Council as a model for the Benedictines was now subjected to poignant criticism. The voice of the abbot of Cîteaux was but feebly heard in distant territories and the pyramidal interdependency of the French houses was sorely tested. The efforts of Jean de Cirey to publicize the plight of the Order in the courts of kings and popes were expensive and were bankrupting an already impoverished Order.[74] His too frequent fiscal demands met resistance and provoked even a threat of schism. His methods appeared arbitrary and authoritarian, and Pierre de Virey, abbot of Clairvaux could not reconcile them with the institutes of the Order. In 1482 Virey made accusations before the general chapter.[75] There followed an investigation which exonerated Jean de Cirey and condemned Virey's *libellus* to burning. But the matter dragged on. The abbot of Clairvaux appealed from the Order's judgment to the Parlement of Paris. He went so far as to declare a Congregation of Clairvaux and its affiliations.[76] The controversy evoked scandal that reached

73. Charles VIII dismissed the complaints of the clergy, refusing to answer them "because of the opposition made to some of the articles . . . by my lords the cardinals and prelates." *Ibid.*, p. 704.

74. Jean de Cirey elaborated his plans in a lengthy *diffinitio* which was published in place of a general chapter in 1477; *Statuta*, vol. 5, pp. 357ff (n. 1–2).

75. *Ibid.*, pp. 445–46 (n. 52).

76. The "schism" lasted six years; there is a summary of events in Martène and Durand, vol. 4, p. 164; the details can be found in *Statuta*, vol. 5, p. 454–56 (n. 16); pp. 457–58 (n. 20); pp. 470–71 (n. 81); pp. 481–83 (n. 37); pp. 517–23 (n. 70–72); p. 607 (n. 79); pp. 652–53 (n. 59).

the Holy See, and Pope Innocent VIII summoned both abbots in 1485. More drastically, in 1489, he issued the bull *Ad sacrum apostolatus* which united Cîteaux and Clairvaux under the one abbot Jean de Cirey.[77] The prestige of the Order had been greatly tarnished. The breakdown of Cistercian monasticism was evident everywhere. There was enough scandal to arouse princes and prelates. If Cirey attempted to govern as a general abbot, his influence was limited to few houses. The commendatories ignored the regular abbots; the regulars tried to evade capitular reformers and commissioners. Worse, even the latter were derelict, and they had to be cited for their failure to keep and report records and receipts to the Order.[78]

During the controversy between the abbots of Cîteaux and Clairvaux, Pope Innocent VIII directed the bull *Meditatio cordis nostri* to the general chapter of 1487.[79] This was a stern rebuke to correct the widespread abuses in Cistercian monasteries or suffer suppression. Innocent said that the papal court had been buffeted with complaints from kings, princes, and other lords evoked by scandals in the Order, and he warned the general chapter to initiate remedies at once. Jean de Cirey received the menacing challenge vigorously. His action was unprecedented. He decided to convoke a special meeting of regular abbots to review the plight of the Order. In 1493 they convened in assembly at Paris. The act was born of despair. Needless to say, the assembly accomplished nothing. Nevertheless it warrants some observations. It can be considered an epilogue to Cistercian monasticism in the Middle Ages. It marked the end of the religious Order of Cîteaux as it was conceived by the *Charter of Charity*.

There were forty-five abbots at Paris, all of the French "nation."

77. *Ibid.*, pp. 665–67. The author's note is interesting: the original bull is lost and the copy is dated 1602. Virey never attended the Assembly of Abbots at Paris in 1493 as abbot of Clairvaux, but he appears in records of the Order to the end of the century. Overall there is much obscurity surrounding these developments.

78. *Ibid.*, vol. 6, pp. 55–57 (n. 62).

79. J. Paris, *Nomasticon Cisterciense: seu antiquiores ordinis Cistercienses constitutiones,* (nova editio, Paris: apud Sebastianum Mabre-Cramoisy, regis typographum, 1670), pp. 667–73.

N

Their deliberations produced the *Articles of Paris*.[80] They were submitted to the following general chapter for ratification, but oddly, they were rejected on legalistic principles.[81] With their repudiation went any hope of reform. More significant are the number and nationality of attendant abbots. It is obvious that the Order in France had abandoned any notions of reuniting all the houses in a momentous restoration. Jean de Cirey could not conceal his disgust for the innovations that permitted annual, biennial, and triennial abbacies in Italy.[82] In fact within a few years, Pope Alexander VI published the bull which united the monasteries of Tuscany and Lombardy in the Congregation of St Bernard in Italy.[83] It is impossible to determine how strong the ties were between the mother-houses in France and the affiliations in England, Spain, and Germany.[84] It is certain that the bull of Innocent VIII was corroborated by royal letters of Charles VIII which summoned Jean of Cîteaux and Jean of Bonport to Tours (12 November 1492) "with some reverend fathers, lord bishops, abbots, renowned and learned men, doctors and legal advisors" to deal with the reform of the monastic state in the kingdom.[85] So the assembly of Paris became a national concern and did not affect the foreign abbeys.

Here too there are questions. Wars, pestilence, roving marauders, *commendes*, desertion, union of houses, poverty, all these had eroded the magnificent system of Cistercian monasticism for more than a

80. *Nomasticon Cisterciense*, pp. 673ff.

81. *Ibid.*, pp. 673–74; also Helyot, vol. 5, p. 361.

82. *Defensorium Pacis*, 2, 32, fol. 126*v*: "Preterea inutilem nonnullorum transalpinorum novitatem qui ordinis fundamenta quantum in eis fuit evertentes, non contenti forma ipsius ordinis, induxerunt abbates annales, alii biennales, alii triennales ex quo brevi annorum curriculo quilibet eorum abbatis officio fungitur."

83. Franciscus Gaude (ed.), *Bullarum, diplomatum et privilegiorum sanctorum Romanorum pontificum taurinensis editio locupletior* . . . 25 vols. (Turin, 1857–1872), vol. 5, pp. 371–76.

84. There was still communication between the chapter and individual houses in Spain in 1487 and 1489: *Statuta*, vol. 5, pp. 608–610 (n. 80); 681–82 (n. 31); in Scotland in 1496: *ibid.*, vol. 6, pp. 133–34 (n. 16–17).

85. *Nomasticon Cist.*, p. 675.

century. So whom do the forty-five abbots at Paris represent? Are
they all that were left 'of the hundreds, perhaps close to a thous-
and, houses that dotted the French landscape? Or are they all that
obeyed the summons of the abbot of Cîteaux? The latter seems
more likely the case. There were certainly enough abbots at the
general chapter of 1493 to defeat the Articles of Paris. The chance
for reform had been missed, and the Order continued on the path
of decline.

The medieval conception of government, of the monarchy and
state, did not provide for the separation of the spiritual and the
temporal. As long as the papacy was the dominant authority in
Christianity, a universal protection was afforded to ecclesiastical
institutions. But the progress of political theory that became the
basis of the national monarchies challenged the notion of a superior
jurisdiction. The acceptance of the universal Church was altogether
different from the control and appropriation of territorial churches
and their wealth and influence. The first idea was theoretically
sound while the latter was unconditionally rejected by Gallican
interests. Hence, the privileges granted by Rome to the religious
Orders, to Cîteaux in particular, became juridically untenable.

The system of Cîteaux depended upon the ecclesiastical theories
of the Gregorian Church. The prestige and power of the papacy
insured its success. As the one faltered, so did the other. The Order
could not resolve the disturbing dilemma whose alternatives were
both injurious. To defend the universal primacy of the papacy
against the Gallicanists and conciliarists implied the acknowledgment
of the plenary disposition of all benefices, Cistercian abbeys too, by
the popes; on the other hand the support of the Gallican decrees
diminished the effectiveness of papal bulls of protection and led to
the infringement of monastic liberties by bishops and secular lords.
The issues debated by the theorists of popes and kings in the fifteenth
century did not disagree on the theocratic nature of society—
religion and government were inseparable—but on the immediate
exercise of jurisdiction over the affairs of the national churches and
clergy with the consequent diminution of papal authority in fiscal
and judicial matters. It is much too early to conceive of the con-

troversy as one over religious freedom or separation of church and state. As the contestants asserted and exercised their prerogatives, the Cistercians gradually succumbed to the measures resorted to by both. The abbot of Cîteaux was a prominent cleric of the Gallican Church, and he and his fellow French abbots could not maintain control over their foreign dependencies. The movement toward the national congregations had already begun in the fifteenth century. Furthermore, the papal system of reservations made it very difficult to oppose curial nominations to Cistercian abbeys, first outside France, than in the kingdom itself.

The struggle between pope and king to control benefices ignored the whole question of monastic exemption. The abbeys became the prizes of papal or royal favorites, and the general chapters either protested futilely or watched in utter helplessness. For a while, the Order had recourse to one party or another to defend its interests, but with the abrogation of the Pragmatic Sanction of Bourges in 1461 and the Concordat of 1472 the king and pope agreed to share their common hegemony over the Gallican Church, as Paul Ourliac so aptly described it.[86] The number of commendatory abbeys increased at an alarming rate and contributed immeasurably to the acceleration of the Order's decline. Although Jean de Cirey, abbot of Cîteaux from 1475–1501, employed every device possible to save the Order, at most he was only able to retard the deterioration. The final blow at the medieval edifice of Cistercian monasticism was dealt in 1516 when Francis I and Leo X agreed to the Concordat of Bologna. The pope asked only that his prerogatives be respected as he conceded the king the right to nominate to most of the benefices in France. The organizational and interdependent relationship of the abbeys that contributed to the notion of a religious Order was shattered. Furthermore, what houses escaped royal or papal jurisdiction succumbed to the devastation of the wars between Huguenots and Catholics. So many disappeared from the records of the Order in the sixteenth century.

This study attempted to show the plight of the Order of Cîteaux

86. Ourliac, p. 81.

at the close of the Middle Ages. More particularly, it examined the papal-Gallican rivalry that contributed to the circumstances that affected Cistercian monasteries in France in the fifteenth century. As such it is only a small part of the story of the decline of the Order. In many ways the Order of Cîteaux is symptomatic of the general deterioration that affected Christian Europe on the eve of the Reformation. Therefore it is difficult to determine if the commendatory practice, which was so detrimental to the monastic Orders, was a cause or an effect when it is considered in its historical context.

The Order never completely disappeared. The monastic ideal of Cîteaux survived in isolated abbeys that preserved its observances singly until called upon to join subsequent reform movements again. First the Feuillants, then more especially the Trappists, have carried the spirit of the Cistercians into the twentieth century. The system has undergone change; it has adapted to contemporary needs as much as possible. But while it changes, it is more obvious than ever that it remains close to the original form that St Stephen gave it and St Bernard successfully propagated.

William J. Telesca

Le Moyne College

MARTIN LUTHER'S ATTITUDE TOWARD
BERNARD OF CLAIRVAUX

I REGARD BERNARD AS THE MOST PIOUS of all monks and prefer him to all the others, even to St Dominic. He is the only one worthy of the name 'Father,' and of being studied diligently."[1] This assessment of Bernard by Luther is typical of the Augustinian friar's attitude toward the Cistercian monk. It is a remarkable accolade coming from one who displayed an aversion to medieval Christianity with a special hostility reserved for monasticism. It is the purpose of the present study to explore this apparent anomaly.

Luther was convinced that he and his followers stood in the traditions of the ancient and medieval Church. They believed that true Catholic Christianity had become adulterated primarily during the fourteenth and fifteenth centuries, since the great Western schism, and that a return to the Fathers (including Bernard, Bonaventure, and Aquinas) was a return to orthodoxy. During his enforced residence in the Wartburg Luther busied himself with the

---

1. Luther, *Sermons on the Gospel of St John*, in *Luther's Works*, American edition, vol. 22, (Published jointly by Concordia Publishing House, St Louis, and Fortress Press, Philadelphia, 1956–), p. 38. Hereafter Luther references will be from the American Edition (*AE*) unless otherwise indicated. In his *Lectures on Galatians*, AE, vol. 26, p. 460 Luther writes, "(Bernard) was a man so pious, holy, and chaste that I think he deserves to be put ahead of all other monks." Roland Bainton, *Here I Stand* (Nashville: Abingdon Press, 1950), p. 353, "Before Luther wrote on Christ's Nativity he steeped himself in the interpretations by Augustine, Bernard, Tauler, and Ludwig of Saxony."

study of Bernard, and in preparation for the Leipzig debate he supplied himself with numerous passages from the Cistercian's writings. His knowledge of Bernard came chiefly from the mystical writings, especially the sermons on the Song of Songs, *De diligendo Deo*, and his letters. He was also familiar with *De consideratione* and *De praecepto et dispensatione*. Luther's selectivity can be attributed either to the lack of available manuscripts or to a policy of choosing only those works which were congenial with the Reformer's own theology. That theology has often been described in terms of *sola gratia, sola fide*, and *sola Scriptura*, and it is in relation to these issues that Luther most frequently cited Bernard.

On Grace

Luther defined grace as an attitude on the part of God who was willing to save sinners only because of Christ's merits, which were considered to be transferable to the sinner. Although God's justice demanded that man's sin be punished, his anger toward man was intercepted by Christ, and because of this it was possible for man to enjoy forgiveness of sins in this life and paradise hereafter. Man was incapable of changing God's angry disposition toward him by living an upright life. It was only because of Christ's life, death, and resurrection that man could claim eternal rewards.

Melanchthon maintained that Luther was deeply influenced by the following passage from one of Bernard's sermons.

> In addition, you must also believe that through him (Christ) your sins are forgiven. This is the testimony that the Holy Spirit has put into your heart when he says, "Your sins are forgiven you." For this is the meaning of the Apostle, that man without merit is justified through faith.[2]

Melanchthon added that Luther was enlightened and strengthened by this statement, and that it clarified for him the meaning of Rom

2. As quoted by E. G. Schwiebert, *Luther and His Times* (St Louis: Concordia Publishing House, 1950), p. 171. Cf. *Corpus Reformatorum*, vol. 6, p. 159.

3:28. The occasion for these comments by Bernard was his attack against Abelard's moral example theory of the atonement.

Luther was fond of quoting a statement from Bernard uttered at a time when the monk believed he was at the point of death.

> St Bernard himself also had to feel and admit this (helplessness in the sight of God). He had led an extremely ascetic life with prayers, fasts, chastisements, and there was nothing he lacked. He was an example for everyone else, and I know no one among the monks who wrote or lived better than he. And yet when the anguish of death came upon him, he himself had to pronounce this judgment on his whole holy life: "O I have lived damnably and passed my life shamefully." How so, dear St Bernard? Have you not been a pious monk all your life? Are not chastity, obedience, preaching, fasting, and prayer something valuable? "No," he says, "it is all lost and belongs to the devil."[3]

In Luther's sermons on St John he again refers to this selection from Bernard, where the Cistercian speaks of a two-fold claim Christ has to heaven.

> I take comfort in the knowledge that Jesus Christ, my Lord, has a two-fold claim on heaven. In the first place he can lay claim to it for himself because he is the true and natural Son of God, governing with the Father from eternity. Hence he is entitled to heaven as an heir from eternity. But this is not the source of my comfort. In the second place he has gained heaven through his holy suffering and death and then presented this to me. In this manner I too shall fall heir to heaven.[4]

Luther was convinced that, "had St Bernard not died in this faith, he would have gone to the devil and into the abyss of hell."[5] He

---

3. Luther, *Commentary on the Sermon on the Mount*, AE, vol. 21, p. 283, citing Bernard, *Sermones in cantica*, 20, PL 183:867. Luther refers to this incident again in his *Sermons on the Gospel of St John*, AE, vol. 22, pp. 52, 387, 360, and 283, and in his *Lectures on Galatians*, AE, vol. 26, p. 5. It is also found in the *Career of the Reformer*, AE, vol. 31, p. 89.

4. Bernard, *Sermones in cantica*, 20, PL 183:867; Luther, *Sermons on the Gospel of St John*, AE, vol. 22, p. 52.

5. Luther, *Sermons on the Gospel of St John*, AE, vol. 22, p. 52.

again refers to Bernard in his commentary on Hebrews, quoting from his sermon on the Annunciation and his elaboration of Ps 85:9 ("that glory may dwell in our land"):

> In this sermon St Bernard speaks in the following way. "It is necessary for you to believe that God can remit your sins, bestow grace on you and give glory to you. And this is not enough, unless you believe with complete certainty that your sins have been remitted, that grace has been bestowed on you, and that glory is to be given to you."[6]

Bernard's statements on the Incarnation are frequently cited by Luther in his commentaries on grace. "Bernard loved the Incarnation of Christ very much. So did Bonaventure. I praise these men very highly for the sake of that article on which they reflect so gladly and brilliantly, and which they practice in themselves with great joy and godliness."[7] Luther continues by repeating Bernard's explanation of the Devil's fall. Already in the beginning Satan foresaw God's plan to save man by permitting Christ to assume humanity. This conferred a great dignity on man, greater indeed than that of the angels, and Satan, moved by envy, raged against God with the result that he was expelled from heaven. Luther concludes that, "these thoughts of Bernard are not unprofitable, for they flow from admiration for the boundless love and mercy of God."[8] Luther approves of Bernard's interpretation of the creedal statement, "and was made man."

> As St Bernard deliberated on these words, he derived some very comforting thoughts from them. He said: "Now I can see that God, my Lord, is not angry with me; for he is my flesh and blood and sits at the right hand of the heavenly Father as Lord over all

6. Luther, *Commentary on Hebrews*, AE, vol. 29, p. 171, citing Bernard, *Sermo in festo Annunciationis Beatae Mariae Virginis*, 1:3, PL 183: 383–84.

7. Luther, *Lectures on Genesis*, AE, vol. 5, p. 221.

8. *Ibid.*, citing Bernard, *Sermones de tempore*, 1, PL 183:36. On Lucifer's fall see also Luther, *Lectures on Genesis*, AE vol. 4, p. 256; vol. 1, p. 23; *Sermons on the Gospel of St John*, AE, vol. 22, p. 103.

creatures. If he were ill-disposed toward me, he would not have
taken on my flesh and blood.[9]

Both Bernard and Luther interpret the story of Jacob's ladder as
prefiguring the Incarnation, and in his treatment of this mystery
in his commentary on Ps 110:1 ("The Lord said to my lord, 'Sit
at my right hand,' ") Luther repeats Bernard's conviction that, "if
my flesh and blood sits in heaven above I expect he will not be my
enemy."[10] Luther was especially impressed by the deep humility
Bernard displayed in his reflections on the Incarnation, a humility
enhanced by the fact that Bernard, "had amounted to something
in the world. He had been rich enough, noble, learned, and holy."[11]
If such a one professed no merit in God's sight, it was certain that
the average believer could make no claims on God's grace.

Both theologians, reflecting twelfth and sixteenth-century
Christianity, had a vivid sense of hell and damnation. Luther was
especially intrigued by the fifth book of *De consideratione*, where
Bernard spoke of the impossibility of hiding from God's justice,
and in his devotional writings he alludes to Bernard's warning
against feeling too secure in God's grace.[12]

In gratitude for receiving God's grace, Christians are under
obligation to display a similar attitude of love toward their fellow
men. Luther maintained that Potiphar's wife, while attempting to
seduce Joseph, was not only breaking the sixth commandment but
was also tempting him to the sin of ingratitude. For had he succumbed, he would have rewarded the kindness of Potiphar, his

---

9. Luther, *Lectures on Psalms*, AE, vol. 22, p. 105, citing Bernard, *Sermones
in cantica*, 2:6, PL 183:792.

10. Luther, *Lectures on Psalms*, AE, vol. 13, p. 245, citing Bernard as above.
11. *Ibid.*

12. Luther, *Commentary on Hebrews*, AE, vol. 29, p. 165, citing Bernard,
De consideratione 5:11, PL 182:802; Luther, *Devotional Writings*, AE, vol. 42,
pp. 9–10. *Lectures on Genesis*, AE, vol. 3, p. 225, "If you divide all Scripture it
contains two topics: promises and threats, or benefits and punishments. And
as Bernard states, hearts that are neither softened by kindness nor improved
by blows are properly called hard," citing *De consideratione*, 1:2, PL 182:
730–31.

host, with evil. He continues by referring to Bernard's statement, "No voice is more pernicious than ingratitude, because it dries up the fountain of goodness."[13] Luther further recommended that a charitable attitude be displayed toward fellow Christians who may succumb to temptations. "It is our duty," he writes, "to ascribe his fall not to wickedness but to a lack of caution or even to weakness, just as Bernard taught his followers that if one was unable in any way to excuse a brother's sin, at least one should say it was a great and insuperable temptation by which he was overtaken."[14] In this way God's grace was to flow through the Christian to others.

Bernard's theology of grace was more closely associated with the Church's sacraments than was Luther's (Cf. Bernard *De gratia et libero arbitrio*). Whereas the Reformer included the sacraments as channels of grace, he did not limit the term to an effusion of divine power or strength enabling the believer to follow Christ. In this respect he was, together with most other medieval theologians, a disciple of Augustine. Therefore when Luther cites Bernard he ranges beyond the Cistercian's explicit statements on grace, which are not numerous, but nevertheless he discovers Lutheran emphases scattered throughout Bernard's writings. Even Bernard's mysticism, which Luther usually ignored, occasionally found a ready response in Luther's pietism, as indicated by the latter's high regard for the *Sermones in cantica*.

Concerning this three-fold kiss read Bernard at the beginning of the Song of Songs, to find this interpretation: "Kiss the Son, that is, worship Christ as God with the greatest reverence; subject yourselves to Christ the Lord with the greatest humility; and cling to Christ, the Bridegroom, with the greatest love. Behold, love and fear, with humility as the measure and midpoint of both—this is the most perfect worship of God.[15]

13. Luther, *Lectures on Genesis*, AE, vol. 7, p. 83, citing Bernard, *Sermones de diversis* 27, PL 183: 615–16.

14. Luther, *Lectures on Galatians*, AE, vol. 27, p. 387, citing Bernard, *Sermones in cantica* 35:5–7, PL 183:900.

15. Luther, *Commentaries on the Psalms*, AE, vol. 14, p. 347, citing Bernard, *Sermones in cantica*, 4, PL 183:796–97.

On Faith

Luther's teaching on faith was closely allied with his view of grace; the latter was God's gift to all men, who grasped it by the hand of the former. Salvation came to those who denied any merit in good works but who relied solely on grace and faith. Certainly Luther's explicit statements in this regard are in advance of the medievalists; nevertheless, he was able to discern his own views in statements of the Fathers.

> Although the Fathers were often wrong, they ought nevertheless to be honored on account of their testimony to faith. So I venerate Jerome and Gregory and others inasmuch as one can sense from their writings, in spite of everything else, that they believed as we do, as the Church from the beginning believed. So Bernard was magnificent when he taught and preached . . . The Fathers aren't worth much for controversy, but on account of their testimony to faith they ought all to be honored.[16]

Luther's definition of a saint was, "those who are so wise through faith that they depend solely on the mercy of God and regard their works as nothing," and he continues by holding up Bernard as the exemplary saint, who was said to have encouraged a faint-hearted brother: "Brother, go and hold Mass on my faith," and when he did so, he was benefited. Luther continues: "You see that this holy man performed all his acts in faith, which is what prevents anyone from perishing in his error, no matter how great the error may be."[17]

16. Luther, *Table Talks,* AE, vol. 54, p. 105.

17. Luther, *Word and Sacraments,* AE, vol. 36, p. 186, citing Bernard, *Exordium magnum Cisterciense,* 2:6, PL 185:419. *Commentary on Hebrews,* AE, vol. 29, p. 218, "Hence Bernard in his sermons on the Song of Songs admonishes his brothers not to despise their prayers in any way but to believe that they are written and have been written in heaven before they are completed, and that they should expect with the greatest certainty that their wish, namely, that their prayers, have either been heard and are to be fulfilled in their own good time or that it is better if they are not fulfilled." (*Sermones in Quadragesima,* 5:5, PL 183:180). Luther often repeats this anecdote.

At least a dozen references to Bernard's evaluation of faith can be found in Luther's comments on the Annunciation. Typical of these is the following:

> Bernard says concerning the faith of the Virgin Mary when it had been announced to her by the angel that she would be the mother of Christ that the strength of the faith of the Virgin who could believe the words of the angel was no less a miracle than the Incarnation of the Word itself. Therefore the greatest things in the histories of the saints are the words which God speaks with the saints. Although their virtues and deeds should be praised—and God requires these too—yet they, like the feet, should be put in the lowest place. But the head in the life of the saints is the speaking of God itself.[18]

But Luther was also critical of Bernard's devotion to the blessed Virgin. "Bernard filled a whole sermon with praise of the Virgin Mary and in so doing forgot to mention what happened, so highly did he esteem Mary."[19] Elsewhere he chided Bernard for offering excessive devotion to Mary with the result that, "Christ is given to scolding and punishing, but Mary has nothing but sweetness and love. Therefore Christ was generally feared; we fled from him and took refuge with the saints calling upon Mary and others to deliver us from our distress. We regarded them as holier than Christ."[20] In fact, Luther at one time accused the Cistercian of

18. Luther, *Lectures on Genesis*, AE, vol. 5, p. 234, citing Bernard, *In nativitate Domini*, 11:4, PL 183:121.

19. Luther, *Table Talk*, AE, vol. 54, p. 84. See *Nativitate Beatae Mariae Virginis Sermo*, PL 183:441.

20. Luther, *Sermons on the Gospel of St John*, AE, vol. 22, p. 377. Luther, *Commentary on the Psalms*, AE, vol. 13, p. 326, "They taught us to call upon the dear mother of Christ and to urge her, for the sake of the breasts which she gave her son, to plead against his wrath over us and to obtain His grace." Cf. poem ascribed to Bernard, *Oratio devota ad Dominum Jesum et B. Mariam Matrem Eius*, PL 184:1326. *Sermons on the Gospel of St John*, AE, vol. 23, p. 57, "There is a shameful and blasphemous picture or painting of Judgment Day in which we see the Son on his knees before the Father showing him his wounds, and St John and Mary interceding for us at the last judgment, the mother showing the Son the breasts he had sucked. The picture is based on St Bernard's writings, but these words, this picture, and this portrayal are not to St Bernard's credit."

maintaining a double standard in his preaching and disputation. "Bernard was superior to all the Doctors in the Church when he preached, but he became quite a different man in his disputations, for then he attributed too much to law and to free will."[21]

On Scripture

Luther was not a biblicist in the sense that his teaching on the sufficiency of Scripture excluded Catholic tradition. Indeed, his veneration for St Bernard indicates the high regard he held for some Fathers of the Church, and he believed that the decisions of the first four ecumenical councils were normative for the Church. A large part of his argument at the Leipzig debate centered on his belief that he was standing in the continuity of orthodox Catholic tradition. Nevertheless, he also maintained that ecclesiastical tradition must flow from apostolic tradition (i.e. Scripture) or be demonstrably connected with it. In this sense Scripture was the source and norm for all subsequent tradition, and when the latter was neither explicitly traceable to apostolic testimony nor supported by it, it was either suspect or at best *de humano* and changeable. This understanding of *sola Scriptura* is reflected in Luther's commentary on St John.

> You must not only go to St Bernard and St Ambrose, but it is imperative that you take them with you to Christ and see whether they agree with his teaching. If they do not, but have added something to that which Christ has taught, or have evolved something from their own piety and taught this, I shall let them answer for that.[22]

Luther cautions his readers that patristic authority rests upon the degree in which the Fathers reflect Scripture. "We will not listen to this: 'Bernard lived and wrote thus,' but only to this, 'He was supposed to live and write according to the Scriptures.' We are not

21. Luther, *Table Talk,* AE, vol. 54, p. 105.
22. Luther, *Sermons on the Gospel of St John,* AE, vol. 22, p. 255.

consistency which brought them to rely solely on the merits of Christ. "Bernard . . . put all his faith in Christ and despaired absolutely of his own works. He takes no pride in his vow of poverty, obedience, chastity; in fact, he calls his life wasted. All the holy and pious monks must have been like Bernard . . . who were wonderfully saved and in the last resort had to say that their vows were nothing."[37]

Despite his aversion to monasticism, Luther gives grudging recognition to the virtues of some Fathers. "A few may have recognized their error and accepted Christ, the only true Light, by faith, as I previously said about Bernard."[38] He refused to condemn those who admired the works of Francis and Bernard, and confessed that there was as much faith in the monasteries as in Jacob's house, who was considered a patriarch of monasticism.[39] But evidence of such monastic faith was also evidence that God could work miracles under the most adverse conditions.[40]

Luther admired the social concerns of Bernard, whose vow of *stabilitas* was considerably bent as he traveled throughout Europe on his numerous missions.

> We can see the divine work in Bernard and men like him. Bernard, lest he leave his monks in a puerile and narrow love (excessive withdrawal from the world) wrenched them away and thrust them into the midst of all the real concerns of life. He did this so that in these activities love might show its real power, a love poured out and shed on all men, shown to everyone, ready to serve anyone. Moreover, it was by this secret miracle that he saved them so that they did not perish in that damnable institution of narrow and artificial love.[41]

37. Luther, *Christian in Society,* AE, vol. 44, pp. 292–93.

38. Luther, *Sermons on the Gospel of St John,* AE, vol. 22, p. 58.

39. Luther, *Lectures on Genesis,* AE, vol. 7, p. 307.

40. Luther, *Word and Sacrament,* AE, vol. 36, p. 77.

41. Luther, *Christian in Society,* AE, vol. 44, pp. 334–35. "The world admires the holiness of Benedict, Gregory, Bernard, Francis, and men like that, because it hears that they performed works that looked magnificent and unusual. . . . They did not live such an ascetic and horrible life as these others

asking how the saints lived and wrote."[23] He cites with approval a similar statement from Bernard.

> St Bernard declares that he learned his wisdom from the trees, such as oaks and pines, which were his teachers; that is, he conceived his ideas from Scripture and pondered them under the trees. He adds that he regards the holy fathers highly, but does not heed all their sayings, explaining why in the following parable: he would rather drink from the spring itself than from the brook, as do all men, who once they have a chance to drink from the spring forget about the brook, unless they use the brook to lead them to the spring. Thus Scripture too must remain master and judge, for when we follow the brooks too far they lead us away from the spring.[24]

In the matter of interpreting Scripture, Luther both admired and criticized Bernard. The Psalms, for instance, should be read according to the spirit in which they were written, and then applied to one's personal life and to the life of the Church. "I see that St Bernard was an expert in this art and drew from it all the wealth of his learning."[25] Scripture, according to Luther, cannot simply be read for its contents and narration, but the reader ought to meditate upon selected texts. "Thus Bernard's heart and mind gave free play to his reflections on the words of our text (Jn 1:14) and his meditations betoken his wondering delight over them. That is also what he wants to convey and impress on us."[26] As to catechresis (the mixing of metaphors, i.e., "O death, where is thy sting?") he lauds Bernard's "wonderful mastery of this art," for it displays a profound understanding of the totality of Scripture; "nevertheless, one must not do violence to simple grammar."[27]

23. Luther, *Word and Sacraments,* AE, vol. 36, p. 137.

24. Luther, *Church and Ministry III,* AE, vol. 41, p. 20. This analogy cannot be located in Bernard's works. Luther continues this passage by suggesting that too often Bernard regarded the Fathers as the spring itself and equal to Scripture.

25. Luther, *Commentary on the Psalms,* AE, vol. 14, p. 311.

26. Luther, *Sermons on the Gospel of St John,* AE, vol. 22, p. 104.

27. Luther, *Lectures on Genesis,* AE, vol. 8, p. 147.

On the other hand, Luther cautions against accepting everything Bernard wrote. He believed Bernard's interpretation of Ps 91:56 was too subjective, "savoring too strongly of monkishness, and is too feeble for Christians being assailed more for the sake of the Word and faith than for the sake of their life and works." Although different interpretations were permissible, "and we do not want to dissuade others from their views, our interpretation is good too, if not actually the best."[28] He was critical of Bernard's use of allegory, arising from his failure to treat Scripture primarily and in the first instance as historical.[29] This led to a distortion of the true meaning of a given text.

> St Bernard was a man so lofty in spirit that I almost venture to set him above all other celebrated teachers both ancient and modern. But note how often he plays (spiritually to be sure) with the Scriptures and twists them out of their true sense.[30]

On Monasticism and Vows

Luther was sharply critical of monasticism and the vows of poverty, celibacy, and obedience. His most forthright statement against this institution was his *De votis monasticis* of 1522, in which his primary concern was the irreconcilability of monasticism with the doctrine of grace. Vows, he insisted, are contrary to the Word of God, to faith, to evangelical liberty, to God's commandments, and to reason. He suggests that good and saintly men, including Augustine and Bernard, observed ascetical practices "for the purpose of being exalted above others in the kingdom of heaven,"[31] and that abstinence from meat and the like was required to be a good Christian, which in effect "made of Christ a liar."[32] And even

---

28. Luther, *Word and Sacrament*, AE, vol. 35, p. 217.

29. Luther, *Lectures on Genesis*, AE, vol. 2, p. 164.

30. Luther, *Christian in Society*, AE, vol. 45, p. 363.

31. Luther, *Lectures on Genesis*, AE, vol. 8, p. 7.

32. Luther, *Word and Sacrament*, AE, vol. 35, p. 134. Regarding Bernard's asceticism, Luther is fond of repeating this anecdote. "Even though St Bernard

---

when monks' lives were exemplary in externals, Luther cites Bernard to prove that in matters of thought and intention there were sins enough.[33]

It was axiomatic with Luther that all Christians, including monks, were equal in the sight of God.

> I love St Bernard as the one who, among all writers, preached Christ most charmingly. I follow him wherever he preached Christ, and I pray to Christ in the faith in which he prayed to Christ. But I will not consent to wearing his cowl, his hair shirt, and his monkish garb; for by so doing I would be condemning all other Christians, as if their stations were not as good, honorable, and dignified as that of the monk, Bernard. A father, mother, or child, a hired man or maid, may believe exactly what St Bernard believed. They share his baptism and his faith; they also have the same Christ and the same God he had. This puts them on a level with St Bernard.[34]

The reason many Christians were attracted to monasteries, according to Luther, was ignorance and a childish naiveté. They, including Bernard, are like the two hundred men who accompanied Absalom in his effort to overthrow King David (2 Sam 15:1-11). They followed him in simple trust, unaware of his treasonous plans.[35] Other monks were "like children who are deceived by the outward appearance and who save the gilded shells of nuts as gold and admire them."[36] Fortunately many of them were saved by the in-

---

was a saintly man, he too was afflicted for a time with such folly (ascetical practices). He denied his body so much that his breath stank and he could not associate with people. Later, however, he came to his senses and also told his brothers not to hurt the body too much. For he realized that he had made himself unable to serve his brothers." *Catholic Epistles*, AE, vol. 30, p. 27.

33. Luther, *Lectures on Genesis*, AE, vol. 5, p. 323.

34. Luther, *Sermons on the Gospel of St. John*, AE, vol. 22, p. 268. "The monks extol the legends of their fathers, Benedict and Bernard, but surely God speaks at far greater length and associates far more intimately with any Christian whatever than they boast about their fathers," *Lectures on Genesis*, AE, vol. 3, p. 165.

35. Luther, *Christian in Society*, AE, vol. 44, pp. 288-93.

36. Luther, *Lectures on Genesis*, AE, vol. 2, pp. 268-69.

Luther was especially impressed with Bernard's sermons to the brothers. "By this one work he restored the old institution of Paul and saved himself and his brethren with him. If there were men of Bernard's caliber in the monasteries (today) they could be tolerated, because they would in part be observing the institution of Paul in all seriousness."[42]

Although Luther acknowledged that the monks of the past had often lived exemplary lives, he maintained that in his own day only the shell of external observances remained without the true spirit of monasticism. "With their rules the monks did not follow the faith of St Bernard or Francis; instead they paid respect to Francis' cowl and outward life, to the rope which he wore, to his poverty."[43] The greatness of Bernard lay in the special gifts God had given to him, but monks who came after him lacked his gifts so they stressed the observance of rules. "They employed their own gifts to establish sects and almost to blot out the name of Christ. They placed their trust not in their Christianity and their baptism but in their dedication, whether to Francis or Bernard."[44]

Luther was critical of monastic vows, whose binding nature he considered contrary to the freedom of the Gospel. He interpreted Bernard's *De praecepto et dispensatione* as mitigating the vows. Since this treatise supports the idea that every part of the Rule is in the hands of the superior, who has the privilege of granting dispensations, it follows that, "these particular rules sometimes hold good and sometimes do not hold good."[45] He maintained that Bernard lived up to the vows, "not because the vows compelled him to do

---

but remained in human society, eating ordinary food, drinking wine, and wearing fine and decent clothing," *Lectures on Galatians,* AE, vol. 27, p. 84.

42. Luther, *Christian in Society,* AE, vol. 44, p. 325.

43. Luther, *Sermons on the Gospel of St John,* AE, vol. 22, p. 273.

44. Luther, *Lectures on Genesis,* AE, vol. 2, p. 269. "The saints used evil (vows) to produce good. But nobody (today) vows to live in the spirit in which Bernard lived. They ought, but this cannot be brought under the control of a vow," *Christian in Society,* AE, vol. 44, p. 354. Luther's extended criticism of monasticism is in his *De votis monasticis.*

45. Luther, *Christian in Society,* AE, vol. 44, p. 343.

so, but from a free choice of spirit."[46] This may be the basis for Luther's statement that, "even St Bernard asserts that a monk is not obliged to obey even his abbot if he commands him other than his Rule allows."[47] Although Luther was able to defend Bernard's freedom under the Gospel to choose a life under vows, he believed that few of his followers understood vows in this sense. Instead, they followed the letter of the Rule rather than its spirit, and so lapsed back into a legalism which was contrary to the Gospel.[48]

On the Fathers

As stated above, Luther was convinced that he stood in the Catholic tradition of the Church, but at the Leipzig debate it was not difficult for John Eck to indicate where the Reformer was at variance with some Fathers and councils.[49] Some time after the debate Luther praised the doctors of the Church and confessed himself to be small and insignificant in comparison. He continued, "Now I admit that the holy Fathers Ambrose and Bernard were believers and elect; but Christ himself declares that even the saints may err and the elect may be led astray. It does not follow by any means that everything they said and did was holy and good and

46. *Ibid.*, p. 309. "He who is free can, just as the apostle Paul (Acts 16:3), submit himself to all laws, and to the dominion of all men, in the same way in which St Bernard and others who were monks in the truest sense of the word surrendered themselves to living under a vow," *Letters*, AE, vol. 48, p. 298.

47. *Ibid.*, p. 266.

48. *Ibid.*, p. 316, "Consequently St Bernard and others kept vows of chastity, obedience, and poverty, not because of the vows. Instead, they observed the ancient example of the Fathers and of the Gospel. . . . Their followers upheld this error by a wrong understanding of their example."

49. Luther, *Commentary on Genesis*, AE, vol. 2, p. 55, "The wretched papists assail us today with this one argument saying, 'Do you think, that all the Fathers were in error?' It is indeed painful to maintain this, especially about the better ones—Augustine, Ambrose, Bernard, and that entire company of excellent men who ruled the Church by the Word, who have been adorned with the distinction and lofty name 'Church Father,' and for whose labors we have both praise and admiration."

must be accepted and taught. For they too were human."[50] The ultimate criterion for patristic authority was Scripture.

> Holiness does not make a man infallible, and it does not imply that one must rely and depend on all the dicta of the Fathers or approve and believe all their teachings. Rather, take the touchstone of God's Word into your hands. Let this be your criterion for testing, trying, and judging all that the Fathers have preached, written, and said.[51]

Although even saints fall and err, they do so through ignorance. In this way Luther explains Bernard's adherence to the papacy and the monastic order, but he rejoices that forgiveness is offered to them as well as to all believers. In his *Commentary on Deuteronomy* he finds occasion to fault several Fathers for their errors, including Bernard for his doctrine of free-will, and he concludes: "Thus none of the saints hitherto has put off the whole flesh or killed its feelings, and there is no hope other than that both judge and teacher act in the fear of God, always suspicious of themselves, lest perhaps they handle the Law of God and his Word improperly."[52]

Luther on Bernard—An Analysis

There can be no doubt that Luther approached Bernard subjectively, determined to discover support for his own theology in the

50. Luther, *Sermons on the Gospel of St John,* AE, vol. 22, p. 259.

51. *Ibid.,* p. 254. "Be careful therefore to stay on the track. Don't let anyone pull you away from the Word through any statement of man, be it Augustine, Jerome, Bernard, or even an angel (Gal 1:8). 'The elect will be led astray,' says Christ (M 24:24). Therefore we cannot build on the mere word of one of the elect saints without Scripture," *Word and Sacrament,* AE, vol. 36, p. 289.

52. Luther, *Lectures on Deuteronomy,* AE, vol. 9, p. 164. "I have observed this in St Bernard. Whenever he begins to speak of Christ it is pure pleasure to follow; but when he goes beyond this and talks of rulers or works, then it is no longer St Bernard. The same thing happens to St Augustine, Gregory, and all the rest; when Christ is not in them, they are nothing but secular professors, like philosophers or lawyers." *Commentaries on the Psalms,* AE, vol. 14, p. 38.

writings of the Cistercian. That such support was present in Bernard is certain, but Luther often failed to appreciate the historical context from which Bernard's statements issued. It was patently unhistorical to use the most exemplary monk of the twelfth century and the most ardent champion of monasticism as a witness against this institution. Bernard's apparent mitigation of the vows was not due to a Lutheran doctrine of grace, but rather to the monk's insistence that the spirit of the vows be maintained against their letter. Luther acknowledged Bernard's support of monasticism, but he tended to idealize the twelfth century and held up Bernard as a symbol of everything noble and Christian in the religious life. But monasticism was never dispensable for Bernard, and he was far from asserting the type of Christian liberty which was characteristic of Lutheran thought.

A similarly unhistorical approach was followed when Luther found support in Bernard for his anti-papal attitude. Although Bernard did not hesitate to reproach the papacy for its abuses, denouncing papal preoccupation with "Justinian's law, not the Lord's,"[53] he never conceived of the possibility of eliminating the institution itself. Luther found Bernard's admonitions to Pope Eugenius III in *De consideratione* in harmony with his own critical attitude toward the papacy, but to continue the simile, "the music would have ended in discord if Luther had taken hold of the theme instead of staying on one bar only."[54]

---

53. Geoffrey Barraclough, *The Medieval Papacy* (London: Thames and Hudson, 1968), p. 101.

54. W. Koehler, *Luther und die Kirchengeschichte nach seinen Schriften* (Erlangen: Verlag von Fr Junge, 1900), p. 327. However, Luther was willing to acknowledge papal primacy *de humano*, as a useful arrangement, but he denied to it a theological basis of authority. On the papacy he writes, "If Bernard felt sorry for Eugenius at a time when the Roman See, which though even then very corrupt, was ruled with better prospects for improvement, why should not we complain who for three hundred years have had such a great increase of corruption and wickedness," *Career of the Reformer*, AE, vol. 31, p. 337; "Therefore Bernard writes admirably to Pope Eugenius: 'Of necessity you have no knowledge of many things, and of necessity you pretend not to know many things you do know.' " *Lectures on Genesis*, AE, vol. 4, p. 82; "Christians are taught that the pope, in granting indulgences, needs

It is certainly true that Bernard spoke in lofty terms of the authority of Scripture, but such utterances were commonplace among the medieval writers. For Bernard as well as his contemporaries, Scripture "was to the medieval mind wide enough to encompass the works of the Fathers and those of subsequent Doctors. . . . Holy Writ and the commentaries thereon formed one uncleft whole which was kept together by the continuity of the Church's life."[55] From the fourteenth century on, however, Scripture and Tradition had often been viewed as two disparate entities, and by Luther's time Scripture was in contention with the Church for primacy of authority. To cite Bernard as a witness for Scripture under these circumstances was to ignore four centuries of intervening history. Luther recognized the authority of the Fathers, but only in a derivative sense. The Fathers, (including Bernard) constituted a body of authority only insofar as they could be said to reflect Scripture, a distinction unknown in Bernard's day.

The heart of Luther's theology was his emphasis on justification by grace through faith because of Christ. It is here that Luther's pietism and Bernard's mysticism came closest to agreement. Bernard's passages on salvation correspond very closely to Luther's, and in both cases salvation was a gift of grace centering on Christ's passion. In both theologians Christ's death was viewed as a theological center. In the twelfth century Bernard's statements were called forth by Abelard's insistence on the ethical dimension of Christ's life to the exclusion of its salvatory role. For Luther it appeared as though contemporary ecclesiastical practices (monasticism, masses for the dead, indulgences) likewise lessened the value of Christ's work, and he attempted to restore the passion to the

---

and thus desires their devout prayers more than their money. The pope's heart must be nourished by devout prayer. St Bernard has written about this matter in a most attractive way to Pope Eugenius." *Career of the Reformer,* AE, vol. 31, p. 204; "Papal religion gave such an appearance of holiness that great men like Gregory, Bernard, and others were deceived by it for a while." *Lectures on Galatians,* AE, vol. 27, p. 89.

55. George H. Tavard, "Holy Church or Holy Writ: A Dilemma of the 14th Century," *Church History,* 23 (September 1954), p. 195.

center of Christian life. Luther, however, was critical of the type of mystical devotion characterized by union with God through contemplation and ecstatic experience.

Luther was not oblivious to the differences which existed between his theology and several of the Fathers. He was critical of them when their statements appeared to be at variance with his understanding of grace. He cannot be accused of deliberately ignoring those aspects of their writings which contradicted his theology, but he attributed these differences to a deficiency of understanding on their part due to their sinful human nature. He firmly believed, on the basis of his considerable knowledge of patristic thought, that he stood in a direct continuum with the mainstream of Catholic thought and piety.

Carl Volz

Concordia Seminary
St Louis

BIBLIOGRAPHY OF STUDIES BY JEREMIAH F. O'SULLIVAN

Medieval Europe. With John F. Burns. New York, Appleton-Century-Crofts. 1943.

Cistercian Settlements in Wales and Monmouthshire, 1140–1540. New York, Fordham University Press. 1947.

The Writings of Salvian the Presbyter. Translation. New York, Cima Publishing Co., 1947. (The Fathers of the Church).

The Register of Eudes of Rouen. Translated by Sidney F. Brown. Edited by Jeremiah F. O'Sullivan. New York. Columbia University Press. 1964. (Records of Civilization, LXXII).

"Old Ireland and Irish Monasticism," *Old Ireland,* edited by Robert McNally, New York, Fordham University Press. 1965. Pp. 90–119.

IN PREPARATION

Monastic Customs. Columbia University Press. (Records of Civilization).

The Writings of Stephen of Salley. Translation. Cistercian Publications. Cistercian Fathers Series 27).

Cistercians and Cluniacs. Cistercian Publications. (Cistercian Studies Series 25).

CISTERCIAN FATHERS SERIES

Under the direction of the same Board of Editors as the CISTERCIAN STUDIES SERIES, the CISTERCIAN FATHERS SERIES seeks to make available the works of the Cistercian Fathers in good English translations based on the recently established critical editions. The texts are accompanied by introductions, notes and indexes prepared by qualified scholars.